10⁰⁰

#1 Best Seller

14ᵗʰ Blue Book
Dolls & Values®
by Jan Foulke
Photographs by Howard Foulke

Antique Section — Pages 21 to 206.

Modern Section — Pages 207 to 311.

Published by

Hobby House Press™

Hobby House Press, Inc.

Grantsville, MD 21536

ACKNOWLEDGEMENTS

For their encouragement and support, we again wish to thank our friends, customers, fellow dealers and fans, as well as doll collectors around the world.

Special thanks to:

Those who allowed us to use photographs of their dolls or who provided special information for use in this edition. Terri & Kathy's Dolls, Rosemary Kanizer, Victoria's Dolls, Norman & June Verro, Sidney Jeffrey (My Dolly Dearest), Miriam Blankman, George Humphrey, Peggy Bealefield (Doodlebug Dolls), Rae-Ellen Koenig (The Doll Express), Susan Babkowski, Edward R. Pardella, Joanna Ott, Carol Corson, Mimi Hiscox, Becky Lowe, Andy Ourant, Dorothy Hunt & Jeremy (Sweetbriar), Shelia Thall (Cobwebs), Elliott Zirlin, Delores Gilbert, Joan & Larry Kindler, Kay & Wayne Jensen, Mary Barnes Kelly, Nancy A. Smith, Jay Lowe, Fritzi Bartlemay, Richard W. Withington, Inc., McMasters Doll Auctions, and H&J Foulke, Inc.

Those who shared their doll collections but wished to remain anonymous.

The Colemans, who allowed some marks to be reproduced from their book, *The Collector's Encyclopedia of Dolls.*

Gary Ruddell of Hobby House Press, Inc., with whom we have worked for 25 years and Carolyn Cook, editor.

Howard, for his beautiful photographs.

All of these people helped make this book possible.

Jan Foulke
June 1999

Additional copies available @ $19.95 plus postage
from
HOBBY HOUSE PRESS, INC.
www.hobbyhouse.com
1 Corporate Drive
Grantsville, MD 21536
1-800-554-1447
E-mail: hobbyhouse@gcnet.net

©1999 by Jan and Howard Foulke

ISBN: 0-87588-550-0

Using This Book

Doll collecting continues to increase in popularity every year. The great number of collectors entering the field has given rise to larger and more frequent doll shows, more dealers in dolls, more books on dolls, thicker doll magazines and more doll conventions and seminars, as well as an overwhelming offering of new dolls by mass-production companies and individual artists. This explosion has also increased the demand for old dolls and discontinued collectors' dolls, causing prices to rise as more collectors vie for the same dolls.

With the average antique or collectible doll representing a purchase of at least several hundred dollars, today's collectors must be as well informed as possible about the dolls they are considering as additions to their collections. Since the first *Blue Book of Dolls & Values* was published in 1974, our objectives have remained the same:

- To present a book that will help collectors to identify and learn more about dolls.
- To provide retail prices as a guide for buyers and sellers of dolls.

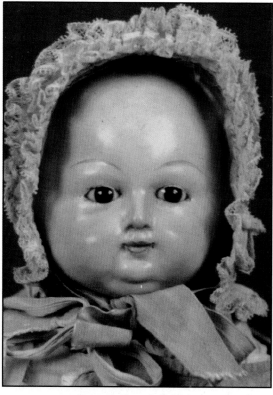

21in (53cm) papier-mâché Sonneberg täulfing. *H & J Foulke, Inc.* For additional information see page 195.

Since every edition of the *Blue Book* has sold more copies than the previous one, we can only conclude that these objectives are in line with the needs of the doll lovers, collectors, dealers and appraisers who keep buying the latest editions of our book.

For convenience in locating a doll more quickly, this book has been divided into two sections: *Antique* and *Modern*. Where certain dolls, such as *Raggedy Ann* and *Kewpie*, were made over very long periods, the modern examples are included with the main entry in the *Antique* Section in order to keep the whole production history of a doll in one place.

The dolls presented in this book are listed alphabetically by maker, material or the trade name of the individual doll. An extensive index has been provided to help in locating a specific doll. For the most part, dolls are listed in chronological order within a main entry.

For the listed dolls we have

9½in (24cm) brown-eyed china head doll with Greiner-style hairdo. *H & J Foulke, Inc.* For additional information see page 73.

included historical information, physical description, marks and labels, and the retail selling price. Photographs are also included for many dolls; however, since every doll cannot be pictured in each edition, previous **Blue Books** should be consulted for additional photographs.

In some cases the doll sizes given are the only ones known to have been made, but in the cases of most of the French and German bisque, china, papier-mâché and wood dolls, sizes priced are chosen at random and listed sizes must not be interpreted as definitive. It is impossible to list every doll in every possible size, especially for dolls that range from 6 to 42 inches (15 to 106cm). The user will need to call a little common sense into play to interpolate a price for an unlisted size.

The historical information given for some of the dolls would have been much more difficult to compile were it not for the original research already published by Dorothy S., Elizabeth A. and Evelyn J. Coleman; Johana G. Anderton; Jürgen and Marianne Cieslik; and Pam and Polly Judd.

The data for retail prices was gathered during 1998 and 1999 from antique shops and shows, auctions, doll shops and shows, advertisements in collectors' periodicals, lists from doll dealers, and purchases and sales reported by both collectors and dealers. This information, along with our own valuations and judgments, was computed into the range of prices shown in this book. When we could not find a sufficient number of dolls to be sure of giving a reliable range, we marked those prices with two asterisks ("**").

The price for a doll listed in this guide is the retail value of a doll if purchased from a dealer. In setting a price for each doll, we use a range to allow for the variables of originality, quality and condition that must be reflected in the price. Fine examples of a doll, especially those which are all original or boxed with original tags or never played with, can bring a premium of at least 50% more than prices quoted for ordinary examples. Sometimes a doll will bring a premium price because it is particularly cute, sweet, pretty or visually appealing, making an outstanding presentation. There is no way to factor this appeal into a price guide.

The international market continues to be an important factor in the antique doll world. International interest has added a whole new dimension to the American doll market as increasing awareness of antique dolls in Germany, France, Switzerland, Holland, Denmark and other countries is causing a great exodus and a depletion of our supply of

16in (41cm) J.D. Kestner 257 character baby. *H & J Foulke, Inc.* For additional information see page 122. See page 126 for mold mark.

antique dolls.

Of particular interest in the international arena are German bisque character children, German bisque babies by Kestner, Kämmer & Reinhardt, and Hertel, Schwab & Co., German bisque "dolly" faces (particularly small sizes) by Kestner, Kämmer & Reinhardt, and Handwerck, Käthe Kruse dolls and

6

German celluloid dolls. This interest continues to keep prices in these categories strong.

All prices given for antique dolls are for those of good quality and condition, but showing some normal wear and aging. They should be appropriately dressed in old clothing or new clothing made from old fab-

16in (41cm) German bisque shoulder head doll with molded hair. *H & J Foulke, Inc.* For additional information see page 51.

ply and can easily cost more than $85 each if purchased separately.

Prices given for composition dolls are for those in overall good to excellent condition with original hair and clothing, except as noted. Composition may be lightly crazed, but should be colorful. Hard plastic and vinyl dolls must be perfect, with hair in original set and crisp, original clothes. A never-played-with doll in original box with labels would bring a premium price.

The users of this book must keep in mind that no price guide is the final word. It cannot provide an absolute answer as to what to pay. This book should be used only as an aid in purchasing a doll. The final decision must be yours, for only you are on the scene, actually examining the specific doll in question. No book can take the place of actual field experience. Doll popularity can cycle; prices can fluctuate; regional variations can occur. Before you buy, do a lot of looking. Ask questions. Most dealers and collectors are glad to talk about their dolls and pleased to share their information with you.

rics. Bisque or china heads should not be cracked, broken or repaired, but may have slight making imperfections such as speckling, surface lines, darkened mold lines and uneven coloring. Bodies may have repairs but should be old and appropriate to the head. A doll with original old dress, shoes and wig will generally be valued at higher than quoted prices because these items are in scarce sup-

Investing In Dolls

With the prices of the average antique or collectible doll representing a purchase of at least several hundred dollars in today's doll market, the assembling of a doll collection becomes rather costly. Actually, very few people buy dolls strictly as an investment; most collectors buy a doll because they like it. It has appeal to them for some reason: perhaps as an object of artistic beauty, perhaps because it evokes some kind of sentiment, perhaps because it fills some need that they feel or speaks to something inside them. It is this personal feeling toward the doll which makes it of value to the collector.

However, most collectors expect to at least break even when they eventually sell their dolls. Unfortunately, there is no guarantee that any particular doll will appreciate consistently year after year; however, the track record for old or antique dolls is fairly good. If you are thinking of the future sale of your collection, be wary of buying expensive new or reproduction dolls. They have no track record, and most have little resale value. Collectible dolls of the last 30 years are a risky market. Alexander dolls are a case in point. After many years of doubling their value the minute they were carried from the toy store shelves, dolls of the 1960s to 1990s have slid in price so that many are now bringing only 25-50% of their cost to collectors.

Because most collectors have only limited funds for purchasing dolls, they must be sure they are spending their dollars to the best advantage. There are many factors to consider when buying a doll, and this chapter will provide some suggestions about what to look for and what to consider. Probably the primary tenet is that a collector who is not particularly well-informed about a doll should not consider purchasing it unless he or she has confidence in the person selling the doll.

6in (15cm) 208 Kestner all-bisque child with swivel neck. *H & J Foulke, Inc.* For additional information see page 125.

Marks

Fortunately for collectors, most of the antique bisque, some of the papier-mâche, cloth and other types of antique dolls are marked or labeled. Marks and labels give the buyer confidence because they identify the trade name, the maker, the country of origin, the style or mold number, or perhaps even the patent date.

Most composition and modern dolls are marked with the maker's name and sometimes also the trade name of the doll and the date. Some dolls have tags sewn on or into their clothing to identify them; many still retain original hang tags.

Of course, many dolls are unmarked, but after you have seen quite a few dolls, you begin to notice their individual characteristics and can often determine what a doll possibly is. When you have had some experience buying dolls, you begin to recognize an unusual face or an especially fine quality doll. Then there should be no hesitation about buying a doll marked only with a mold number or no mark at all. The doll has to speak for itself, and the price must be based upon the collector's frame of doll reference. That is, one must relate the face and quality to those of a known doll maker and make price judgments from that point.

9in (23cm) Armand Marseille 253 googly. *H & J Foulke, Inc.* For additional information see page 149.

Quality

The mark does not tell everything about a doll. Two examples from the same mold could look entirely different and carry vastly different prices because of the quality of the work done on the doll, which can vary from head to head, even with dolls made from the same mold by one firm. To command top price, a bisque doll should have lovely bisque, decoration, eyes and hair. Before purchasing a doll, the collector should determine whether the example is the best available of that type. Even the molding of one head can be much sharper with more delineation of such details as dimples or locks of hair. The molding detail is especially important to notice when purchasing dolls with character faces or molded hair.

The quality of the bisque should be smooth; dolls with bisque which is pimply, peppered with tiny black specks or unevenly colored, or which has noticeable firing lines on the face, would be second choices at a lower price. However, collectors must keep in mind that porcelain factories sold many heads with small manufacturing defects because companies were in business for profit and were producing expendable play items, not works of art. Small manufacturing defects do not devalue a doll. It is perfectly acceptable to have light speckling, light surface lines, firing lines in inconspicuous places, darkened mold lines, a few black specks, or cheek rubs. The absolutely perfect bisque head is a rarity.

Since doll heads are hand-painted, the artistry of the decoration should be examined. The tinting of the complexion should be subdued and even, not harsh and splotchy.

14in (35cm) Simon & Halbig 939 child with open mouth and square cut teeth. *H & J Foulke, Inc.* For additional information see page 187. See page 188 for mold mark.

Artistic skill should be evident in the portrayal of the expression on the face and in details such as the lips, eyebrows and eyelashes, and particu-

12in (31cm) Georgene Novelties (Averill) cloth child, all original. *H & J Foulke, Inc.* For additional information see page 41.

Furthermore, an especially fine example will bring a premium over an ordinary but nice model.

Condition

Another important factor when pricing a doll is the condition. A bisque doll with a crack on the face or extensive professional repair involving the face would sell for one-quarter or less than a doll with only normal wear. An inconspicuous hairline would decrease the value somewhat, but in a rare doll it would not be as great a detriment as in a common doll. As the so-called better dolls are becoming more difficult to find, a hairline is more acceptable to collectors if there is a price adjustment. The same is true for a doll which has a spectacular face—a hairline would be less important to price in that doll than in one with an ordinary face.

Sometimes a head will have a factory flaw which occurred in the making, such as a firing crack, scratch, piece of kiln debris, dark specks, small bubbles, a ridge not smoothed out or light surface lines. Since the factory was producing toys for a profit and not creating works of art, heads with slight flaws were not all discarded, especially if flaws were inconspicuous or could be covered. If factory defects are not detracting, they have little or no effect on the value of a doll.

larly in the eyes, which should show highlights and shading when they are painted. On a doll with molded hair, individual brush marks to give the hair a more realistic look would be a desirable detail.

If a doll has a wig, the hair should be appropriate if not old. Dynel or synthetic wigs are not appropriate for antique dolls; a human hair or good quality mohair wig should be used. If a doll has glass eyes, they should be old with natural color and threading in the irises to give a lifelike appearance.

If a doll does not meet all of these standards, if should be priced lower than one that does.

It is to be expected that an old doll will show some wear. Perhaps there is a rub on the nose or cheek, a few small "wig pulls" or maybe a chipped earring hole; a Schoenhut doll or a Käthe Kruse may have some scuffs; an old papier-mâché may have a few age cracks; a china head may show wear on the hair; an old composition body may have scuffed toes or missing fingers. This wear is to be expected and does not necessarily affect the value of a doll. However, a doll in exceptional condition will bring more than "book" price.

Unless an antique doll is rare or you particularly want that specific doll, do not pay top price for a doll that needs extensive work: restringing, setting eyes, repairing fingers, replacing body parts, new wig or dressing. All of these repairs add up to a considerable sum at the doll hospital, possibly making the total cost of the doll more than it is really worth.

Composition dolls in perfect condition are becoming harder to find. Because their material is so susceptible to the atmosphere, their condition can deteriorate literally overnight. Even in excellent condition, a composition doll nearly always has some fine crazing or slight fading. It is very difficult to find a composition doll in mint condition and even harder to be sure that it will

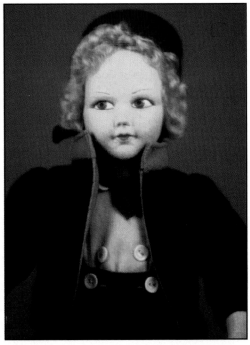

15in (38cm) Norah Wellings cloth child, all original. *H & J Foulke, Inc.* For additional information see page 203.

stay that way. However, in order for a composition doll to bring "book" price, there should be a minimum of crazing, very good coloring, original uncombed hair and original clothes in very good condition. Pay less for a doll that does not have original clothes and hair or that is all original but shows extensive play wear. Pay even less for one with heavy crazing and cracking or other damages. For composition dolls that are all original, unplayed with, in original boxes and with little or no crazing, allow a premium of about 50% over "book" price.

Hard plastic and vinyl dolls must be in excellent condition if they are at "book" price. The hair should be perfect in the original set: clothes should be completely original, fresh and unfaded. Skin tones should be natural with good cheek color. Add a premium of 25-50% for mint dolls never removed from their original boxes.

Body

In order to command top price, an old doll must have the original or an appropriate old body in good condition. If a doll does not have the cor-

rect type of body, the buyer ends up not with a complete doll but with parts that may not be worth as much as one whole doll. As dolls are becoming more difficult to find, more are turning up with "put together" bodies. Many dolls are now entering the market from old collections assembled years ago. Some of these contain dolls which were "put together" before there was much information available about correct heads and bodies. Therefore, the body should be checked to make sure it is appropriate to the head, and all parts of the body should be checked to make sure that they are appropriate to each other. A body with mixed parts from several makers or types of bodies is not worth as much as one with correct parts.

Minor damage or repair to an old body does not affect the value of an antique doll. An original body carefully repaired, recovered or even, if necessary, completely repainted is preferable to a new one. An antique head on a new body would be worth only the value of its parts, whatever the price of the head and new body, not the full price of an antique doll. A rule of thumb is that an antique head is generally worth about 40-50% of the price

8in (20cm) Virga hard plastic *Lucy*, all original. *H & J Foulke, Inc.* For additional information see page 274.

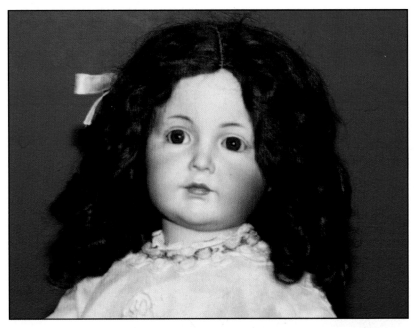

25in (63cm) Kämmer & Reinhart 117a character child. *Fritzi Bartlemay Collection.* For additional information see page 120.

of the complete doll. A very rare head could be worth up to 80%.

If there is a choice of body types for the same bisque head, a good quality ball-jointed composition body is more desirable than a crudely made five-piece body or stick-type body with only pieces of turned wood for upper arms and legs. Collectors prefer jointed composition bodies over kid ones for dolly-faced dolls, and pay more for the same face on a composition body.

Occasionally the body adds value to the doll. In the case of bisque heads, a small doll with a completely jointed body, a French fashion-type with a wood-jointed body, a Tête Jumeau head on an adult body or a character baby head on a jointed tod-dler-type body would all be higher in price because of their special bodies.

As for the later modern dolls, a composition doll on the wrong body or with a body that is cracked, peeling and in poor condition would have a greatly reduced value. The same is true of a vinyl doll with replaced parts, body stains or chewed-off fingers.

Clothing

It is becoming increasingly difficult to find dolls in old clothing because, as the years go by, fabrics continue to deteriorate. Consequently, collectors are paying more than "book" price for an antique doll if it has original old clothes, shoes, and

14

4in (10cm) **Tiny Town** girl with jump rope, all original. *H & J Foulke, Inc.* For additional information see page 306.

hair. Even faded, somewhat worn, or carefully mended original or appropriate old clothes are preferable to new ones. As collectors become more sophisticated and selective, they realize the value of old doll clothing and accessories. Some dealers are now specializing in these areas. Good old leather doll shoes will bring more than $85 per pair; a lovely Victorian white-work doll dress can easily cost $95; an old dress for a French fashion lady, $300 and more. Good old doll wigs can bring from $25 to $250.

However, when clothing must be replaced and appropriate old clothing cannot be obtained, new

clothes should be authentically styled for the age of the doll and constructed of fabrics that would have been available when the doll was produced. There are many reference books and catalog reprints showing dolls in original clothing, and doll supply companies offer patterns for dressing old dolls.

To bring top price, a modern doll must have original clothes. It is usually fairly simple to determine whether or not the clothing is original and factory made. Some makers even placed tags in the doll's clothing. Replaced clothing greatly reduces the price of modern dolls. Without the original clothing, it is often impossible to identify a modern doll because so many were made using the same face mold.

Total Originality

Today totally original dolls are becoming rare. It is often difficult to determine whether the head and body and all other parts of a doll, including wig, eyes and clothes, have always been together. Many parts of a doll may have been changed and clothing and accessories could have been added over the years. Many dolls labeled "all original" are simply wearing contemporary clothing and wigs. Some collectors and dealers are "embellishing" more expensive dolls by taking original clothing and wigs from cheaper dolls to further enhance the value of the more costly ones.

Dolls with trunks of clothing should be examined to determine whether or not the clothes actually go with the doll or are an assembled wardrobe. A little common sense goes a long way in deciding whether the clothes are of the proper fit, fabric and style for the dolls. The same is true for accessories.

Boxed sets of dolls and accessories should be examined very carefully as some very charming sets of newly assembled old items are being offered as totally original for very, very high prices. Of course, when these ensembles are genuine, they are the ultimate in doll collecting.

Age

The oldest dolls do not necessarily command the highest prices. A lovely old china head with exquisite decoration and very unusual hairdo would bring a price of several thousand dollars but not as much as a 20th century German bisque character child. Many desirable composition dolls of the 1930s and *BARBIE®* dolls of the 1960s are selling at prices higher than older bisque dolls of 1890 to 1920. So, in determining price, the age of the doll may or may not be significant.

Size

The size of a doll is usually taken into account when determining a

14in (36cm) Hedwig/DeAngeli *Suzanne*, all original with tag. *H & J Foulke, Inc.* For additional information see page 251.

price. Generally, the size and price for a certain doll are related: a smaller size is lower, a larger size is higher. However, there are a few exceptions. The 11in (28cm) *Shirley Temple* and tiny German dolly-faced dolls on fully-jointed bodies are examples of small dolls that bring higher prices than their larger counterparts.

Availability

The price of a doll is directly related to its availability in most cases. The harder a doll is to find, the higher will be its price. Each year brings more new doll collectors than newly discovered, desirable old dolls; hence, the supply of old dolls is diminished. As long as the demand for certain antique and collectible dolls is greater than the supply, prices will rise. This explains the great increase in prices of less common dolls, such as the K & R and other German character children, early china heads and papier-mâchés, composition personality dolls, Sasha dolls and some Alexander dolls that were made for only a limited period of time. Dolls that are fairly common, primarily the German dolly faces and the later china head dolls made over a long period of production, show a more gentle increase in price.

25in (63cm) unmarked German bisque child. *H & J Foulke, Inc.* For additional information see page 53.

Popularity

There are fads in dolls just as in clothes, food and other aspects of life. Dolls that have recently risen in price because of their popularity include the early Jumeaus, all-bisques, German character children, *Patsy* family dolls, *Shirley Temples,* early *BARBIE®* dolls, composition personality dolls, hard plastic dolls of the 1950s, vinyl fashion dolls and Nancy Ann storybook dolls. Some dolls are popular enough to tempt collectors to pay prices higher than the availability factor warrants. Although *Shirley Temples, Tête Jumeaus, Bye-Los, Hildas,* K & R 117, and some plastic Alexander dolls are not rare, the high prices they bring are due to their popularity. American cloth dolls, Schoenhuts, Heubachs, Greiners and closed-mouth shoulder head dolls are in a soft period, so many bargains can be found in these categories.

18in (46cm) Emma Clear bisque "Gibson Girl," 1949. *H & J Foulke, Inc.* For additional information see page 228.

Desirability

Some very rare dolls do not bring a high price because they are not particularly desirable. There are not many collectors looking for them. Falling into this category are the dolls with shoulder heads made of rubber or rawhide and the Springfield jointed wood dolls. While an especially outstanding example will bring a high price, most examples bring very low prices in relationship to their rarity.

Uniqueness

Sometimes the uniqueness of a doll makes price determination very difficult. If a collector has never seen a doll exactly like it before, and it is not cited in a price guide or even shown in any books, deciding what to pay can be a problem. In this case, the buyer has to use all available knowledge as a frame of reference for the unknown doll. Perhaps a doll marked "A.M. 2000" or "S & H 1289" has been found, and the asking price is 25% higher than for the more commonly found numbers by that maker. Or perhaps a black *Kamkins* is offered for twice the price of a white one, or a French fashion lady with original wardrobe is offered at 60% more than a redressed one. In cases such as these, a collector must use his or her own judgment to determine what the doll is worth.

Visual Appeal

Perhaps the most elusive aspect in pricing a doll is its visual appeal. Sometimes, particularly at auction,

we have seen dolls bring well over their "book" value simply because of their look. Often this is nothing more than the handiwork of someone who had the ability to choose just the right wig, clothing and accessories to enhance the doll's visual appeal and make it look particularly cute, stunning, beautiful or otherwise especially outstanding.

Sometimes, though, the visual appeal comes from the face of the doll itself. It may be the way the teeth are put in, the placement of the eyes, the tinting on the face or the sharpness of the molding. Or it may not be any of these specific things; it may just be what some collectors refer to as the "presence" of the doll, an elusive indefinable quality which makes it the best example known!

12in (31cm) Ideal all-vinyl **Betsy Wetsy**, all original and boxed. *Terri & Kathy's Dolls.* For additional information see page 283.

Selling A Doll

So many times we are asked, "How do I go about selling a doll?," that it seems a few paragraphs on the topic are in order. The first logical step is to look through the **Blue Book** to identify the doll and to ascertain a retail price. Work from there to decide what you might ask for your doll. It is very difficult for a private person to get a retail or "book" price for a doll.

Be realistic about the condition. If you have a marked 18in (46cm) *Shirley Temple* doll with combed hair, no clothing, faded face with crazing and a piece off of her nose, do not expect to get the "book" price of $1,000 for her because that would be a retail price for an excellent doll, all original, in pristine unplayed-with condition if purchased from a dealer. Your very used doll is probably worth only $50 to $75 because it will have to be purchased by someone who wants to restore it.

If you have an antique doll with a perfect bisque head but no wig, no clothes and unstrung, but with all of its body parts, you can probably expect to get about half of its retail value depending upon how desirable the particular doll is. If your doll has a perfect bisque head with original wig, clothing and shoes, you can probably get up to 75% of its retail value.

As to actually selling the doll, there are several possibilities. Possibly the easiest is to advertise in your local paper. You may not think there are any doll collectors in your area, but there probably are. You might also check your local paper to see if anyone is advertising to purchase dolls; many dealers and collectors do so. Check the paper to find out about antique shows in your area. If a dealer has dolls, ask if he would be interested in buying your doll. Also, you could inquire at antique shops in your area for dealers who specialize in dolls. You will probably get a higher price from a specialist than a general antique dealer because the former are more familiar with the market for specific dolls. A roster of doll specialists is available from The National Antique Doll Dealers Association, Inc., P.O. Box 81143, Wellesley Hills, MA 02181-0001.

You could consign your doll to an auction. If it is a common doll, it will probably do quite well at a local sale. If it is a more rare doll, consider

*The first logical step is to look through the **Blue Book** to identify the doll and to ascertain a retail price.*

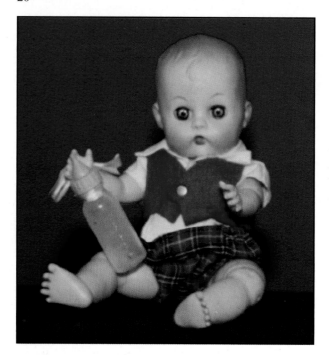

8in (20cm) Vogue vinyl *Jimmy*, all original. *Rosemary Kanizer.* For additional information see page 309.

sending it to one of the auction houses that specialize in selling dolls; most of them will accept one doll if it is a good one, and they will probably get the best price for you.

If you are online, you can try selling your doll on one of the auction services, such as eBay™. You will need to have a digital camera or scanner to provide photographs, which are very important to online selling. You should decide on a reserve, a minimum price you will accept, just in case it's a slow auction week. Of course, you will have to ship the doll. If it has a bisque head with glass or sleeping eyes, you will have to stuff the head to protect the eyes. Improper packing of the head is the most common cause of damage during shipping.

It would probably be worth your while to purchase a doll magazine from your local book store, doll shop or newsstand; most doll magazines include ads from auction houses, doll shows and leading dealers. You could advertise in doll magazines, but you might have to ship the doll and guarantee return privileges if the buyer does not like it.

If you cannot find your doll in the *Blue Book*, it might be a good idea to have it professionally appraised. This will involve your paying a fee to have the doll evaluated. We provide this service and can be contacted through the publisher. Many museums and auction houses also appraise dolls.

For more detailed information about collecting and selling dolls, consult my book *Doll Buying and Selling*, available from Hobby House Press.

ANTIQUE & VINTAGE

Values given in this section are retail prices for clean dolls in very good overall condition with no cracks, chips or repairs in porcelain heads and with proper bodies and appropriate wigs and clothes. Naked, wigless, dirty, unstrung "attic dolls" are worth 40-65%, depending upon the rarity of the doll.

Pair of felt children by Margarete Steiff, all original. *Nancy A. Smith Collection.*

ALABAMA

Early Alabama Indestructible Doll: All-cloth painted with oils, tab-jointed shoulders and hips, flat derriere for sitting; painted hair with circular seam on head, molded face with painted facial features; applied ears; painted stockings and shoes (a few with bare feet); appropriate clothes; all in good condition, some wear acceptable, no repaint or touch up.

11-15in (28-38cm)   **$1,400-$1,600**
21-24in (53-61cm)   **$2,500-$3,000**
Black: 14-19in (36-48cm)
                                  $6,600**
Wigged: 24in (61cm)
                          $3,000-$3,500**

Later doll, molded ears, bobbed hairdo:
14-15in (36-38cm)   **$800-$1,000**
21-24in (53-61cm)   **$2,000-$2,500**
Black: 14-19in (36-48cm)   **$3,000**
**Not enough price samples to compute a reliable average.

Mark: Various stamps, including:

PAT. NOV. 9, 1912
NO. 2
ELLA SMITH DOLL CO.

FACTS

Ella Smith Doll Co., Roanoke, Ala., 1899-1925.

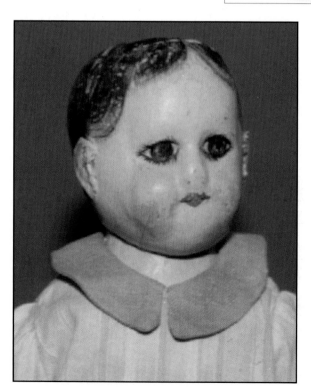

11½in (29cm)
Alabama Baby.
Nancy A. Smith Collection.

ALEXANDRE

H.A. Bébé: 1889-1891. Perfect bisque socket head, closed mouth, paperweight eyes; jointed composition and wood body; lovely clothes; all in good condition.

Mark:

H ⅍ A

17-19in (43-48cm) **$5,800-$6,800****

Bébé Phénix: 1889-1900. As above; composition body sometimes with one-piece arms and legs.

Mark: Red Stamp Incised

PHÉNIX
★ 95

17-18in (43-46cm)	**$3,800-$4,200**
22-23in (56-58cm)	**$4,700-$5,200**

Open mouth:

17-19in (43-48cm)	**$2,300-$2,500**

**Not enough price samples to compute a reliable average.

FACTS

Henri Alexandre, Paris, France, 1888-1892; Tourrel 1892-1895; Jules Steiner and successors 1895-1901.
Designer: Henri Alexandre.
Trademark: Bébé Phénix.

25in (51cm) *Phénix Bébé *94. H & J Foulke, Inc.*

ALL BISQUE
(So-called FRENCH)

All-Bisque French Doll: Ca. 1880. Jointed at shoulders and hips, swivel neck, slender arms and legs; solid dome head, good wig, glass eyes, closed mouth; molded shoes or boots and stockings; appropriately dressed; all in good condition, with proper parts.

5in (13cm)	**$1,550-$1,650***
6in (15cm)	**$2,100-$2,350***
8in (20cm)	**$5,000****

With bare feet:

5in (13cm)	**$2,150-$2,350***
6in (15cm)	**$2,500-$2,650***

With jointed elbows and knees:

5½in (14cm)	**$4,500***

With jointed elbows:

5½in (14cm)	**$4,200***

*Allow extra for original clothes.
**Not enough price samples to compute a reliable average.

5½in (14cm) French all-bisque by Simon & Halbig with smiling face. *H & J Foulke, Inc.*

Oriental: 5½in (14cm)   **$1,650-$1,850**
Black: 5½in (14cm)   **$1,650-$1,850**
Painted eyes:
  4-4½in (10-12cm), all original
                              $750-$850
  2½in (6cm), blue boots,
    all original   **$225-$275**

Later French Dolls: 1910-1920
S.F.B.J., long tan stockings, swivel neck, glass eyes
  6in (15cm)   **$500-$600**
J.V., tall black boots, swivel neck, glass eyes
  6in (15cm)   **$450-$500**

Mark: None, sometimes numbers.

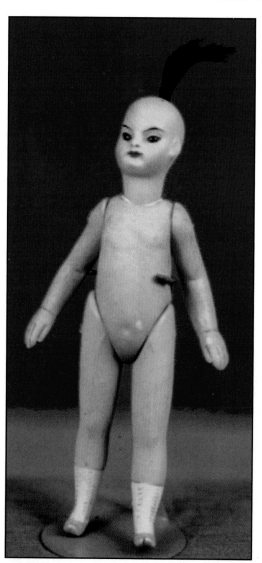

FACTS
Various French and/or German firms. Ca. 1880-on. Smiling-faced dolls made by Simon & Halbig for the French trade.

5½in (14cm) French all-bisque Oriental. *H & J Foulke, Inc.*

ALL-BISQUE DOLLS
GERMAN

All-Bisque with molded clothes: Ca: 1890-on. Good quality work; all in good condition, with proper parts.

Children:

3½-4in (9-10cm)	**$115-$150**
5-6in (13-15cm)	**$175-$225**
7in (18cm)	**$250-$275**

All-Bisque Slender Dolls: Ca. 1900-on. Stationary neck, slender arms and legs, glass eyes, molded shoes or boots and stockings; many in regional costumes; all in good condition, proper parts.

3¾-4in (9-10cm)	**$165-$185***
5-6in (13-15cm)	**$275**

Swivel neck:

4in (10cm) 10a or 39/11	**$225-$250**
5½in (14cm) 13a	**$450-$500**

Black or Mulatto:

4-4½in (10-12cm)	**$325-$375**
Swivel neck, 5in (13cm)	**$500**

Round face: swivel neck, 2-strap heeled shoes, pegged shoulders and hips

4½-5½in (11-14cm) redressed	**$375-$425**
4½-5½in (11-14cm) original clothes	**$500-$550**

*Allow extra for original child clothes.

All-Bisque with painted eyes: Ca. 1880-1910. Stationary neck, painted eyes, molded and painted shoes and stockings; fine quality work; all in good condition, with proper parts.

1¼in (3cm) crocheted clothes	**$85**
1½-2in (4-5cm)	**$75-$85**
4-5in (10-13cm)	**$175-$225**
6-7in (15-18cm)	**$250-$300**

Swivel neck, 4-5in (10-13cm) **$250-$275**
Early style, bootines, yellow boots or shirred hose:

4-5in (10-13cm)	**$300-$350**

3¾in (9cm) all-bisque with molded riding clothes; 4in (10cm) Campbell Kid-type with molded clothes. *H & J Foulke, Inc.*

3¾in (9cm) slender all-bisque with painted stocking legs. *H & J Foulke, Inc.*

6-6½in (15-16cm)	**$400-$450**
8in (20cm)	**$750-850**
Black stockings, tan slippers:	
6in (15cm)	**$450**

All-Bisque with glass eyes: Ca. 1890-1910. Stationary neck, glass eyes, molded and painted shoes and stockings; all in good condition, with proper parts, fine quality.

3in (8cm)	**$275-325***
4½-5in (11-13cm)	**$275-$325***
6in (15cm)	**$350-$375***
7in (18cm)	**$400-$450***
8in (20cm)	**$500-$550***
9in (23cm)	**$700-$800**
10in (25cm)	**$900-$1,000**
12in (31cm)	**$1,300-$1,400**

Early style model, stiff hips, shirred hose or bootines:

3in (8cm)	**$325**
4½in (11cm)	**$325-$350**
6in (15cm)	**$500-$550**
7in (18cm)	**$650-$700**
8½in (21cm)	**$950-$1,000**
Long black or white stockings, tan shoes:	
5in (13cm)	**$500-$550**
7½in (19cm)	**$800-$850**

*Allow $50-$100 extra for yellow boots or unusual footwear and/or especially fine quality.

All-Bisque with swivel neck and glass eyes: Ca. 1880-1910. Swivel neck, glass eyes, molded and painted shoes or boots and stockings; all in good condition, with proper parts, fine quality.

3-1/4in (8cm)	**$350-$375**
4-4½in (10-12cm)	**$375-425***
5-6in (13-15cm)	**$550-$650**
7in (18cm)	**$750-$800***
8in (20cm)	**$900-$1,000***
9in (23cm)	**$1,100-$1,200***
10in (25cm)	**$1,300-$1,500**
Early Kestner or S&H-type:	
4½-5in (12-13cm)	**$1,650-$1,850**
6in (15cm)	**$1,650-$1,850**
8in (20cm)	**$2,300-$2,500**
10in (25cm)	**$3,000-$3,200**
With swivel waist:	
5½-6in (14-15cm)	**$5,000****
With jointed knee:	
8in (20cm)	**$5,000-$5,500**
#102 (so-called "Wrestler"):	
5-1/2in (14cm)	**$1,500-$1,800**
8½-9in (22-23cm)	**$3,000-$3,500**
#120 (Bru-type face):	
8½in (22cm)	**$3,200-$3,600**
Bare feet:	
5½-6in (14-15cm)	**$2,000-$2,250**
8in (20cm)	**$3,000-$3,500**
12in (31cm)	**$5,000****
Round face, bootines:	
6in (15cm)	**$1,250-$1,350**

8in (20cm)   **$1,850-$2,100**
Long black stockings, tan slippers:
7½in (19cm)   **$1,050-$1,250**

Simon & Halbig 886 and **890:** See page 188.
*Allow $100-$150 extra for yellow boots or unusual footwear.
**Not enough price samples to compute a reliable average.

All-Bisque Baby: Ca. 1900-on. Jointed at shoulders and hips, curved arms and legs, molded hair, painted features; all in good condition, with proper parts.

2½-3½in (6-9cm)   **$75-$95**
4-5in (10-13cm)   **$125-$175**
Fine early quality, blonde molded hair:
3½-4½in (9-11cm)   **$160-$185**
6-7in (15-18cm)   **$250-$300**
13in (33cm)   **$900-$1,000**
Immobile:
5-6in (13-15cm)   **$160-$195**

All-Bisque Character Baby: Ca. 1910. Jointed at shoulders and hips, curved arms and legs; molded hair, painted eyes, all in good condition, with proper parts, very good quality.

3½in (9cm)   **$95-$110**
4½-5½in (11-14cm)   **$175-$225**
7in (18cm)   **$275-$325**
8in (20cm)   **$375-$425**

Mark: Some with "Germany" and/or numbers; some with paper labels on stomachs.

8in (20cm) early all-bisque with stiff hips and shirred hose. *H & J Foulke, Inc.*

4¼in unmarked all-bisque with stationary neck. *H & J Foulke, Inc.*

FACTS

Various firms including Hertwig; Alt, Beck & Gottschalkck; Kestner; Kling; Simon & Halbig; Hertel, Schwab & Co.; Bähr & Pröschild; Limbach; Ca. 1880-on.

6in (15cm) early Simon & Halbig. Prices are on page 26. *H & J Foulke, Inc.*

#830, #391, and others with glass eyes:

4-5in (10-13cm)	**$275-$325**
6in (15cm)	**$400-$450**
8in (20cm)	**$600-$650**
11in (28cm)	**$850-$950**

Swivel neck, glass eyes:

6in (15cm)	**$625-$675**
8in (20cm)	**$800-$850**
10in (25cm)	**$1,000-$1,100**

Swivel neck, painted eyes:

5-6in (13-15cm)	**$325-$375**
8in (20cm)	**$575-$625**
11in (28cm)	**$800-$900**

Mildred, the Prize Baby:

5in (13cm) at auction	**$4,600**

Baby Darling #497:

6in (15cm)	**$850**

Limbach (clover mark):

4-5in (10-13cm)	**$55-$85**
7in (18cm)	**$110-$135**
11-12in (28-31cm) fine quality	**$550-$650**

All-Bisque Character Dolls with Glass Eyes: Ca. 1910. Excellent quality with proper parts.

#150, 155, 156:

5-6in (13-15cm)	**$400-$500**
7in (18cm)	**$650**

#602, swivel neck:

5½-6in (14-15cm)	**$550-$650**

#79, pierced nose:

4½in (12cm)	**$500**

#609, 22

4½in (12cm)	**$425-$450**

All-Bisque Character Dolls: 1913-on. Painted eyes; all in good condition with proper parts.

Pink bisque:

2-3in (5-8cm)	**$50-$60**
5in (13cm)	**$95**

9in (23cm) early Kestner. Prices are on page 26. *H & J Foulke, Inc.*

Glass eyes, wig:

2¾in (7cm)	**$85-$95**

Thumbsucker:

3in (8cm)	**$225-$250**

Girl with molded hair bow loop:

2½in (6cm)	**$65-$75**

Chubby:

4½in (11cm)	**$210-$240**
6in (15cm)	**$325-$375**

HEbee, SHEbee:

5in (13cm)	**$600**
7in (18cm)	**$800**

Peeterkin:

5-6in (13-15cm)	**$275-$375**

Little Imp:

5in (13cm)	**$125-$150**

Orsini girls, Glass eyes:

5in (13cm)	**$1,500-$1,700**

Painted eyes:

5in (13cm)	**$900-$1,100**

Happifats:

4in (10cm) boy and girl	**$500-$600 pair**

Happifats Baby:

3¾in (10cm)	**$275-$300**

Wide Awake:

5in (13cm)	**$225**

Little Annie Rooney:

4in (10cm)	**$300**

September Morn, Grace Drayton:

7in (18cm) at auction	**$4,000**

Max-Moritz:

3¾in (9cm)	**$1,750 pair**
4½in (11cm) molded	
clothes	**$2,300 pair**

#222 Our Fairy, glass eyes:

5in (13cm)	**$650-$700**
8½in (22cm)	**$875-$900**
11in (28cm)	**$1,800**

#790, 791, 792:

5½-6in (14-15cm)	**$450-$500**

#160:

5-1/2-6in (14-15cm)	**$300-$350**

Later All-Bisque with painted eyes: Ca. 1920. Many by Limbach (clover mark) and Hertwig; some of pretinted bisque; mohair wig or molded hair, molded and painted one-strap shoes and white stockings; all in good condition, with proper parts.

3½in (9cm)	**$70-$80**
4½-5in (12-13cm)	**$100-$110**
6in (15cm)	**$160-$185**
7-8in (18-20cm)	**$225-$250**

All-Bisque "Flapper" (tinted bisque): Ca. 1920. Molded bobbed hair with loop for bow, painted features; long yellow

6in (15cm) 830 all-bisque character baby, all original. *H & J Foulke, Inc.*

4-1/2in (11cm) 22/10 all-bisque toddler. *H & J Foulke, Inc.*

5in (13cm) all-bisque Orsini *DiDi.* *H & J Foulke, Inc.*

3¾in (9cm) *Max & Moritz,* all original. *H & J Foulke, Inc.*

stockings, one-strap shoes with heels; all in good condition, with proper parts, very good quality.

5in (13cm)	**$300-$325**
6-7in (15-18cm)	**$400-$450**

Standard quality:

4-5in (10-13cm)	**$135-$165**

All-Bisque Baby: Ca. 1920. Pink bisque, curved arms and legs; all in good condition, with proper parts.
Candy Baby, original factory clothes:

2½in-3in (6-8cm)	**$85-$95**

2-face, swivel neck:

4in (10cm)	**$150-$175**

All-Bisque "Flapper:" Ca. 1920. Pink bisque with molded bobbed hair; original factory clothes, all in good condition, with proper parts.

3in (8cm)	**$75-$95**
Molded hats	**$225-$250**
Molded bunny ears cap	**$350**
Aviatrix	**$225-$250**

Swivel waist:

3½in (9cm)	**$350**

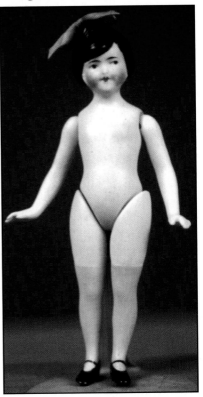

6¼in (16cm) tinted bisque "flapper" with molded hair. *H & J Foulke, Inc.*

All-Bisque Nodder Characters: Ca. 1920-on. Many made by Hertwig & Co. Nodding heads, elastic strung, molded clothes; all in good condition.

3-4in (8-10cm)	**$35-$50**
Comic characters	**$45 up***
Dressed Animals	**$150-$175**
Dressed Teddy Bears	**$200-$225**
Santa	**$200-$225**

Dutch Girl:

6in (15cm)	**$150-$165**

All-Bisque Immobiles: Ca. 1920. Molded clothes, in good condition.

Adults and **children:**

1½-2¼in (4-6cm)	**$35-$45**

Children:

3¼in (8cm)	**$55-$65**

Santa:

3in (8cm)	**$125-$135**

Children with animals on string:

3in (8cm)	**$165-$185**

Jointed Animals: Ca. 1910-on. All-bisque animals, wire-jointed shoulders and hips; original crocheted clothes, in good condition.
Rabbit:

2-2¾in (5-7cm)	**$475-$525**

Bear:

2-2½in (5-6cm)	**$450-$500**
Frog, Monkey, Pig	**$600-$700**

Bear on all fours:

3¼in (8cm)	**$225-$275**

*Depending on rarity.

ALL-BISQUE DOLLS
MADE IN JAPAN

Baby:

White, 4in (10cm)	$30-$33
All original elaborate outfit	$50-$65
Two-face, crying and sleeping	$150-$175
Black, 4-5in (10-13cm)	$55-$65

Betty Boop-type:

4-5in (10-13cm)	$20-$25
6-7in (15-18cm)	$32-$38

Black Character Girl:

Molded hair bow loop:

4½in (12cm)	$40-$50

Bride & Groom, boxed set:

4in (10cm)	$70-$75

Buster Brown:

2¾in (7cm)	$40

Child:

4-5in (10-13cm)	$32-$35
6-7in (15-18cm)	$40-$50

With animal on string:

4½in (12cm)	$38-$42

Cho-Cho San:

4½in (12cm)	$70-80

Circus Set, boxed:

11 pieces	$150-$175

Comic Characters:

3-4in (8-10cm)	$30 up*
Mickey Mouse	$175-$225

"Nippon" Characters

4-5in (10-13cm)	$85-$95

Nodders:

4in (10cm)	$25-$35

Old Woman in Shoe:

Boxed set	$225-$250

Orientals:

3-4in (8-10cm)	$20-$25

Queue San:

4in (10cm)	$70-$80

Shirley Temple:

5in (13cm)	$95-$110

Skippy:

5½in (14cm)	$75-$100

Snow White:

Boxed set	$350-$450

Stiff Characters:

3-4in (8-10cm)	$5-$10
6-7in (15-18cm)	$30-$35

Teddy Bear:

3in (8cm)	$40-$50

Three Bears:

Boxed set	$250-$300

Three Little Pigs $40-$50 each

Wedding Set, boxed, 3 pieces:

4½in (13cm)	$125-$135

*Depending upon rarity.

FACTS
Various Japanese firms. Ca. 1915-on.
Mark: "Made in Japan" or
"NIPPON."

6in (15cm) Made in Japan all-bisque baby. *H & J Foulke, Inc.*

ALT, BECK & GOTTSCHALCK

China Shoulder Heads: Ca. 1880. Black or blonde-haired china head; old cloth body with china limbs; dressed; all in good condition. Mold numbers such as 784, 1000, 1008, 1028, 1046, 1142, 1210 and others.

Mark: *1008 ✕ 9*

16-18in (41-46cm)	**$350-$400**
22-24in (56-61cm)	**$475-$525**
28in (71cm)	**$600-$650**

Bisque Shoulder Head: Ca. 1880. Molded hair, closed mouth; cloth body with bisque lower limbs; dressed; all in good condition. Mold numbers such as 890, 990, 1000, 1008, 1028, 1064, 1142, 1254, 1288, 1304.

Painted eyes:

15-17in (38-43cm)	**$425-$475**
22-23in (56-58cm)	**$575-$625**

Glass eyes:

14-16in (36-41cm)	**$600-$700***
22in (56cm)	**$1,100***

#926, molded pink and white scarf on head:

16in (41cm)	**$2,000**

#990, pink mob cap, #998, white mob cap:

20in (51cm)	**$850-$950**

#894, blue scarf, glass eyes:

21in (52cm)	**$1,650-$1,750**

#1024, molded orange bonnet:

17½in (44cm)	**$2,100**

*Allow extra for unusual or elaborate hairdo or molded hat.

FACTS

Alt, Beck & Gottschalck, porcelain factory, Nauendorf near Ohrdruf, Thüringia, Germany. 1854-on.

25in (64cm) unmarked china shoulder head, 784-type mold, unusual brown eyes. *H & J Foulke, Inc.*

18½in (42cm) unmarked ABG-type bisque shoulder head with molded hat. *H & J Foulke, Inc.*

6in (15cm) all-bisque 83/100 girl. *H & J Foulke, Inc.*

#1022, short blonde curly hair, molded blue hairband, molded necklace with orange pendant, glass eyes:

22in (56cm)	**$1,650**

Bisque Shoulder Head: Ca. 1885-on. Turned shoulder head, wig, glass eyes, closed mouth; kid or cloth body; dressed; all in good condition. Mold numbers, such as **639, 698, 1032, 1123, 1235.**

Mark:

639 ⅍ 6

with DEP after 1888

17-19in (43-48cm)	**$750-$850**
23-25in (58-64cm)	**$1,100-$1,200**
With open mouth:	
16-18in (41-46cm)	**$475-$525**
21-23in (53-58cm)	**$600-$675**

#911, 916, swivel neck, closed mouth:

20-23in (51-58cm)	**$1,500-$1,650**
#912:	
21-23in (53-58cm)	**$1,400-$1,500**

Child Doll: Perfect bisque head; open mouth; ball-jointed body; all in good condition; appropriate clothes.

Mark:

2 ½
A B & G
Made in Germany

#1362 Sweet Nell*:

14-16in (36-41cm)	**$425-$475**
19-21in (43-53cm)	**$525-$550**
23-25in (58-64cm)	**$650-$750**
29-30in (74-76cm)	**$1,000-$1,100**
36in (91cm)	**$1,600-$1,700**

*Allow 10-15% extra for Flapper body.

#630, closed mouth:

23in (58cm)	**$1,900-$2,200**
#911, closed mouth:	
16in (41cm)	**$1,500-$1,600**
#938, closed mouth:	
20in (51cm) at auction	**$4,500**

All-Bisque Girl: 1911, Chubby body, molded white stockings, blue garters, black Mary Janes.

Mold #83 over **#100, 125, 150,** or **225:**

5-6in (13-15cm)	**$225-$250***
7in (18cm)	**$300-$325***
8in (20cm)	**$450-$475***

All-Bisque Baby:

8½in (21cm) swivel

   neck   **$850-$900****

**Not enough price examples to compute a reliable average.

*Allow extra for real eyelashes.

Character: Ca. 1910-on. Perfect bisque head, good wig, sleep eyes, open mouth; some with open nostrils; composition body; all in good condition; suitable clothes.

Mark:

#1322, 1352, 1361:

10-12in (25-31cm) **$400-$450***

16-18in (41-46cm) **$575-$625***

22-23in (56-58cm) **$850-$900***

Toddler:

10in (25cm) 5-piece body **$750-$800**

14-16in (36-41cm) **$900-$1,000**

#1357

16-18in (46-51cm) **$1,250-$1,500**

#1407 Baby BoKaye:

8in (20cm) **$1,350-$1,500**

#1431 Orsini, earthenware baby:

24in (61cm) **$900-$1,100**

#1450, smiling girl:

14in (36cm) **$14,000-$15,000**

*Allow $50 extra for flirty eyes.

10in (25cm) 1361 Toddler, all original. *H & J Foulke, Inc.*

LOUIS AMBERG & SON

Newborn Babe, Bottle Babe, My Playmate: Ca. 1914-on. Perfect bisque head, painted hair, sleep eyes, soft cloth body; appropriate clothes; all in good condition. Mold 886 by Recknagel. Mold 371 with open mouth by Marseille.

Mark:

L·A·&·S·
371·3/0 D·R·G·M·
Germany

THE ORIGINAL
NEWBORN BABE
(C) Jan 9th 1914 - No. G 45520
AMBERG DOLLS
The World Standard

Length:

9-10in (23-25cm)	**$375-$425**
13-14in (33-36cm)	**$500-$600**
17in (43cm)	**$700-$750**

Bottle Babe, all original with playpen:

7in (18cm) **$425-$450**

Charlie Chaplin: 1915. Composition portrait head molded mustache; straw-filled cloth body with composition hands; original clothes; all in good condition with wear.

Mark: cloth label on sleeve:

14in (36cm) **$600-$650**

Mibs: 1921. Composition shoulder head designed by Hazel Drucker with wistful expression, molded blonde or reddish hair; cloth body with composition arms and legs with painted shoes and socks; appropriate old clothes; all in good condition.

Mark: None on doll; paper label only:

"Amberg Dolls
Please Love Me
I'm Mibs"

16in (41cm) **$950-$1,050**

Baby Peggy: 1923. Composition head, molded brown bobbed hair, smiling closed mouth; appropriately dressed; all in good condition.

20in (51cm) **$650-$750****

Baby Peggy: 1924. Perfect bisque head by Armand Marseille with character face; brown bobbed mohair wig,

---

FACTS

Louis Amberg & Son, New York, N.Y., U.S.A. 1907-on.

8½in (22cm) long 886 *My Playmate* baby, all original. *H & J Foulke, Inc.*

brown sleep eyes, closed mouth; composition or kid body, fully-jointed; dressed or undressed; all in very good condition.

Mark:

"19 © 24"
LA & S NY
Germany
—50—
982/2"

#982 or 983 shoulder head:
  20in (51cm)   **$1,800-$2,000**

#972 or 973 socket head:
  18-22in (46-56cm)   **$2,200-$2,500**

**Not enough price samples to compute a reliable range.

All-Bisque Character Children: 1920s. Made by a German porcelain factory; pink pretinted bisque.

4in (10cm)	**$125**
5-6in (13-15cm)	**$160-$185**

Girl with molded bow:

6in (15cm)	**$375-$425**

Girl with downward gaze, glass eyes, wig:

5½in (14cm)	**$475-$525**
7in (18cm)	**$600-$650**

Mibs:

3in (8cm)	**$300-$325**
4¾in (12cm)	**$400-$425**
6in (15cm)	**$575**

Baby Peggy:

3in (8cm)	**$325-$350**
5½in (14cm)	**$500-$550**
4½in (12cm) wigged	**$475-$525**

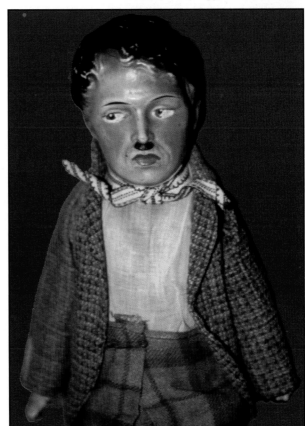

14in (36cm)
Charlie Chaplin,
all original.
H & J Foulke, Inc.

7in (18cm) all-bisque girl with molded hairbow. *H & J Foulke, Inc.*

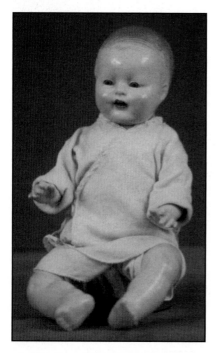

Mibs-type girl with molded flowers in hair:
    4¾in (12cm)   **$225**

Vanta Baby: 1927. A tie-in with Vanta baby garments. Composition or bisque head with molded and painted hair, sleep eyes, open mouth with two teeth, suitably dressed; all in good condition.
Mark: Bisque Head

√anta Baby
L ABS · ³⁄₀ D·R·G·M·
Germany.

Bisque head:
    20-22in (51-56cm)   **$1,100-$1,250**
Composition head:
    18-20in (46-51cm)   **$325-$375**

Sue, Edwina or **It:** 1928. All-composition with round ball joint at waist, appropriate clothes.
    14in (36cm)   **$475-$525**

Tiny Tots Body Twists: 1928. All-composition with large round ball joint at the waist.
    8in (20cm)   **$165-$195**
    All original with paper label,
        at auction   **$420**

Sunny Orange Maid: 1924. Composition/cloth. Molded "orange" hat, orange dress.
    14in (36cm)   **$750****
****Not enough price samples to compute a reliable average.

16in (41cm) *Vanta Baby* with composition head. *H & J Foulke, Inc.*

GEORGENE AVERILL
(MADAME HENDREN & GEORGENE NOVELTIES, INC.)

Bonnie Babe: 1926. Bisque heads by Alt, Beck & Gottschalck; cloth bodies by K & K Toy Co.; distributed by George Borgfeldt, New York. Perfect bisque head with smiling face, open mouth with two lower teeth; cloth body with composition arms (sometimes celluloid) and legs often of poor quality; all in good condition. Mold #1386 or 1402.

Mark:

Copr. by Georgene Averill Germany 1005/3652 1386

Length:

12-13in (31-33cm)	$1,000-$1,100
16-18in (41-46cm)	$1,400-$1,600
22-23in (56-58cm)	$1,800-$1,900

Composition body:

8in (20cm) tall	$1,250**

Celluloid head:

16in (41cm) tall	$550-$650**

All-Bisque Bonnie Babe: 1926.

5in (13cm)	$750-$850
7in (18cm)	$1,100-$1,200

Sunny Boy and Girl: Ca. 1927. Celluloid "turtle" mark head; stuffed body with composition arms and legs; appropriate or original clothes; all in good condition.

15in (38cm)	$425-$500

**Not enough price samples to compute a reliable range.

FACTS

Averill Mfg. Co. and Georgene Novelties, Inc., New York, N.Y. U.S.A. 1915-on.
Designer: Georgene Averill.
Trademarks: Madame Hendren, Georgene Novelties.

5½in (14cm) all-bisque *Bonnie Babe* with label. *H & J Foulke, Inc.*

Composition Dolls: All appropriately dressed in good condition.

Mme. Hendren Character: Ca. 1915-on. Original tagged felt costume, including Dutch children, Indians, cowboys, sailors:

    10-14in (25-36cm)　　**$150-$200**

Mama and Baby Dolls: Ca. 1918-on. Composition with cloth bodies, names such as Baby Hendren and Baby Georgene:

    15-18in (38-46cm)　　**$250-$300**

    22-24in (56-61cm)　　**$400-$450**

Dolly Reckord: 1922. Record-playing mechanism in torso, with records:

    26in (66cm)　　**$600-$700**

Grace Drayton: 1920s. Black Chocolate Drop with yarn pigtails:

    14in (36cm)　　**$575**

Whistling Doll: 1925-1929. Doll whistles when feet are pushed up or head is pushed down.

Dan, sailor or cowboy:

    14-15in (36-38cm)　　**$300-$350**

Black Rufus or **Dolly Dingle** **$450-$475**

Little Brother and **Little Sister:** 1927. Grace Corry (Rockwell):

    14in (36cm)　　**$450-$500**

Snookums: 1927.

    14in (36cm)　　**$350-$375**

Body Twists: 1927. Dimmie and Jimmie with a large round ball joint at waist:

    14½in (37cm)　　**$475-$525**

Patsy-type Girl: 1928.

    14in (36cm)　　**$325-$350**

    17-18in (43-46cm)　　**$400-$450**

Lenci-type Girl: Ca. 1930. Lenci-style, composition face, original felt and organdy clothes:

    19in (48cm)　　**$400-$500**

Little Cherub: 1937. Designed by Harriet Flanders.

    16in (41cm)　　**$300-$350**

    12in (31cm) painted eyes **$200-$250**

17in (43cm) *Madame Hendren* infant with composition head. *H & J Foulke, Inc.*

12in (31cm) cloth Grace Drayton *Chocolate Drop,* all original. *H & J Foulke, Inc.*

19in (48cm) vinyl and cloth *Baby Dawn,* all original. *H & J Foulke, Inc.*

Cloth Dolls: Original clothes; all in excellent condition, clean with bright color.

Children or Babies:

12in (31cm)	**$125-$150**
24-26in (61-66cm)	**225-$275**

Girl Scout:

13½in (35cm)	**$250-$275**

Brownie:

13½in (35cm)	**$250-$275**

International and Costume Dolls:

12in (31cm)	**$90-$100**
Mint in box with wrist tag	**$115-$135**

Becassine, mint in box:

13in (33cm) at auction	**$925**

Uncle Wiggily or Nurse Jane:

18-20in (46-51cm)	**$575-$650**

Characters, 14in (36cm):

Little Lulu	**$500**
Nancy, boxed	**$850**
Sluggo, boxed	**$775**
Tubby Tom, boxed	**$800**

Characters, 10in (25cm):

Topsy & Eva	**$175-$200**

Maud Tousey Fangel, 1938. Snooks, Sweets, Peggy-Ann. Marked "M.T.F." Bright color, all original.

12-14in (31-36cm)	**$600-$700**
17in (43cm)	**$850-$900**
22in (56cm)	**$1,100-$1,250**

Grace G. Drayton: good clean condition, some wear acceptable.

Chocolate Drop, 1923. Brown cloth with three yarn pigtails:

11in (28cm)	**$450-$500**
16in (41cm)	**$750-$850**

Dolly Dingle, 1923:

11in (28cm)	**$400-$450**
16in (41cm)	**$600-$650**
10in (25cm) double face	**$750**

Vinyl Dolls:

Baby Dawn, Ca. 1950. Vinyl and cloth, all original and excellent.

19in (48cm)	**$350**

BABY BO KAYE

Baby Bo Kaye: Perfect bisque head with flange neck marked as below; molded hair, glass eyes, open mouth with two lower teeth; cloth torso with composition limbs; dressed; all in good condition.

    16-19in (41-48cm)   **$2,400-$2,800**
Celluloid head:
    16in (41cm)   **$750**
#1407 (ABG) bisque head, composition body:
    7½in (19cm)   **$1,350-$1,500**

All-Bisque Baby Bo Kaye: Molded hair, glass sleep eyes, open mouth with two teeth; swivel neck, jointed shoulders and hips; molded pink or blue shoes and socks; unmarked but may have sticker on torso.

    5in (13cm)   **$1,400-$1,500**
    6in (15cm)   **$1,800-$1,900**

FACTS
Bisque heads made in Germany by Alt, Beck & Gottschalck; bodies by K & K Toy Co., New York, N.Y. U.S.A. 1925.
Designer: J.L. Kallus.
Distributor: George Borgfeldt Co., N.Y.
Mark: "Copr. by J.L. Kallus Germany 1394/30"

8½in (21cm) ABG 1407 ***Baby Bo Kaye.*** *H & J Foulke, Inc.*

BABYLAND RAG

Babyland Rag: Cloth face with hand-painted features, sometimes mohair wig; cloth body jointed at shoulders and hips; original clothes.

Early face:
　13-15in (33-38cm)
　　Very good　　$750-$850*
　　Fair　　　　$400-$500
　22in (56cm)
　　Very good　$1,000-$1,200*
　　Fair　　　　$550-$600
　30in (76cm)
　　Very good　$2,000-$2,200
Topsy Turvey:
　13-15in (33-38cm)
　　Very good　　$700-$800*
Buster Brown:
　30in (76cm)
　　Very good　　　$2,200
Black:
　15in (38cm)
　　Fair　　　　$650-$700*
　20-22in (51-56cm)
　　Very good　$1,200-$1,400
Life-like face (printed features):
　13-15in (33-38cm)
　　Very good　　$600-$650*

Topsy Turvey:
　14in (36cm)
　　Good　　　　$700-$800*
Babyland Rag-type (lesser quality):
　14in (36cm) White
　　Good　　　　$375-$475
Brückner Rag Doll:
Mark:

PAT'D. JULY 8ᵀᴴ 1901

Stiffened mask face, cloth body, flexible shoulders and hips; appropriate clothes; all in good condition.
　12-14in (31-36cm)
　　White　　　　$210-$235
　　Black　　　　$275-$300
　　Topsy Turvy　$500-$550
　　Dollypop　　　$250**

*Allow more for mint condition doll.
**Not enough price samples to compute a reliable range.

FACTS
E. I. Horsman, New York, NY., U.S.A. Some dolls made for Horsman by Albert Brückner. 1901-on.
Mark: None

21in (53cm) black *Babyland Rag Dinah* with handpainted face. *H & J Foulke, Inc.*

BÄHR & PRÖSCHILD

17in (43cm) 204 Belton-type child with closed mouth. *H & J Foulke, Inc.*

23in (58cm) 289 child with open mouth. *H & J Foulke, Inc.*

Marked Belton-type Child Doll: Ca. 1880. Perfect bisque head, solid dome with flat top having two or three small holes, paperweight eyes, closed mouth with pierced ears; wood and composition jointed body with straight wrists; dressed; all in good condition. Mold numbers in **200** series.

Mark: 204

12-14in (30-36cm)	**$1,750-$2,000**
18-20in (46-51cm)	**$2,500-$2,800**
24in (61cm)	**$3,600**

Marked Child Doll: Ca. 1888-on. Perfect bisque socket head, set or sleeping eyes, open mouth with four or six upper teeth, good human hair or mohair wig; jointed composition body (many of French-type); dressed; all in good condition. Mold numbers in **200** and **300** series.

Mark: 224
      dep

#204, 239, 273, 275, 277, 289, 297, 300, 325, 340, 379, 394 and other socket heads:

12-13in (30-33cm)	**$600-$700**
16-18in (41-46cm)	**$800-$900**
22-24in (56-61cm)	**$1,150-$1,250**

#224 (dimples):

14-16in (36-41cm)	**$875-$925**
22-24in (56-61cm)	**$1,250-$1,500**

#246, 309 and other shoulder heads on kid bodies:

16-18in (41-46cm)	**$525-$575**
22-24in (56-61cm)	**$675-$725**

#302, 325, swivel neck, kid body:

17in (43cm)	**$650-$675**
20in (51cm)	**$750-$800**

All-Bisque Girl, yellow stockings (Heart mark):

5in (13cm)	**$325-$350**
7in (18cm)	**$450**

#513, possibly by **B.P.:**

22-26in (56-66cm)	**$850-$900**

Marked B.P. Character Baby: Ca. 1910-on. Perfect bisque socket head, solid dome or good wig, sleep eyes, open mouth; composition bent-limb baby body; dressed; all in good condition. Mold #585, 604, 624, 678, 619, 620 and 587.

Mark:

585
5
B&P
Germany

10-12in (25-31cm)	**$400-$500**
15-17in (36-43cm)	**$650-$750**
20-21in (51-53cm)	**$800-$900**

Toddler, fully jointed body:

12-13in (31-33cm)	**$950-$1,150**
22in (56cm)	**$1,650**

Toddler, 5-piece body:

10-12in (25-31cm)	**$675-$750**
14in (36cm)	**$850-$950**

#425, All-bisque baby:

5½-6in (13-15cm)	**$250-$300**

#642, Character child

17in (43cm) at auction	**$2,700**

FACTS

Bähr & Pröschild, porcelain factory, Ohrdruf, Thüringia, Germany. Made heads for Bruno Schmidt, Heinrich Stier, Kley & Hahn and others. 1871-on.

12in (31cm) **585** character toddler. *H & J Foulke, Inc.*

BELTON-TYPE
(SO-CALLED)

17in (43cm) Belton-type girl with German-style face. *H & J Foulke, Inc.*

Belton-type Child Doll: Perfect bisque socket head, solid but flat top with two or three small holes for stringing; paper-weight eyes, closed mouth, pierced ears; wood and composition ball-jointed body with straight wrists; dressed; all in good condition.

TR 809:

17in (43cm)	**$1,600-$1,650**

Bru-type face:

12-14in (30-35cm)	**$2,500-$2,700**

Fine early quality, French-type face (some mold #137 or #183):

13-15in (33-38cm)	**$2,400-$2,700**
18-20in (46-51cm)	**$3,100-$3,400**
22-24in (56-61cm)	**$3,600-$4,000**

Good quality, German-type face:

12in (31cm)	**$1,250-$1,450**
15-17in (38-43cm)	**$1,600-$1,800**
20in (51cm)	**$2,200-$2,400**

Tiny with 5-piece body (pretty):

8-9in (20-23cm)	**$850-$950**

#200 Series, see **Bähr & Pröschild**, page 44.

FACTS
Various German firms, such as Bähr & Pröschild. 1875-on.
Mark: None, except sometimes numbers.

16in (41cm) 137 Belton-type girl with French-style face. *Private Collection.*

C. M. BERGMANN

Bergmann Child Doll: Ca. 1889-on. Marked bisque head, composition ball-jointed body, good wig, sleep or set eyes, open mouth; dressed; all in nice condition. Heads by **A.M.** and unknown makers:

10in (25cm)	**$400**
14-16in (36-41cm)	**$375-$425**
20in (51cm)	**$475-$525**
23-24in (58-61cm)	**$550**
28-29in (71-74cm)	**$700-$800**
32-33in (81-84cm)	**$1,100-$1,200**
35-36in (89-91cm)	**$1,400-$1,600**
39-42in (99-111cm)	**$2,200-$2,600**

Heads by **Simon & Halbig:**

10in (25cm)	**$500-$600**
13-15in (33-38cm)	**$400-$450**
18-20in (46-51cm)	**$525-$575**
23-24in (58-61cm)	**$650-$700**
29-30in (81-91cm)	**$1,000-$1,100**
35-36in (81-91cm)	**$1,600-$1,800**
39in (99cm)	**$2,500**

Eleonore:

25in (64cm)	**$800-$900**
24in (61cm) all original, boxed	**$1,200**

#612 Character Baby, open closed mouth:
    14-16in (36-41cm)   **$2,200-$2,400**

#B4 Character Toddler:
    12in (31cm)   **$950**

FACTS

C. M. Bergmann doll factory of Waltershausen, Thüringia, Germany; heads manufactured for this company by Armand Marseille, Simon & Halbig, Alt, Beck & Gottschalck and perhaps others. 1888-on.
Distributor: Louis Wolfe & Co., New York
Trademarks: Cinderella Baby (1897), Columbia (1904), My Gold Star (1926).
Mark: CM BERGMANN
A-41-M·
Made in Germany

C. M. Bergmann
Waftershausen
Germany
1916
6½a

20in (51cm) S & H/Bergmann with 550-mold face. *H & J Foulke, Inc.*

12in (31cm) B4 Goebel/Bergmann character toddler. *H & J Foulke, Inc.*

BISQUE
ENGLISH

English Bisque Doll: Perfect bisque socket or shoulder head model, glass or painted eyes, molded hair or wigged; cloth or composition body; appropriate clothing; all in good condition.

12in (31cm)	**$200-$300***
18-20in (46-51cm)	**$300-$350***

*Allow extra for especially pretty doll with glass eyes on a composition body.

FACTS

Various porcelain factories, such as Nottingham Toy Industry, Ltd., Nottingham; Doll Pottery Co., Goss & Co., and S. Hancock & Sons, Stoke-on-Trent as well as others. Ca. 1914-on.

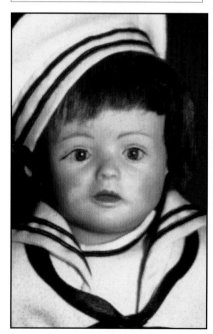

12in (31cm) NTI Boy, 5 piece composition body. *Rhoda Shoemaker Collection.*

BISQUE
FRENCH

(Unmarked or Unidentified Marks and Unlisted Small Factories)

Marked A.L. Bébé: Ca. 1875. Possibly Alexander Lefebvre & Cie. Perfect pressed bisque socket head, closed mouth, paperweight eyes; French wood and composition jointed body; appropriate clothing; all in good condition.

22in (56cm) at auction	**$35,000**

Marked B.M. Bébé: 1880-1895. Alexandre Mothereau. Perfect pressed bisque socket head, closed mouth, paperweight eyes; French wood and composition jointed body; appropriate clothing; all in good condition.

16in (41cm)	**$15,000-$18,000****
27-29in (69-74cm)	**$25,000****

Marked C.P. Bébé: Ca. 1875. Possibly Pannier. Perfect pressed bisque socket head, closed mouth, paperweight eyes; French wood and composition body; appropriate clothing; all in good condition.

20in (51cm) at auction	**$58,500**

Marked H Bébé: Ca. late 1870s. Possibly by A. Halopeau. Perfect pressed bisque socket head of fine quality, paperweight eyes, pierced ears, closed mouth, cork pate, good wig; French wood and composition jointed body with straight wrists; appropriate clothing; all in excellent condition.

Mark:

2 • H

Size:	
	0 = 16-1/2in (42cm)
	2 = 19in (48cm)
	3 = 21in (56cm)
	4 = 24in (61cm)

21-24in (53-61cm) **$65,000-$75,000**

Huret Child: Ca. 1878. Maison Huret. Perfect bisque head; appropriate clothing; all in excellent condition. Gutta-percha body:

18in (46cm)	**$70,000-$80,000**
Wood body, 18in (46cm)	**$34,000**

Marked J. Bébé: Ca. 1880s. Joseph Louis Joanny. Perfect pressed bisque socket head, paperweight eyes; closed mouth; French wood and composition body; appropriate clothing; all in good condition.

15-16in (38-41cm)	**$5,000-$6,000**
22in (56cm)	**$7,500-$8,500**

Marked J.M. Bébé: Ca. 1880s. Perfect pressed bisque socket head, paperweight eyes, closed mouth, pierced ears, good wig; French composition and wood body; appropriate clothing; all in good condition.

Mark:

5

♂ ♀ ♏

13in (33cm) at auction	**$7,500**
19-21in (48-53cm)	**$20,000****

Marked M. Bébé: Mid 1890s. Perfect bisque socket head, closed mouth, paperweight eyes, pierced ears, good wig; French jointed composition and wood body; appropriate clothing; all in good condition. Some dolls with this mark may be **Bébé Mascottes.**

Mark:

M

4

18-21in (46-53cm)	**$3,500-$4,000**

Marked Bébé Mascotte: 1890-97, May Freres Cie; 1898-on Jules Nicholas Steiner. Perfect bisque socket head, closed mouth, paperweight eyes; pierced ears; jointed composition and wood body; appropriate clothing; all in good condition.

11-12in (28-31cm)	**$2,250-$2,500**
17-19in (42-48cm)	**$3,800-$4,000**
24-26in (61-66cm)	**$5,300-$5,800**

**Not enough price samples to compute a reliable average.

23in (58cm) *Bébé Mascotte. Private Collection*

Marked P.G. Bébé: Ca. 1880-1899. Pintel & Godchaux, Montreuil, France. Perfect bisque socket head, paperweight eyes, closed mouth, good wig; jointed French composition and wood body; appropriate clothing; all in good condition.

Trademark: Bébé Charmant
Mark:

B	A
P9G	P7G

20-22in (51-56cm)	**$3,000-$3,200**
Open mouth:	
18-20in (46-51cm)	**$1,600-$1,800**

Marked PAN Bébé: Ca. 1887. Henri Delcroix, Paris and Montreuil-sous-Bois (porcelain factory). Perfect bisque socket head, paperweight eyes, closed mouth, pierced ears, good wig; French composition and wood body; appropriate clothes; all in good condition.

Mark:

PAN
2

Size:	2 = 12in (31cm)
	10 = 27in (68cm)
	11 = 28½in (72cm)

29in (74cm) at auction   **$16,500**

Unmarked Bébé: Ca. 1880-1890. Perfect bisque socket head, paperweight eyes; closed mouth; jointed French composition and wood body; appropriate clothing; all in good condition.

Jumeau quality:	
12-14in (31-36cm)	**$3,100-$3,400**
20-22in (51-56cm)	**$4,400-$4,600**

*For lady and fashion dolls *(poupées)* see pages 87-88.

22in (56cm) J Bébé.
Kay & Wayne
Jensen Collection.

BISQUE
GERMAN
(Unmarked or Unidentified Marks and Unlisted Small Factories)

Shoulder head with molded hair: Ca. 1880. Tinted bisque shoulder head with beautifully molded hair (usually blonde), closed mouth; original kid or cloth body; bisque lower arms; appropriate clothes; all in good condition.

American Schoolboy:

12-14in (31-36cm)	**$550-$650**
17-20in (43-51cm)	**$750-850**

Composition body:

11-12in (28-31cm)	**$650-$750**

Boy or girl, painted eyes:

14-16in (36-41cm)	**$300-$350**

Boy or girl, glass eyes:

16in (41cm)	**$700-$750**

Lady, painted eyes:

12-14in (31-36cm)	**$325-$375**

bisque arms and legs; good old clothes or nicely dressed; all in good condition.

Standard quality:

8-9in (20-23cm)	**$210-$265**
11-13in (28-33cm)	**$325-$375**
15in (38cm)	**$450**

Fine quality:

18-22in (46-56cm)	**$1,000 up***

All bisque:

4½in (12cm)	**$175-$195***
7in (18cm)	**$250-$300***

*Allow extra for unusual style.

Doll House Doll: Ca. 1890-1920. Man or lady bisque shoulder head; cloth body, bisque lower limbs; original clothes or suitably dressed; all in nice condition.

Hatted or Bonnet Doll: Ca. 1880-1920. Bisque shoulder head, molded bonnet; original cloth body with

11in (28cm) hatted bisque with molded butterfly bonnet. *H & J Foulke, Inc.*

5in (13cm) 1920s doll house maid, all original. *H & J Foulke, Inc.*

4½-7in (12-18cm)
Victorian man with mustache **$175-$225**
Victorian lady, all original **$200**
Lady with glass eyes and wig **$350-$400**
Man with mustache, original military
   uniform **$750 up**
Molded hair, glass eyes,
   ca. 1870 **$450-$500**
Girl with bangs, ca. 1880,
   all original **$210**
Chauffeur with molded cap **$350-$400**
Black man **$650-$700**
Soldier, molded hat, goatee
   and mustache **$1,250-$1,500**
Maid, all original **$150-$175**
1920s man or lady **$100-$125**

Child Doll with closed mouth: Ca. 1880-1890. Perfect bisque head; glass eyes; good wig; nicely dressed; all in good condition, excellent quality. Kid or cloth body.
   17-19in (43-48cm) **$750-$850**
   23-25in (58-64cm) **$1,100-$1,200***
#50 shoulder head:
   14-16in (35-41cm) **$1,100-$1,200**
*Allow 30% extra for swivel neck fashion-type model.

#132, 120, 126 Bru-type face:
   13-14in (33-36cm) **$2,500-$2,800**
   19-21in (48-53cm) **$3,800-$4,000**
#51 swivel neck shoulder head:
   17-19in (43-48cm) **$1,550-$1,750**

FACTS
Various German firms. 1860s-on. **Mark:** Some numbered, some "Germany," some both.

11in (28cm) hatted bisque so-called "Kate Greenaway." *H & J Foulke, Inc.*

#86, Bru-type Nurser:
13in (33cm) at auction   **$1,000**
*Allow 30% extra for swivel neck fashion-type model.

Composition body:

11-13in (28-33cm)	**$1,450-$1,650**
16-19in (41-48cm)	**$1,950-$2,250**

#136:

12-15in (31-38cm)	**$2,200-$2,400**
19-21in (48-53cm)	**$2,800-$3,200**

Child Doll with open mouth "Dolly Face": 1888-on. Perfect bisque head, ball-jointed composition body or kid body with bisque lower arms; good wig, glass eyes, open mouth; dressed; all in good condition. Very good quality; including dolls marked **G.B.**, and **K** inside **H, L.H.K., P.Sch., D&K.**

12-14in (31-35cm)	**$400-$450***
18-20in (46-51cm)	**$600-$700***
23-25in (58-64cm)	**$800-$900***
30-32in (76-81cm)	**$1,300-$1,500**

#50, 51, square teeth:

14-16in (36-41cm)	**$950-$1,050**

#444, 478:

23-25in (58-64cm)	**$900-$1,000**
35in (81cm)	**$1,800-$2,000**

Standard quality; including **My Sweetheart, Princess, My Girlie, My Dearie, Pansy, Viola, Goebel, G & S, MOA,** and **A.W.**

14-16in (35-41cm)	**$350-$400**
20-23in (51-58cm)	**$525-$550**
30-32in (76-81cm)	**$1,000-$1,100**

*Allow extra for square cut teeth.

Small Child Doll: 1890 to World War I. Perfect bisque socket head, 5-piece composition body, set or sleep eyes, cute clothes; all in good condition.

Very good quality (**Simon & Halbig** type):

5-6in (13-15cm)	**$300-$350**
8-10in (20-25cm)	**$400-$450**

11in (28cm) 126 with Bru-type face. *Jensen's Antique Dolls.*

Fully-jointed body:

7-8in (18-20cm)	**$550-$600**

Closed mouth:

4½-5½in (12-14cm)	
all original	**$500**
8in (20cm)	**$750-$850**

Standard quality:

5-6in (13-15cm)	**$100-$125**
8-10in (20-25cm)	**$175-$225**

#39-13, 5-piece mediocre body, original clothes:

5in (13cm) glass eyes	**$200-$225**
Painted eyes	**$90-$100**

Globe Baby: 1898. Carl Hartmann.

8in (20cm)	**$325-$375**
8in (20cm) all original clothes and wig	**$400-$450**
12in (31cm)	**$450-$550**

Character Baby: Ca. 1910-on. Perfect bisque head, good wig or solid dome with painted hair, sleep eyes, open mouth; composition bent-limb baby body; suitably dressed; all in good condition. Including dolls marked **G.B., S&Q, Geobel,** and **F.B.**

9-10in (23-25cm)	**$300-$350**
14-16in (35-41cm)	**$500-$550***
19-21in (48-53cm)	**$600-$700***

15in (38cm) 110 A. Wislizenus character toddler. *H & J Foulke, Inc.*

15in (38cm) 435.7 character baby. *H & J Foulke, Inc.*

23-24in (58-61cm)	**$800-$900***

Toddler:

12-14in (31-35cm)	**$650-$850**

My Sweet Baby:

23in (58cm) toddler	**$1,000-$1,200**

#110, A. Wislizenus toddler:

15in (38cm)	**$1,250-$1,350**

#126, molded hair, painted eye toddler:

15in (38cm) at auction	**$1,500**

*Allow extra for a toddler body.

Character Child: Ca. 1910-on. Perfect bisque head, jointed composition body; dressed; all in good condition.

#820, PM shoulder head:

12in (31cm)	**$350**

#2-22, black molded hair:

18in (46cm) at auction	**$2,400**
#111, 18-20in (46-51cm)	**$20,000****
#128, 18-20in (46-51cm)	**$25,000****

#129, wide smile with molded teeth:

16in (41cm) at auction	**$9,250**
#159, 23in (58cm)	**$1,150**
#660, PR, 23in (58cm) at auction	**$2,100**

#125, smiling:

13in (33cm) at auction	**$6,380**

#500 G.H. Erste Steinbacher:

15in (38cm) at auction	**$1,700**

Boy with holes behind ears to accommodate eyeglasses:

12in (31cm)	**$1,800****

Infant, unmarked or unidentified maker: Ca. 1924-on. Perfect bisque head; cloth body; dressed; all in good condition.

10-12in (25-31cm) long	**$325-$375***
15-18in (38-46cm) long	**$525-$625***
#800, 11-12in (28-31cm)	**$550-$600**

HvB:

15in (38cm) long	**$450**

Gerling Baby:

17in (43cm) long	**$550-$600**

#697, 12in (31cm) at auction	**$1,200**

*Allow extra for an unusual face.
**Not enough price samples to compute a reliable average.

BISQUE
JAPANESE
(CAUCASIAN DOLLS)

Character Baby: Perfect bisque socket head with solid dome or wig, glass eyes, open mouth with teeth, dimples; composition bent-limb baby body; dressed; all in good condition.

9-10in (23-25cm)	**$110-$125***
13-15in (33-38cm)	**$150-$200***
19-21in (48-53cm)	**$250-$275***
24in (61cm)	**$300-$400***

Hilda look-alike:

19in (48cm)	**$750-$850***

Child Doll: Perfect bisque head, mohair wig, glass sleep eyes, open mouth; jointed composition or kid body; dressed; all in good condition.

14-16in (36-41cm)	**$200-$250**
20-22in (51-56cm)	**$300-$350**

*Do not pay as much for doll with inferior bisque head.

FACTS

Various Japanese firms; heads were imported by New York distributors such as Morimura Brothers, Yamato Importing Co., and others. 1915-on.
Marks:

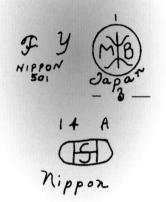

13in (33cm) Morimura Brothers character baby.
H & J Foulke, Inc.

BLACK DOLLS*

Black Bisque Doll: Ca. 1880-on. Various French and German manufacturers from their regular molds or specially designed ones with Negroid features. Perfect bisque socket head either painted dark or with dark coloring mixed in the slip, running from light brown to very dark; composition or sometimes kid body in a matching color; cloth bodies on some baby dolls; appropriate clothing; all in good condition.

French Makers—
  Bru, Circle Dot:
    17in (43cm)   **$30,000**
  E.D., open mouth:
    16in (41cm)   **$2,200**
  F. Gaultier, child, scroll mark:
    18in (46cm)   **$4,500-$5,000**
  Jumeau,
    Early E. J.:
      19in (48cm) at auction**$31,000**
    Bébé, open mouth:
      15in (38cm)   **$2,700-$2,900**

Depose 8, closed mouth:
  18in (46cm) at
    auction   **$17,600**
Exhibition Doll (1876):
  25in (64cm) at auction **$88,000**
Lanternier,
  18-20in (46-51cm)
    $950-$1,250
Paris Bébé, closed mouth:
  15½in (39cm)   **$4,800-$5,000**
Poupée shoulder head, jointed
  wood body, original
  ethnic clothes   **13,000**
SFBJ, fully jointed body:
  11in (28cm)   **$1,300**
Steiner, Figure A, open mouth:
  21in (53cm)   **$4,000-$4,200**
Van Rozen, all original:
  15in (38cm) at auction   **$17,000**
  With crack behind ear   **$5,100**

German Makers—
  Bähr & Pröschild #277:
    10in (25cm)   **$800**
    12in (30cm)   **1,000**
  Belton-type, 179:
    14in (36cm)   **$2,700**
  Gebr. Heubach #7671:
    18in (46cm)   **$3,500**
  H. Handwerck:
    12in (31cm)   **$1,000**
    18in (46cm)   **$1,600-$1,800**

*Also see entry for specific maker of doll or for material of doll.

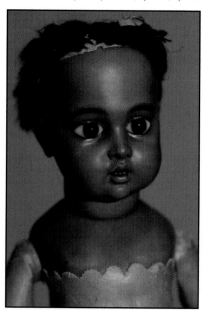

17in (43cm) Circle Dot/Bru Jne 4.
Private Collection.

E. Heubach, #399, 414, 452:

7½in (19cm) toddler $425-$450
10-12in (25-30cm) **$500-$550**
#444, 13in (33cm) **$650**
#463, 12in (30cm) **$700**
#300, 6in (15cm) **$450-$500**
#316, 18in (46cm) **$1,925**
#418, 14in (38cm) **$1,100**

Kämmer & Reinhardt:

Child, 16in (41cm) **$1,500-$1,800**
#100 Baby, 14in (36cm) **$1,200**
#101, 13-14in (33-36cm)
$4,000-$4,500
#126, toddler,
8-9in (20-23cm) **$1,250**
#192, 21in (53cm) **$2,500-$2,650**

J. D. Kestner:

Child, 16in (41cm)**$1,600-$1,900**
Hilda, 12-13in (31-33cm)
$3,000-$3,200

Kuhnlenz #34:

7-8in (18-20cm) fully jointed
$500-$600
8½in (21cm) 5-piece body all
original Mammy with baby **$700**
21in (53cm) **$5,500-$6,500**

Armand Marseille:

#341, cloth body:
10-12in (25-31cm)**$400-$425**
#351, composition body:
8-12in (20-31cm) **$500-$525**
14-16in (38-41cm)**$650-$750**
#362, composition body:
15in (38cm) **$900**

Recknagel:

#126, infant,
10½in (26cm) **$375**

10in (25cm) Ernst Heubach 399 character toddler. *H & J Foulke, Inc.*

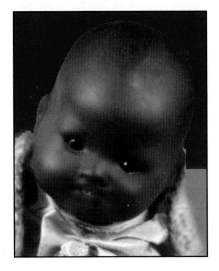

8in (20cm) Armand Marseille 351 character baby. *H & J Foulke, Inc.*

21in (53cm) Kämmer & Reinhardt 192 child. *H & J Foulke, Inc.*

20in (51cm) early 20th century black cloth doll. *Joan & Larry Kindler Antiques.*

S PB H:
Hanna, 7-8in (18-20cm)
$375-$425
#1923 child, 19-20in
(48-51cm)   **$900-$1,000**
Simon & Halbig:
#739, 19-22in (48-56cm)
$2,900-$3,100
#949, open mouth,
16in (41cm)   **$2,600-$2,900**
#970, 16½in (42cm)
$1,600-$1,700
#1009, 18in (46cm)
$2,100-$2,200
#1249, 20in (51cm)
$1,900-$2,100
#1349 Jutta, 13in (33cm)   **$1,750**
#1358, 19-20in
(48-51cm)   **$8,000-$9,000**
Franz Schmidt 1272:
22½in (57cm)   **$2,600**
TR809, closed mouth,
19in (48cm)   **$1,500**
Unmarked Child:
10-13in (25-33cm) jointed body
$400-$500
8-9in (20-23cm) 5-piece body
$300-$350
4-5in (10-14cm) S & H quality
$450-$500
All-Bisque:
5in (14cm) glass eyes   **$500-$550**
6in (15cm) Kestner, swivel neck,
bare feet   **$1,650**
2½in (6cm) French,
swivel neck   **$250**
7in (18cm) S & H 886
$1,000-$1,200

Cloth Black Doll*: Ca. 1880-on. American-made cloth doll with black face, painted, printed or embroidered features; jointed arms and legs; original clothes; all in good condition.

Primitive, painted or embroidered
face: **$1,000-$2,000+**
Stockinette (so-called Beecher-type),
20in (51cm) **$3,000**
1930s Mammy:
18-20in (46-51cm) **$350+**

*Also check under manufacturer if known.
+Greatly depending on appeal.

WPA, molded cloth face:
22in (56cm) **$1,100-$1,200**
Alabama-type, 24in (61cm)
$2,500-$3,500
Chase Mammy, 26in (66cm) **$10,000****

**Not enough price samples to compute a
reliable average.

Golliwogg: Ca. 1925-1930. English cloth
character; all original; very good condition.
18in (46cm) **$425-$525**
Ca. 1950:
16-18in (41-46cm) **$225-$325**

Black Papier-Mâché Doll: Ca. 1890. By
various German manufacturers. Papier-
mâché character face, arms and legs, cloth
body; glass eyes; original or appropriate
clothes; all in good condition.
12-14in (31-36cm) **$350-$450**
18-20in (46-51cm) character with
broad smile **$1,200**

Black Low-Fired Pottery: Ca. 1930.
English and German. Molded curly hair.
16in (41cm) **$850**
K&R, 24in (61cm) flirty eyes **$1,250**

BRU

Poupée (Fashion Lady): Ca. 1866-on.
Perfect bisque swivel head on shoulder
plate, cork pate, appropriate old wig,
closed mouth, paperweight eyes, pierced
ears; gusseted kid lady body; original or
appropriate clothes; all in good condition.
Smiling face, sizes A (11in, 28cm) to O
(36in, 91cm):
14-16in (35-41cm) **$3,200-$3,800***
20-21in (51-53cm) **$5,500-$6,000***
13in (33cm) original regional
costume, boxed **$11,500**
Wood arms:
13-14in (33-35cm) **$3,800-$4,000***
Wood body, naked:
15-17in (38-43cm) **$6,000-$6,800***
21in (53cm) **$9,000**
*Allow extra for original clothes.

FACTS
Bru Jne. & Cie, Paris, and Montreuil-
sous-Bois, France. 1866-1899.

16in (41cm) early Bru *poupée*. *Delores
Gilbert.*

Oval face, incised with numbers only. Shoulder plate sometimes marked "B. Jne & Cie."

12-13in (31-33cm)	**$2,500-$2,800***
15-17in (38-43cm)	**$3,200-$3,600***
20-21in (51-53cm)	**$4,200-$4,700***
Wood body, naked:	
16in (41cm)	**$5,000-$5,200**

Candy Container: 1867. 2 faces (crying and smiling):

14in (36cm) at auction   **$7,400***

All-Bisque: 1867. 2 faces:

9½in (24cm)   **$4,500-$5,500****

*Allow extra for original clothes.

**Not enough samples to compute a reliable range.

Marked Breveté Bébé: Ca. 1879-1880. Perfect bisque swivel head on shoulder plate, cork pate, skin wig, paperweight eyes with shading on upper lid, closed mouth with white space between lips, full cheeks, pierced ears; gusseted kid body pulled high on shoulder plate and straight cut with bisque lower arms (no rivet joints); original or appropriate old clothes; all in good condition.

Mark: Size number only on head. Oval sticker on body:

or rectangular sticker like Bébé Bru one, but with words "Bébé Breveté."

Size 5/0	= 10-1/2in (27cm)
Size 2/0	= 14in (36cm)
Size 1	= 16in (41cm)
Size 2	= 18in (46cm)
Size 3	= 19in (48cm)

11in (28cm)	**$12,000**
14-16in (35-41cm)	**$14,000-$16,000**
19-22in (48-56cm)	**$19,000-$22,000**
Head only, size 3/0	**$4,750**
12in (31cm) body only	**$1,000**

Bébé Modele: Ca. 1880. Breveté face, wood body:

21in (31cm)   **$22,500**

Marked Crescent or Circle Dot Bébé: 1879-1884. Perfect bisque swivel head on a deep shoulder plate with molded breasts, cork pate, attractive wig, paperweight eyes, closed mouth with slightly parted lips, molded and painted teeth, plump cheeks, pierced ears; gusseted kid body with bisque

13½in (35cm) *Bébé Breveté*, all original. *H. Jay Lowe Collection.*

lower arms (no rivet joints); original or appropriate old clothes; all in good condition.

Mark:

Sometimes with "BRU Jne"

Approximate size chart:
0 = 11in (28cm)
1 = 12in (31cm)
2 = 13in (33cm)
5 = 17in (43cm)
8 = 22in (56cm)
10 = 26in (66cm)
12 = 30in (76cm)
14 = 35in (89cm)

10½in (26cm)	**$12,000**
13-14in (33-35cm)	**$13,000-$15,000**
18-19in (46-48cm)	**$18,000-$20,000**
24in (61cm)	**$24,000-$25,000**

Marked Nursing Bru (Bébé Têteur): Ca. 1878-1898. Perfect bisque head, shoulder plate, open mouth with hole for nipple, mechanism in head sucks up liquid, operates by turning key; nicely clothed; all in good condition.

Early model:
  13-15in (33-38cm) **$8,500-$9,500**
Later model:
  13-15in (33-38cm) **$5,500-$6,500**

Marked Bru Jne Bébé: Ca. 1884-1889. Perfect bisque swivel head on deep shoulder plate with molded breasts, cork pate, attractive wig, paperweight eyes, closed mouth, molded tongue, pierced ears; gusseted kid body with scalloped edge at shoulder plate, bisque lower arms with lovely hands, kid over wood upper arms, hinged elbow, all kid or wood lower legs (sometimes on a jointed wood body); original or appropriate clothes; all in good condition (for body photograph see *6th Blue Book*, page 79).

Mark: "BRU Jne"
Body Label:

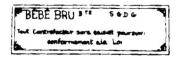

14in (36cm) Bébé Bru, size 3, all original.
H. Jay Lowe Collection.

12-13in (31-33cm) **$16,500-$18,500***
15-17in (38-43cm) **$16,500-$18,500***
23-24in (58-61cm)**$20,000-$22,000***
27in (69cm)   **$25,000-$27,500***
Late model, no molded tongue:
   18-20in (46-51cm) **$12,500-$13,500**

Marked Bru Shoes: **$800-$900**

Bru factory dress and hat:$1,700-$2,000
*Allow extra for original clothes.

Marked Bru Jne R Bébé: Ca. 1889-1899.
Perfect bisque head on a jointed composition body.

Mark:

BRU J^n R
11

Body Stamp: "Bebe Bru" with size number.

Closed mouth:
   11-13in (28-33cm)   **$2,200-$2,600**
   19-21in (48-53cm)   **$6,000-$7,000**
   27in (69cm)   **$9,000**
Open mouth:
   12in (31cm)   **$1,500-$1,800**
   20-21in (51-53cm)   **$3,000-$4,000**

14in (36cm) Bébé Bru, size 3, all original. *H. Jay Lowe Collection.*

BUCHERER

Saba Figures: Composition character head sometimes with molded hat; metal ball-jointed body with large composition hands and composition molded shoes; original clothes, often felt; all in good condition.

8in (20cm) average:

Man and woman in provincial costumes **$200 each**

Fireman, clown, black man, aviator, military, baseball player. Becassine, Pinocchio, Mr. & Mrs. Peter Rabbit and others **$275-$325**

Characters: *Mutt, Jeff, Maggie, Jiggs, Katzenjammers, Happy Hooligan, Charlie Chaplin, Aggie, Jimmy Dugan, Puddin' head* and others. **$400-$500**

FACTS
A. Bucherer, Amriswil, Switzerland. 1921.
Mark: "MADE IN SWITZERLAND PATENTS APPLIED FOR"

Happy Hooligan, all original. *Wayne Jensen Collection.*

BYE-LO BABY

Bisque Head Bye-Lo Baby: Ca. 1923. Perfect bisque head, cloth body with curved legs (sometimes with straight legs), composition or celluloid hands; sleep eyes; dressed. Made in seven sizes, 9-20in (23-51cm). "Bye-Lo Baby" stamp on front of body. Sometimes Mold #1373 (ABG).

Mark: © 1923 by Grace S. Putnam MADE IN GERMANY

Head circumference:

7½-8in (19-20cm)	**$500-$525***
9-10in (23-25cm)	**$475-$500***
12-13in (31-33cm)	**$550-$600***
15in (38cm)	**$900***
17in (43cm)	**$1,100-$1,300***
18in (46cm)	**$1,400-$1,600***

Toddler with wardrobe:

12in (31cm) tall, at auction **$2,500**

Tagged Bye-Lo gown: **$50**

Bye-Lo pin: **$95**

Bye-Lo type, incised "45," open mouth:

12in (31cm) h.c. **$800**

*Allow extra for original tagged gown and button.

FACTS
Bisque heads—J.D. Kestner; Alt, Beck & Gottschalck; Kling & Co.; Hertel, Schwab & Co.; all of Thüringia, Germany.
Composition heads—Cameo Doll Company, New York, N.Y.
Celluloid heads—Karl Standfuss, Saxony, Germany.
Wooden heads (unauthorized)— Schoenhut of Philadelphia, Pa.
All-Bisque Baby—J.D. Kestner.
Cloth Bodies and Assembly—K & K Toy Co., New York, N.Y.
Composition Bodies—König & Wernicke, 1922-on.
Designer: Grace Storey Putnam.
Distributor: George Borgfeldt, New York, N.Y., U.S.A.

Mold #1369 (ABG) socket head on composition body, some marked "K&W."

12-13in (30-33cm) long   **$700-$900**

Painted eyes:

12-13in (30-33cm) long   **$800**

Mold #1415, smiling with painted eyes:

13½in (34cm) h.c.   **$4,000****

Composition head, 1924:

12-13in (31-33cm) h.c.,

all original   **$400-$425**

Celluloid head:

10in (25cm) h.c.   **$350-$375**

Painted bisque head, late 1920s:

12-13in (31-33cm) h.c.   **325-$350**

Wooden head, (Schoenhut), 1925:

$1,700-$2,000

**Not enough price samples to compute a reliable average.

12¾in (32cm) *Bye-Lo Baby* with socket head on composition body.
H & J Foulke, Inc.

Vinyl head, 1948:
  16in (41cm)   **$150-$200**
Wax head, 1922:
  16in (41cm)   **$700-$800**

Baby Aero or **Fly-Lo Baby,** bisque head,
Mold #1418:
  11in (28cm)   **$3,800-$4,200**
Composition head, original costume:
  12in (31cm)   **$800-$900**

Marked All-Bisque By-Lo Baby: Ca.
1925-on. Solid head with molded hair and
painted eyes, jointed shoulders and hips:
  4-5in (10-13cm)   **$325-$395**
  6in (15cm)   **$475-$525**
  8in (20cm)   **$675-$725**
Solid head with swivel neck, glass eyes,
jointed shoulders and hips:
  4-5in (10-13cm)   **$550-$625**
  6in (15cm)   **$725-$825**
  8in (20cm)   **$1,100-$1,200**
Head with wig, glass eyes,
jointed shoulders and hips:
  4-5in (10-13cm)
            $650-$750
  6in (15cm)   **$850-$950**
  8in (20cm)
            $1,250-$1,450
Action Bye-Lo Baby, immobile in various positions,
painted features:
  3in (8cm)   **$400**
All-Celluloid:
  4in (10cm)   **$250-$300**

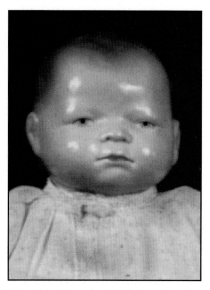

9¾in (24cm) h.c. **Bye-Lo Baby** with celluloid head. *H & J Foulke, Inc.*

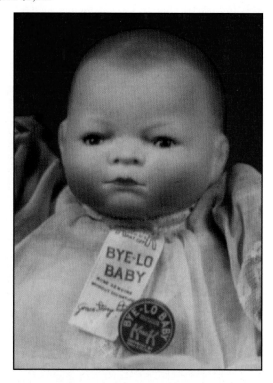

10in (25cm) h.c., 12in (31cm)
long **Bye-Lo Baby,** all original
with tagged gown and pin.
H & J Foulke, Inc.

CATTERFELDER PUPPENFABRIK

C.P. Child Doll: Ca. 1902-on. Perfect bisque head, good wig, sleep eyes, open mouth with teeth; composition jointed body; dressed; all in good condition.

#264 (made by **Kestner**):

17-19in (43-48cm)	**$800-$850**
22-24in (56-61cm)	**$950-$1,000**
35-36in (89-91cm)	**$2,000-$2,500****

C.P. Character Child: Ca. 1910-on. Perfect bisque character face with wig, painted eyes; composition jointed body; dressed; all in good condition.

#207, 219: 15-16in (38-41cm)

	$3,000-$4,000**
#217: 18in (46cm)	**$9,750****
#220: 14in (36cm) glass eyes	**$7,500****
#210: 14in (36cm)	**$5,000****

C.P. Character Baby: Ca. 1910-on. Perfect bisque character face with wig or molded hair, painted or glass eyes; jointed baby body; dressed; all in good condition.

#200, 201, 208:

14-16in (36-41cm)	**$500-$550**
19-21in (48-53cm)	**$750-$850**

#201, toddler:

10in (25cm)	**$700-$900**

#262, 263 (made by **Kestner**):

15-17in (38-43cm)	**$525-$625**
20-22in (51-56cm)	**$800-$900**

#262 toddler, 5-piece body:

18-20in (46-51cm)	**$1,000-$1,200**

**Not enough price samples to computer a reliable range.

FACTS

Catterfelder Puppenfabrik, Catterfeld, Thüringia, Germany. Heads by J.D. Kestner and other porcelain makers. 1902-on. Bisque head; composition body.
Trademark: My Sunshine.
Mark:

C. P.
208
45
N

25in (51cm) 262 character toddler.
H & J Foulke, Inc.

CELLULOID DOLLS

Celluloid Shoulder Head Child Doll: Ca. 1900-on. Cloth or kid body, celluloid or composition arms; dressed; all in good condition.

Painted eyes:

16-18in (41-46cm)	**$160-$185**

Glass eyes:

19-22in (48-56cm)	**$225-$250**

Original provincial costume:

12-14in (30-36cm)	**$210-$235**
Boy/girl pair	**$525-$550**

All-Celluloid Child Doll: Ca. 1900-on. Jointed at neck, shoulders, and hips; all in good condition.

Painted eyes:

4in (10cm)	**$55-$65***
7-8in (18-20cm)	**$85-$100***
10-12in (25-31cm)	**$125-$150***
14-15in (36-38cm)	**$175-$225***

Googly:

5in (12cm)	**$175-$200**

Flocked celluloid, Lenci-type:

6½in (17cm)	**$400****

French with original provencial costume by **LeMinor, Poupees Magali** and others:

8in (20cm)	**$75-$85**
12-14in (31-36cm)	**$140-$165**

*Allow extra for unusual dolls.
**Not enough price samples to compute a reliable average.

5in (12cm) German celluloid googly, all original. *H & J Foulke, Inc.*

16in (41cm) Polish celluloid shoulder head, cloth body, all original. *H & J Foulke, Inc.*

SNF pair with molded provincial costumes:

9in (23cm)	**$250**

Tommy Tucker-type character:

12-14in (31-36cm)	**$225-$250**

Glass eyes:

12-13in (31-33cm)	**$200-$225***
15-16in (38-41cm)	**$275-$300***
18in (46cm)	**$375-$425***
21in (53cm)	**$475-$500***

*Allow extra for unusual dolls.

Marie-France, by Petitcolin, smiling character, all original:

18in (46cm)	**$350**
Boxed in child's dress	**$565**

K*R 717 or 728:

14-16in (36-41cm)	**$700-$750**

All-Celluloid Baby: Ca. 1910-on. All in good condition.

6-8in (15-20cm)	**$65-$85**
10-12in (25-31cm)	**$110-$135***
15in (38cm)	**$175-$200***
21in (53cm)	**$250-$300***

SNF black with African features:

10in (25cm)	**$450**

*Allow $25-$35 extra for glass eyes.

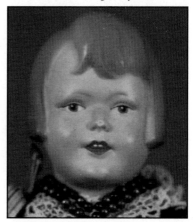

7in (18cm) French celluloid baby by (Le Minor), all original. *H & J Foulke, Inc.*

17in (43cm) German celluloid girl with turtlemark, all original. *H & J Foulke, Inc.*

All-Celluloid, Made in Japan: Ca. 1920s.
Molded clothes:

4-5in (10-12cm)	**60-$80**
8-9in (20-23cm)	**$150-$175**

Child with pedestal legs, jointed arms:

3-4in (8-10cm)	**$15-$20**
6-7in (15-18cm)	**$25-$35**

Baby:

4-5in (10-13cm)	**$20-$30**
8-10in (20-25cm)	**$85-$110**
13in (33cm)	**$150-$175**
24in (61cm)	**$350-$400**

Occupied Japan, chubby toddler character:

6½in (17cm)	**$85-$95**

Parsons-Jackson, Stork Mark:

11½in (29cm) baby	**$165-$185***
14in (36cm) toddler	**$300-$350***

*Allow extra for molded shoes and socks.

Celluloid Head Infant: Ca. 1920s-on. Baby head with glass eyes, cloth body, appropriate clothes; all in good condition.

12-15in (31-38cm)	**$175-$225**

Celluloid Socket Head Doll: Ca. 1910-on. Wig, glass eyes, sometimes flirty, open mouth with teeth; ball-jointed or bent-limb composition body; dressed; all in good condition.

K*R 701 child:

12-13in (31-33cm)	**$900-$1,100**

K*R 717 child, flapper body:

16-18in (41-46cm)	**$750-$800**
17in (43cm) with trunk and wardrobe	**$1,250**

K*R 700 baby:

14-15in (36-38cm)	**$325-$375**

K*R 728:

12-13in (31-33cm)	**$350-$400**
20in (51cm) toddler	**$650**
18in (46cm) flapper	**$850**

F.S. & Co. 1276:

20in (51cm) baby	**$550-$600**

CHAD VALLEY

Chad Valley Doll: All-cloth, usually felt face and velvet body, jointed neck, shoulders and hips; mohair wig, glass or painted eyes; original clothes; all in excellent condition.

Characters, painted eyes:

10-12in (25-31cm)	**$85-$115**

Characters, glass eyes:

17-20in (43-51cm)	**$1,000-$2,000***

Children, painted eyes:

9in (23cm)	**$135-$150**
13-14in (33-36cm)	**$375-$475**
16-18in (41-46cm)	**$550-$650**

Smiling face:

14-15in (36-38cm)	**$425-$475**

Children, glass eyes:

16-18in (41-46cm)	**$700-$800**

Royal Children, glass eyes:

16-18in (41-46cm)	**$1,350**

Mabel Lucie Attwell, glass inset side-glancing eyes, smiling watermelon mouth:

15-17in (38-43cm)	**$750-$850**

Snow White Set:

Dwarfs, 10in (25cm)	**$250-$275 each**

Snow White, 16in (41cm) and seven 6¼in (16cm) dwarfs, all excellent and boxed, at auction **$4,500**

Long John Silver:

20in (51cm) excellent and boxed at auction **$1,380**

*Depending on rarity.

FACTS

Chad Valley Co. (formerly Johnson Bros., Ltd.), Birmingham, England. 1917-on.
Mark: Cloth label usually on foot: "HYGIENIC TOYS Made in England by CHAD VALLEY CO. LTD."

15in (38cm) smiling child with Mabel Lucie Atwell face. *H & J Foulke, Inc.*

MARTHA CHASE

Chase Doll: Head and limbs of stockinette, treated and painted with oils, large painted eyes with thick upper lashes, rough-stroked hair to provide texture, cloth bodies jointed at shoulders, hips, elbows and knees, later ones only at shoulders and hips; some bodies completely treated; appropriate clothing; showing wear, but no repaint.

Baby:

9in (23cm)	**$6,000****
13-15in (33-38cm)	**$575-$675***
17-20in (43-51cm)	**$750***
24-26in (61-66cm)	**$850***

Hospital Baby:

19-20in (49-51cm)	**$750**

Child:

12-15in (31-38cm)	**$1,200**
20in (51cm)	**$1,600**

Lady:

13-15in (33-38cm)	**$1,500-$1,600**

*Allow extra for a doll in excellent condition or with original clothes.

**Very rare. Not enough price samples to compute a reliable average.

Man:

15-16in (38-41cm)	**$3,000****
Black, Mammy or **child:**	**$10,000****

Boy with side part and side curl:

15-16in (38-41cm)	**$3,000**

Hospital Lady:

64in (163cm)	**$900-$1,200**

Alice in Wonderland character set:

Six dolls	**$67,000**

**Not enough price samples to compute a reliable average.

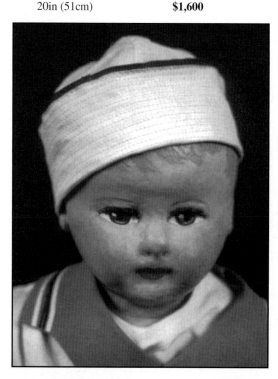

FACTS

Martha Jenks Chase, Pawtucket, R.I., U.S.A. 1889-on.

Designer: Martha Jenks Chase.

Mark: "Chase Stockinet Doll" stamp on left leg or under left arm, paper label on back (usually gone).

24in (61cm) Chase baby. *H & J Foulke, Inc.*

CHINA HEADS

FRENCH

ENGLISH

French China Head Fashion-type Doll (Poupée): China shoulder head, glass or beautifully painted eyes, painted eyelashes, feathered eyebrows, closed mouth, open crown, cork pate, good wig; shapely kid fashion body (may have china arms curved to above elbow); appropriately dressed; all in good condition.

16-17in (41-43cm)	**$3,200-$3,700**
15-16in (38-41cm), naked	
	$2,200-$2,500

Rohmer *poupée:*
18in (46cm)	**$5,500**

Huret *poupée:*
17in (43cm)	**$9,500**
With gutta percha body	**$14,000**

Blampoix *poupée* with wardrobe and trunk:
18in (46cm) at auction	**$5,900**

Painted black hair:
9-11in (23-28cm)	
	$850-$950
11in (28cm) in original	
box, at auction	**$1,400**
16in (41cm)	**$2,500**

Jacob Petit, head only, wigged:
4½in (11cm)	**$1,500**

FACTS

Various French doll firms; some heads sold through French firms may have been made in Germany. 1850s.
Mark: None.

20in (51cm) French
Rohmer *poupée.*
Elliott Zirlin.

English China Doll: Flesh-tinted shoulder head with bald head (some with molded slit for inserting wig), painted features, closed mouth; human hair wig. Cloth torso and upper arms and legs, china lower limbs with holes to attach them to cloth, bare feet. Appropriately dressed; all in good condition.

19-22in (48-56cm)	**$2,500-$3,000**
without china limbs	**$1,200**

FACTS

Unidentified English firm, possibly Rockingham area. Ca. 1840-1860.
Mark: None.

CHINA HEADS
GERMAN

1840s Hairstyles: China shoulder head with black molded hair; may have pink tint complexion; old cloth body; (may have china arms); appropriate old clothes; all in good condition.

Hair swept back into bun:

7½in (19cm)	**$650-$750**
13-15in (33-38cm)	**$2,000-$2,600**
18-21in (46-53cm)	**$3,000-$5,500**

Fancy braided bun:

22-24in (56-61cm)	**$5,000-$6,000**

Long curls, early face:

21in (53cm)	**$3,400**

Bun with exposed ears, head only:

4in (10cm)	**$3,900**

K.P.M.:

Brown hair with bun:

16-18in (41-46cm)	**$5,000**

Young man, brown hair:

16-18in (41-46cm)	**$4,000**
23in (58cm) at auction	**$7,000**

Kinderkopf (child head):

10½in (27cm)	**$800-$900**
18-22in (46-56cm)	**$2,200-$2,800**

Head only:

7in (18cm)	**$1,700**

Wood jointed body, china lower limbs:

5-6in (13-15cm)	**$1,600-$1,800**
11in (28cm)	**$3,500-$4,000**

*Depending upon quality, hairdo, and rarity.

13in (33cm) early china head with molded bun. *H & J Foulke, Inc.*

22in (56cm) so-called *Jenny
Lind* china lady, side and back
view. *H & J Foulke, Inc.*

22in (56cm) so-called *Jenny
Lind* china lady, front view.
H & J Foulke, Inc.

1850s Hairstyles: China shoulder head
(some with pink tint), molded black hair
(except bald), painted eyes; old cloth body
with leather or china arms; appropriate old
clothes; all in good condition.

Bald head, some with black areas on top,
proper wig. Allow extra for original human
hair wig in fancy style.
Fine quality:

12in (31cm)	$700-$750
15-17in (38-43cm)	$1,000-$1,200
22-24in (56-61cm)	$1,700-$1,900

Standard quality:

13in (33cm)	$500-$550
16-17in (41-43cm)	$750-$800

20-22in (51-56cm)	**$900-$1,000**

Covered wagon with blue eyes:

15-17in (38-43cm)	**$675-$775**
21-23in (53-58cm)	**$1,000-$1,100**

Covered wagon with brown eyes:

20-22in (51-56cm)	**$1,300-$1,400**

Greiner-style with brown eyes:

14-15in (36-38cm)	**$1,000-$1,200**
19-22in (48-56cm)	**$,1700-$2,000**

Greiner-style with glass eyes:

15-16in (38-41cm)	**$3,850****
22in (56cm)	**$4,800****

**Not enough price samples to compute a
reliable average.

Waves, framing face, brown eyes:
20-21in (51-53cm)   **$1,700-$2,000**
With glass eyes:
18-21in (46-53cm)**$3,000-$3,500**
Alice Hairdo, with molded headband:
22-24in (56-61cm)   **$950**
29in (73cm)   **$1,550**

Child or Baby, flange swivel neck; taüfling body with china or papier-mâché shoulder plate and hips, china lower limbs; cloth midsection (may have voice box) and upper limbs.
10in (25cm)   **$3,000-$3,500****
Child with Alice Hairstyle:
8-11in (20-28cm)   **$4,000****
**Not enough price samples to compute a reliable range.

1860s and 1870s Hairstyles: China shoulder head with black molded hair (a few blondes); old cloth body may have leather arms or china lower arms and legs; appro-

So-called *Morning Glory* china head with molded flowers in her hair. *Private Collection.*

22in (56cm) so-called *Dolley Madison* with molded hair ribbon and pierced ears. *H & J Foulke, Inc.*

priate old clothes; all in good condition. Plain style with center part (so-called flat top and high brow):

6-7in (15-18cm)	**$110-$115***
14-16in (36-41cm)	**$265-$295***
19-22in (48-56cm)	**$375-$400***
24-26in (61-66cm)	**$425-$525***
28in (71cm)	**$625-$650***
34-35in (86-89cm)	**$900-$950**

Molded necklace:

22-24in (56-61cm)	**$600-$700**

Blonde hair:

18in (46cm)	**$425-$475**

Brown eyes:

20-22in (51-56cm)	**$600-$700**

Swivel neck:

15½in (40cm)	**$2,000****

*Allow more for all original body and clothes.
**Not enough price samples to compute a reliable range.

19½in (50cm) china lady with molded and painted snood. *H & J Foulke, Inc.*

Mary Todd Lincoln, with snood:

18-21in (46-53cm)	**$900-$1,000**

Blonde hair, blue ruffled snood:

21in (53cm)	**$1,300**

Conta and Boehme:

19in (48cm)	**$700-$800**

Molded bonnet, applied flowers, poor quality:

20in (51cm)	**$500**

Young Man:

16in (41cm)	**$900-$1,100**

Dolley Madison, with molded bow:

14-16in (36-41cm)	**$425-$475**
21-24in (53-61cm)	**$625-$700**

Blonde hair, pierced ears:

22in (56cm)	**$750-$800**

Adelina Patti:

13-15in (33-38cm)	**$425-$475**
19-22in (48-56cm)	**$650-$725**

Dagmar-type:

18in (46cm)	**$800**

Jenny Lind:

21-24in (53-61cm)	**$1,600-$1,800**

Curly Top:

14in (36cm) black hair	**$600**
19in (48cm) tan hair	**$900**

Grape Lady:

18in (46cm)	**$2,200-$2,500**

Spill Curl:

19-22in (48-56cm)	**$900-$1,100**

Morning Glory:

21in (53cm)	**$7,500-$8,500****
24in (61cm) at auction	**$10,250**

Fancy hairdo with pierced ears, all original:

21in (53cm)	**$2,000**

Fancy hairdo with molded rose, brown eyes, pierced ears:

20in (51cm)	**$2,425**

Hair pulled back into cascading curls, brown eyes:

    22in (56cm)   **$2,000**

Braid across top of head and braided coiled bun in back:

    23in (58cm)   **$2,700**

Fancy hairdo with molded gold beads:

    21in (53cm)   **$2,500**

Long blonde hair with ornate snood:

    17in (43cm)   **$2,700**

1880s Hairstyles: China shoulder head with black or blonde molded hair; appropriate old clothes; all in good condition.

Many made by Alt, Beck & Gottschalck or Kling & Co.

    14-16in (36-41cm)   **$325-$375**
    21-23in (53-58cm)   **$500-$550**
    28in (71cm)   **700-$750**

Black boy with molded hat:

    10in (25cm) at auction   **$2,000**

Youth and Old Age, double-faced:

    10in (25cm)   **$1,600**

    Head only:

        3in (8cm)   **$700**

Bawo and Dotter, "Pat. Dec. 7/80":

    18-20in (46-51cm)   **$400-$450**

24in (61cm) 1860s china lady with high forehead. *H & J Foulke, Inc.*

Dressel & Kister: Ca. 1890-1920. China shoulder head with varying hairdos and brush stroked hair; delicately painted features; cloth body with china arms having beautifully molded fingers. Often used as ornamental dolls in only half form as for a boudoir lamp or candy box.

13in (33cm) tall	**$1,500 up****
Heads only	**$675-$750**

1890s Hairstyles: China shoulder head with black or blonde molded wavy hair; appropriate clothes; all in good condition.

8-10in (20-25cm)	**$100-$125**
13-15in (33-38cm)	**$150-$195**
19-21in (48-53cm)	**$235-$285**
24in (61cm)	**$350**
Molded bonnet:	
8-10in (20-25cm)	**$165-$185**
Molded "Jewel" necklace:	
22in (56cm)	**$400-$425**
8½in (21cm)	**$150-$165**

Dressel & Kister china shoulder head lady. *Private Collection.*

Pet Name: Ca. 1905. Made by Hertwig & Co. for Butler Bros., N.Y. China shoulder head, molded yoke with name in gold; black or blonde painted hair (one-third were blonde). Used names such as **Agnes, Bertha, Daisy, Dorothy, Edith, Esther, Ethel, Florence, Helen, Mabel, Marion,** and **Pauline.**

12-14in (30-36cm)	**$200-$250**
18-21in (46-53cm)	**$350-$400**
24in (61cm)	**$450**

****Not enough price samples to compute a reliable average.

22in (56cm) 1890s china with blonde hair. *H & J Foulke, Inc.*

CLOTH
PRINTED

Cloth, Printed Doll: Names such as Dolly Dear, Merry Marie, Improved Foot Doll, Standish No Break Doll, and others:

7-9in (18-23cm)	**$60-$70**
16-18in (41-46cm)	**$110-$125**
22-24in (56-61cm)	**$135-$165**

Uncut sheet, bright colors:

13in (33cm) doll	**$110-$125**
20in (51cm) doll	**$135-$165**

Brownies: Ca. 1892. Designed by Palmer Cox; marked on foot:

8in (20cm)	**$75-$85**
Uncut sheet of six	**$250**

Boys and Girls with printed outer clothes. Ca. 1903:

12-13in (31-33cm)	**$100-$125**
17in (43cm)	**$150-$175**

Darkey Doll, Cocheco, made up:

16in (41cm)	**$225-$250**

Aunt Jemima Family:

Four dolls	**$65-$75 each**

Punch & Judy	**$350 pair**
Pitti Sing, uncut	**$65**
Hen and Chicks, uncut sheet	**$65**
Tabby Cat	**$70-$80**
Tabby's Kittens	**$45-$55**
Ball, uncut	**$250-$275**
Peck 1886 Santa	**$225**

Black Child, Art Fabric:

18in (46cm)	**$250**

Topsy, uncut:

8½in (22cm) two dolls on sheet	**$195**

E.T. Gibson, ca. 1912:

Red bathing suit	**$165-$185**

George & Martha Washington **$350 pair**

Pillow-type, printed and hand embroidered, 1920s-1930s:

16in (41cm)	**$65-$85**

Hug-Me-Tight, ca. 1916. Grace Drayton.

Mother Goose Characters:

11in (28cm)	**$225-$250**

Orphan Annie, oil cloth:

17in (43cm)	**$185**
Sandy, oil cloth	**$75-$85**
Smitty, oil cloth	**$60-$70**
Skeezix, oil cloth	**$60-$70**
Buster Brown and Tige	**$325**
Cream of Wheat Rastus	**$90-$110**
Red Riding Hood	**$150**

FACTS

Various American companies, such as Cocheco Mfg. Co., Lawrence & Co., Arnold Print Works, Art Fabric Mills and Selchow & Righter and Dean's Rag Book Company in England. 1896-on.

Mark: Mark could be found on fabric part, which was discarded after cutting.

14in (36cm) embroidered pillow-type doll. *H & J Foulke, Inc.*

CLOTH
RUSSIAN

COLUMBIAN DOLL

Russian Cloth Doll: All-cloth with stockinette head and hands, molded face with hand-painted features; authentic regional clothes; all in very good condition.

6½in (16cm) child	**$50-$55**
11in (28cm) child	**$110-$125**
15in (38cm)	**$200-$250**

Tea Cosy:

20in (51cm)	**$250-$275**

Columbian Doll: All-cloth with hair and features hand-painted on a flat face; treated limbs; appropriate clothes; all in very good condition, no repaint or touch up.

15in (38cm)	**$6,000**
20-22in (51-56cm)	**$7,000-$8,000**

Some wear:

20-22in (51-56cm)	**$4,000-$4,200**

Worn:

20in (51cm)	**$2,200**

FACTS

Unknown craftsmen. Ca. 1930.
Mark: "Made in Soviet Union" sometimes with identification of doll, such as "Ukrainian Woman," "Village Boy," "Smolensk District Woman."

FACTS

Emma and Marietta Adams.
1891-1910 or later.
Mark: Stamped on back of body.
Before 1900: "COLUMBIAN DOLL
EMMA E. ADAMS
OSWEGO CENTRE N.Y."
After 1906: "THE COLUMBIAN
DOLL MANUFACTURED BY
MARIETTA ADAMS RUTTAN
OSWEGO, N.Y."

20in (51cm) Russian Tea Cosy. *H & J Foulke, Inc.*

20-21in (51-53cm) Columbian Doll by Marietta. *Nancy A. Smith Collection.*

DANEL
(LATER JUMEAU)

Marked Paris Bébé: Ca. 1889-1892. Perfect bisque socket head with Jumeau look, good wig, paperweight eyes, closed mouth, pierced ears; composition jointed body; appropriately dressed; all in good condition. This doll was a copy of a Jumeau.

Mark: On Head

TÊTE DÉPOSÉ PARIS BEBE

On Body

16-18in (41-46cm)	$3,800-$4,200
22-24in (56-66cm)	$4,500-$4,800
32in (81cm)	$6,000-$6,200

Marked Paris Bébé: Ca. 1892-on. Character face developed by Jumeau for use with this trademark after he won a lawsuit against Danel. (For photograph see *11th Blue Book,* page 144).

18-19in (46-48cm)	**$5,000-$5,500**
23-25in (58-64cm)	**$6,000-$6,500**

Marked B.F.: Ca. 1891. Bébé Français was used by Jumeau after 1892. Perfect bisque head, appropriate wig, paperweight eyes, closed mouth, pierced ears; jointed composition body; appropriate clothes; all in good condition.

Mark:

B9F

16-19in (41-48cm)	**$4,600-$5,000**
23-25in (58-64cm)	**$5,500-$6,000**

FACTS

Danel & Cie., Paris & Montreuil-sous-Bois, France. 1889-1895. **Trademarks:** Paris Bébé, Bébé Français. Both used by Jumeau after winning an 1892 lawsuit.

22in (56cm) *Bébé Française. H & J Foulke, Inc.*

DEP

DEP Closed Mouth: Ca. 1890. Perfect bisque head, swivel neck, lovely wig, set paperweight eyes, upper and lower painted eyelashes, closed mouth, pierced ears; jointed French composition and wood body (may be stamped Jumeau); pretty clothes; all in good condition.

Mark:

DEP

(size number)

12in (31cm)	**$1,800-$2,000**
15in (38cm)	**$2,350-$2,500***
18-20in (46-51cm)	**$2,900-$3,200***
25-27in (63-68cm)	**$4,200-$4,500***
Open mouth, 22in (56cm)	
	$1,000-$1,200

*Allow more for an especially lovely sample.

Jumeau DEP: Ca. 1899-on. Heads possibly by Simon & Halbig. Perfect bisque socket head (sometimes with Tête Jumeau stamp),

human hair wig, deeply molded eye socket, sleeping eyes, painted lower eyelashes, upper hair eyelashes (sometimes gone), pierced ears; jointed French composition and wood body (sometimes with Jumeau label or stamp); lovely clothes; all in good condition.

Mark:

DEP

8

11½in (29cm)	**$850***
13-15in (33-38cm)	**$900-$950***
18-20in (46-51cm)	**$1,050-$1,200***
23-25in (58-64cm)	**$1,400-$1,700***
29-30in (74-76cm)	**$2,200-$2,500***
35in (89cm)	**$3,000-$3,200**
24in (61cm) all original, in	
Jumeau box, at auction	**$3,200**

*Allow extra for Jumeau flowered shift.

28in (71cm) *DEP* Jumeau. *H & J Foulke, Inc.*

DOOR OF HOPE

Door of Hope lady, all original. *H & J Foulke, Inc.*

Door of Hope: Carved wooden head with painted and/or carved hair; cloth body, some with stubby arms, some with carved hands; original handmade clothes, exact costuming for different classes of Chinese people; all in excellent condition. 25 dolls in the series.

Adult:
11-13in (28-33cm)	**$450-$650**

Child:
7-8in (18-20cm)	**$550-$650**

Amah and Baby:	**$700-$800**
Manchu Lady:	
Carved headdress	**$1,200-$1,300**
Kindergarten Girl:	
6in (15cm)	**$600-$675**
Bride and Groom:	
Old style	**$1,500-$1,600**
New style	**$1,100-$1,250**
Women or Girls with special carving in the hair	**$800-$900**

FACTS

Door of Hope Mission, China; heads by carvers from Ning-Po. 1901-on.
Mark: Sometimes "Made in China" label.

Door of Hope bride, missing headdress. *H & J Foulke, Inc.*

DRESSEL

Marked Holz-Masse: Ca. 1875-on. Papier-mâché or composition shoulder head; cloth/composition body. See page 165.

Child Doll: Ca. 1893-on. Perfect bisque head, good wig, glass eyes, open mouth; suitable clothes; all in good condition.
Marks:

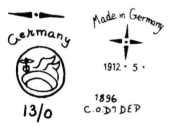

Composition body:

15-16in (38-41cm)	**$375-$400**
19-21in (48-53cm)	**$450-$500**
24in (61cm)	**$525-$550**
32in (81cm)	**$1,100**
38in (96cm)	**$2,000-$2,200**

#93, 1896 Kid body:

19-22in (48-56cm)	**$500-$550**

Character-type face, similar to **K*R 117n.** (For photograph see *12th Blue Book,* page 151):

14in (36cm)	**$1,100-$1,200**
26in (66cm)	**$1,600-$1,800**
41in (66cm)	**$3,100**
23in (58cm) all original, at auction	**$3,100**

FACTS

Cuno & Otto Dressel verlager & doll factory of Sonneberg, Thüringia, Germany. Bisque heads by Armand Marseille, Simon & Halbig, Ernst Heubach, Gebrüder Heubach. 1700-on.
Trademarks: Fifth Ave. Dolls (1903), Jutta (1907), Bambina (1909), Poppy Dolls (1912), Holz-Masse (1875).

15in (38cm) Dressel 1349 *Jutta,* child. *H & J Foulke, Inc.*

Portrait Series: 1896. Perfect bisque heads with portrait faces, glass eyes, some with molded mustaches and goatees; composition body; original clothes; all in good condition. Some marked "S" or "D" with a number.

13in (33cm) Uncle Sam
$1,200-$1,500
15in (38cm) Admiral Dewey and
Officers $1,600-$1,800
11in (28cm) Old Rip $1,200-$1,300
10in (23cm) Farmer $700-$800
10in (23cm) Buffalo Bill $750

Marked Jutta Child: Ca. 1906-1921. Perfect bisque socket head, good wig, sleep eyes, open mouth, pierced ears; ball-jointed composition body; dressed; all in good condition. Head made by Simon & Halbig.
Mold 1348 or 1349
Mark: *1349*
Jutta
S &H
11

14-16in (36-41cm)	$750*
19-21in (43-53cm)	$800-$850*
24-26in (61-66cm)	$1,000-$1,100*
30-32in (76-81cm)	$1,600-$1,800
38-39in (96-99cm)	$3,000-$3,500

*Allow $150 extra for flapper body with high knee joint.

Character Child: Ca. 1909-on. Perfect bisque socket head, ball-jointed composition body; mohair wig, painted eyes, closed mouth; suitable clothes; all in good condition. Glazed inside of head. (For photograph see 10th Blue Book, page 179.)
Mark:

C.O.D.
A/2

10-12in (25-31cm) $1,500-$1,800**
16-18in (41-46cm) $3,000
Limbach 8679 pouty, glass eyes:
14in (36cm) $1,800-$2,000**
Composition head:
19in (48cm) $2,600-$3,000**
13in (33cm) wear on nose
and lips $1,300

Marked C.O.D. Character Baby: Ca. 1910-on. Perfect bisque character face with marked wig or molded hair, painted or glass eyes; jointed baby body; dressed; all in good condition.
12-13in (31-33cm) $350-$375
16-18in (41-46cm) $450-$500
22-24in (56-61cm) $675-$775
**Not enough price samples to compute a reliable range.

14in (36cm) Dressel/Limbach 8679 Character boy.
H & J Foulke, Inc.

Marked Jutta Character Baby: Ca. 1910-1922. Perfect bisque socket head, good wig, sleep eyes, open mouth; bent-limb composition baby body; dressed; all in good condition.

Simon & Halbig:

16-18in (41-46cm)	**$650-$750**
23-24in (58-61cm)	**$1,300-$1,500**

Toddler:

23in (58cm)	**$1,900-$2,100**

Other Makers: (Armand Marseille, E. Heubach):

16-18in (41-46cm)	**$450-$500**
23-24in (58-61cm)	**$700-$800**

Marks:

Heubach 6½ Koppelsdorf
Jutta · Baby
Dressel
Germany
1922
10½

Jutta
1914
8

Toddler:

16-18in (41-46cm)	**$1,150-$1,250**

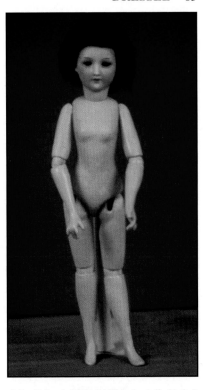

14in (36cm) COD 1469 lady doll. *H & J Foulke, Inc.*

Lady Doll: Ca. 1920s. Bisque socket head with young lady face, good wig, sleep eyes, closed mouth; jointed composition body in adult form with molded bust, slim waist and long arms and legs, feet modeled to wear high-heeled shoes; all in good condition.

Mark:

1469
C O. Dressel
Germany
2

#1469:

14in (36cm) naked	**$2,200-$2,400**
14in (36cm) original clothes	**$3,000-$4,200**

16in (41cm) *Jutta* character toddler, all original. *H & J Foulke, Inc.*

E. D. BÉBÉ

Marked E. D. Bébé: Perfect bisque head, wood and composition jointed body; good wig, beautiful blown glass eyes, pierced ears; nicely dressed; good condition.

Closed mouth:

15-18in (38-46cm)	**$2,800-$3,200***
22-24in (56-61cm)	**$3,600-$4,000***
28in (71cm)	**$4,200-$4,400***

Open mouth:

18-20in (35-51cm)	**$1,800-$2,000***
25-27in (64-69cm)	**$2,500-$2,700***

*For a pretty face.

Note: Dolls with Jumeau look but signed E. D. are Jumeau factory dolls produced when Emile Douillet was director of the Jumeau firm, 1892-1899. They do not have the word "Déposé" under the E. D. They should be priced as Jumeau dolls. (For photograph see *10th Blue Book*, page 181.)

FACTS

Etienne Denamur of Paris, France. 1889-on.

Mark:

E 8 D
DEPOSÉ

26in (66cm) E.D. *Private Collection.*

EDEN BÉBÉ

19in (48cm) *Eden Bébé,* all original. *Jensen's Antique Dolls.*

Marked Eden Bébé: Ca. 1890. Perfect bisque head, fully-jointed or 5-piece composition jointed body; beautiful wig, large set paperweight eyes, closed or open/closed mouth, pierced ears; lovely clothes; all in nice condition.

Closed mouth:

14-16in (36-41cm)	**$2,200-$2,400**
21-23in (53-58cm)	**$2,800-$3,000**
5-piece body:	
12in (31cm)	**$1,200-$1,500**

Open mouth:

19-20in (48-51cm)	**$1,900-$2,000**

FACTS

Fleischmann & Bloedel, doll factory, Paris, France. 1890, then into S.F.B.J. in 1899.
Trademark: Eden Bébé (1890), Bébé Triomphe (1898).
Mark: "EDEN BEBE, PARIS"

FRENCH FASHION-TYPE
(POUPÉE)

French Fashion Lady (Poupée): Perfect unmarked bisque shoulder head, swivel or stationary neck, kid body *poupée peau* or cloth body with kid arms—some with wired fingers; original or old wig, lovely blown glass eyes, closed mouth, earrings; appropriate old clothes; all in good condition. Fine quality bisque.

12-13in (31-33cm)	**$1,800 up***
15-16in (38-41cm)	**$2,500 up***
18-19in (46-48cm)	**$3,200 up***
21in (53cm)	**$3,500 up***
33in (84cm)	**$6,750**

Dainty oval face:

12-14in (31-36cm)	**$2,300-$2,500**

Round face, cobalt eyes (shoulder head):

13-15in (33-38cm)	**$2,300-$2,500**

Fully-jointed wood body *(poupée bois)*, naked:

15-17in (38-43cm)	**$5,000-$5,500+**

Gentleman, molded goatee and mustache:

11in (28cm) at auction	**$2,100**

Portrait face, wood body:

18in (46cm)	**$30,000 up**

Twill-over-wood body (Simon & Halbig-type):

9-10in (23-25cm)	**$4,000**
15-17in (38-43cm)	**$5,000**

Painted eyes, stiff neck:

16-17in (41-43cm)	**$1,600-$1,800**

*Allow extra for fancy original clothing. Value of doll varies greatly depending upon the appeal of the face. Also, allow additional for kid-over-wood upper and bisque lower arms.

+Allow extra for joints at ankle and waist.

E.B. Poupée: E. Barrois 1862-1877. Perfect bisque shoulder head (may have a swivel neck), glass eyes (may be painted with long painted eyelashes), closed mouth; appropriate wig; adult kid body, some with jointed wood arms or wood and bisque arms; appropriate clothing. All in good condition.

Mark:

E . | DÉPOSÉ B .

14-16in (36-41cm)	**$2,500-$3,000**
20-22in (51-56cm)	**$3,200-$3,500**

Child fashion, with trunk and wardrobe:

15in (38cm) at auction	**$10,000**

Marked Huret Poupée: Ca. 1850. China or bisque shoulder head, good wig, painted eyes, closed mouth; kid body; beautifully dressed; all in good condition.

17in (43cm)	**$15,000-$20,000**
Swivel neck	**$32,000**

13in (33cm) *poupée peau* with painted eyes. *H & J Foulke, Inc.*

FACTS
Various French firms. Ca. 1860-1930.
(See also *Bru, Jumeau, Gaultier,* and *Gesland.*)

Gutta-percha body $20,000**
Boots, 2in (5cm) $1,000

Terrene, kid over metal body:
   17in (43cm) $5,500-$6,000

Radiquet and Cordonnier: molded
breasts, bisque arms, one bent at elbow,
bisque lower legs, original signed stand.
   17in (43cm) $13,000-$15,000

Simonne, kid body:
   16in (41cm) $3,200-$3,500
   Wood body:
   18in (46cm) $6,000-$6,500
Period Clothes, Fashion Lady clothing:
   Dress $500-$1,000 up
   Boots $300-$350
   Elaborate wig $300-$400
   Nice wig $150-$250

Rohmer Poupée: Ca. 1857-1880. China
or bisque swivel or shoulder head, jointed
kid body, bisque or china arms, kid or
china legs; lovely wig, set glass eyes,
closed mouth, some ears pierced; fine costuming; entire doll in good condition.
   16-18in (41-46cm) $4,000-$4,500*
Zinc body:
   17in (43cm) at auction $5,100
Mark:

Parasol Doll, original silk outfit:
   18in (46cm) tall $2,200

Rochard Head, with Stanhope necklace
1868:
6-3/4in (17cm) at auction $24,300

A. Dehors, 1860:
   17in (43cm) shoulder head
                 $18,000-$19,000

Dehors & Clement, brown kid body:
   13in (33cm) at auction $9,750
Benoit Martin, wood body, naked:
   18in (46cm) at auction $17,500
**Not enough price samples to compute a
reliable average.

17in (43cm) Terrene *poupée*, kid over
metal body. *Sheila Thall, Cobwebs.*

16in (41cm) Rohmer *poupée*. *Private
Collection.*

FROZEN CHARLOTTE

(Bathing Doll)

Frozen Charlotte: All-china doll, black or blonde molded hair, painted features; hands extended, legs separated but not jointed; no clothes; perfect condition. Good quality.

2-3in (5-8cm)	**$50-$65***
4-5in (10-13cm)	**$140-$165***
6-7in (15-18cm)	**$200-$225***
9-10in (23-25cm)	**$275-$325***
14-15in (36-38cm)	**$550-$600**
17in (43cm)	**$700-$750**

Pink tint, early hairdo:

2½-3½in (6-9cm)	**$225-$250**
5in (13cm)	**$375-$400**
10in (25cm)	**$750**

Pink tint with bonnet:

3½in (9cm)	**$400-$450**
5in (13cm)	**$525-$575**

Black china:

5in (13cm)	**$165-$195**

Black boy, molded turban and pants:

3in (8cm)	**$275-$300**

Black boy, molded shift:

5in (13cm)	**$300-$350**

Blonde hair, molded bow:

5½in (14cm)	**$200-$225**

Wig, lovely boots:

5in (13cm)	**$200-$225**

All-Bisque:

5in (13cm)	**$150-$175**

Parian-type (1860s style):

5in (13cm)	**$225-$250**

Alice style with pink boots:

5in (13cm)	**$325-$350**

Fancy hairdo and boots:

4½in (11cm)	**$275-$300**

Molded clothes:

3-1/4in (9cm)	**$225**

Early boy, blonde hair:

9in (23cm)	**$450**

*Allow extra for pink tint, fine decoration and modeling, unusual hairdo.

FACTS

Various German firms. Ca. 1850s-early 1900s.
Mark: None, except for "Germany," or numbers or both.

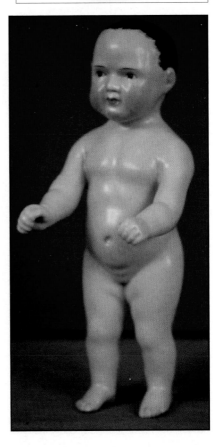

11½in (29cm) pink tint frozen charlotte. *H & J Foulke, Inc.*

FULPER

Fulper Child Doll: Perfect bisque head, good wig; kid jointed or composition ball-jointed body; set or sleep eyes, open mouth; suitably dressed; all in good condition. Good quality bisque.

Kid body:

18-21in (46-53cm) **$375-$425***

Composition body:

16-18in (41-46cm) **$450-$500***

22-24in (56-61cm) **$550-$600***

Fulper Baby:

16-18in (41-46cm) **$550-$650***

22-24in (56-61cm) **$750-$850***

Toddler:

15-17in (38-43cm) **$800-$900**

*Allow more for an especially pretty or cute doll.

FACTS

Heads by Fulper Pottery Co., of Flemington, N.J., for other companies, often Amberg or Horsman. 1918-1921.

Mark: "Fulper-Made in U.S.A."

18in (46cm) Fulper *Colonial Doll* character baby. *H & J Foulke, Inc.*

GAULTIER

Marked F.G. Fashion Lady (Poupée Peau): Ca. 1860-1930. Perfect bisque swivel head on bisque shoulder plate, original kid body, kid arms with wired fingers or bisque lower arms and hands; original or good French wig, lovely glass stationary eyes, closed mouth, ears pierced; appropriately dressed; all in good condition.

Mark: "F.G." on side of shoulder.

12-13in (30-33cm)	**$1,800-$2,100***
16-17in (41-43cm)	**$2,500-$2,600***
20in (51cm)	**$2,800-$2,900***
23in (58cm)	**$3,200-$3,400***
29-30in (71-76cm)	**$5,000-$5,500**
35in (89cm)	**$7,000-$7,400**
37in (94cm)	**$7,900**

Wood body, *(Poupée Bois)*:

16-18in (41-46cm)	**$4,500-$4,750**

Later doll in ethnic costume:

8-9in (20-23cm)	**$750-$850**

Painted eyes:

16-17in (41-43cm)	**$1,600-$1,800**

"Baggy pants," kid over wood arms:

15in (38cm)	**$3,600**

Approximate size chart:

Size 3/0 =	10½in (27cm)
2/0 =	11½in (29cm)
1 =	13½in (34cm)
2 =	15in (38cm)
3 =	17in (43cm)
5 =	20in (51cm)
6 =	22in (56cm)

*Allow extra for original clothes.

FACTS

François Gauthier (name changed to Gaultier in 1875); St. Maurice, Charenton, Seine, Paris, France. (This company made only porcelain parts, not bodies.) 1860 to 1899 (then joined S.F.B.J.)

35in (89cm)
signed F.G.
poupée peau.

Marked F.G. Bébé: Ca. 1879-1887. Perfect bisque swivel head, large bulgy paperweight eyes, closed mouth, pierced ears; dressed; all in good condition. So-called "Block letter" mark.

Mark:

$$F . 7.G$$

Composition body:

13-15in (33-38cm)	**$4,300-$4,600**
18-20in (46-51cm)	**$5,200-$5,700**
22-23in (56-58cm)	**$5,800-$6,100**
27-28in (69-71cm)	**$6,800-$7,200**
33-35in (84-89cm)	**$7,500-$8,000**

Kid body:

13in (33cm)	**$4,200-$5,200**
16in (41cm)	**$5,500-$5,750**
20-22in (51-56cm)	**$6,00-$7,000**

Marked F.G. Bébé: Ca. 1887-1900. Bisque head, beautiful large set eyes; well dressed; all in good condition. So-called "Scroll" mark.

Mark:

Closed mouth, very good quality bisque:

5-6in (13-15cm)
$750-$800
15-17in (38-43cm)
$2,800-$3,100*
22-24in (56-61cm)
$3,600-$3,900*
27-28in(69-71cm)
$4,300-$4,600*

Open mouth:

14-17in (38-43cm)
$1,750-$1,950
20-22in(51-56cm)
$2,100-$2,400
31in (79cm)
$3,300-$3,600

*For grainy or high color bisque, deduct $500-$1,000.

Early Block Mark F.G. Bébé on Kid Body. *Courtesy Dorothy Hunt, Sweetbriar.*

GESLAND

Fashion Lady (Poupée): Perfect bisque swivel head, good wig, paperweight eyes, closed mouth, pierced ears; stockinette body on metal frame with bisque hands and legs; dressed; all in good condition.

Early face:

16-20in (41-51cm) **$5,500–$6,200***

F.G. face:

14in (36cm)   **$3,600–$3,800***
16-20in (41-51cm) **$4,000–$4,500***
28in (71cm)   **$6,000–$6,500**

Body only for 14in (36cm)   **$900**

*Allow extra for original clothes.

Man with molded black hair and hat:

18½in (47cm) at auction   **$22,500**

Bébé: Perfect bisque swivel head; composition shoulder place, good wig, paperweight eyes, closed mouth, pierced ears; stockinette body on metal frame with composition lower arms and legs; dressed; all in good condition.

Beautiful early face:

14-16in (36-41cm)   **$4,900–$5,100**
22-24in (56-61cm)   **$5,900–$6,400**

"Scroll" mark face:

14-16in (36-41cm)   **$2,800–$3,100***
22-24in (56-61cm)   **$4,000–$4,500***

*Deduct 25% for ruddy bisque.

FACTS

Heads: Francois Gaultier, Paris, France.
Bodies: E. Gesland, Paris, France.
1860-1928.
Mark: Head: **F.G**

Body: Sometimes stamped E. Gesland.

16½ (42cm) **Bébé Gesland** with early F.G. block mark. *H & J Foulke, Inc.*

GOOGLY-EYED DOLLS

All-Bisque Googly: Jointed at shoulders and hips, molded shoes and socks; mohair wig, glass eyes, impish mouth; undressed; in perfect condition.

#217, 501, 330 and others:

4½-5in (11-13cm)	**$750-$800**
5½-6in (14-15cm)	**$900-$1,000**

#189, 192 swivel necks:

4½-5in (11-13cm)	**$900-$1,100**
5½-6in (14-15cm)	**$1,150-$1,250**
7in (18cm)	**$1,350-$1,450**

Jointed elbows and knees (Kestner), swivel neck,

5in (13cm)	**$2,850**
6-7in (15-18cm)	**$3,500-$3,850**
Baby, 4½in (12cm)	**$550-$600**

Painted eyes, molded hair:

4½in (12cm)	**$450-$500**
6in (15cm)	**$600-$650**

S.W.C. #405 (glass eyes),

6½in (17cm)	**$1,150**

S.W.C. #408 (painted eyes),

5in (13cm)	**$300**
K & R 131, 7in (18cm)	**$3,500-$3,800**

Painted eyes, composition body: Perfect bisque swivel head; 5-piece composition toddler or baby body; cute clothes; all in good condition.

A.M.,E. Heubach, Goebel, R.A.:

6-7in (15-18cm)	**$500-$550***
9-10in (23-25cm)	**$900-$950***

#252 A.M. Kewpie-type baby,

9in (23cm)	**$1200-$1300**

Gebrüder Heubach:

6-7in (15-18cm)	**$575-$625***
7in (18cm) Winker	**$850-$900**
9in (23cm) with top knot	**$1,350-$1450**

*Allow extra for unusual models.

**Not enough price samples to compute a reliable range.

FACTS

J.D. Kestner; Armand Marseille; Hertel, Schwab & Co.; Heubach; H. Steiner; Goebel and other German and French firms. Ca. 1911-on.

18in (46cm) **Einco** googly baby. *H. Jay Lowe Collection.*

Glass eyes, composition body: Perfect bisque head; original composition body; cute clothes; all in nice condition.

JDK 221:
   12in (30cm)
      $6,500-$6,800
   14in (35cm)
      $8,000-$8,200
   16½in (43cm) largest
      size **$12,000-$13,000**

A.M. #323 and other similar models by H. Steiner, E. Heubach, Goebel and Recknagel:
   6-7in (15-18cm)
      $900-$1,100
   10-11in (25-28cm)
      $1,650-$1,950
   13in (33cm)   **$2,500**
   Baby body,
      10-11in (25-28cm) **$1,400-$1,500**
A.M. #253 (watermelon mouth):
   6-7in (15-18cm)   **$1,000-$1,200**
   9-10in (23-25cm)   **$1,800-$2,000**
A.M. #200:
   8in (20cm)   **$1,200-$1,500**
   11-12in (28-31cm)   **$2,100-$2,300**
A.M. #240:
   10in (25cm) toddler   **$3,000-$3,200**
A.M. #241:
   11in (28cm) at auction   **$4,600**
B.P. 686:
   10½in (26cm) at auction   **$3,900**
Demalcol (Dennis, Malley, & Co. London, England),
   9-10in (23-25cm)   **$750-$850**

E. Heubach:
   #310, 14in (36cm)   **$3,600**
   #322, 8½in (21cm),
      at auction   **$2,400**

15in (38cm) K & R 131 googly. *H. Jay Lowe Collection.*

Hertel, Schwab & Co.:
   #163, baby
      15in (38cm)   **$6,000-$6,500**
   #163, toddler, red molded hair
      16in (41cm)   **$7,000-$7,500**
      12in (31cm)   **$4,000-$4,500**
   #165, baby
      12-13in (31-33cm)   **$3,900-$4,100**
      16in (41cm)   **$4,800-$5,000**
   toddler
      11-12in (28-31cm)   **$4,000**
      16in (41cm)   **$5,500**
   #172, baby
      15in (38cm)   **$6,800-7,200****
   toddler
      18in (46cm)   **$12,000****
   #173, baby
      10-11in (26-28cm) **$3,500-$3,800****
      16in (41cm)   **$6,000-$6,500****
   toddler
      10-12in (26-31cm) **$4,000-$5,000****
      16in (41cm)   **$7,000-$7,500****

G. Heubach:

Einco, 11in (28cm)

5-piece body	**$3,500-$3,800**
14-15in (36-38cm)	**$6,500-$7,000**
18-20in (46-51cm)	
	$14,500-$15,000

Elizabeth,

7-9in (18-23cm)	**$1,650-$1,850**

#8678, 9573:

6-7in (15-18cm)	**$900-$1,100**
9in (23cm)	**$1,250-$1,500**

Handwerck, Max:

Molded hat,

10-13in (25-33cm)	**$2,100-$2,300**
Double-faced	**$2,200-$2,400**

K * R 131:

8in (20cm),

5-piece body	**$3,500-$4,000**
15-16in (38-41cm)	**$12,000**

Kley & Hahn 180,

16½in (43cm)	**$3,500****

Limbach SK, 10in (25cm)   **$1,650**

P.M. 950,

11in (28cm)	**$1,600****

SFBJ #245

8in (20cm), 5-piece body

	$2,100-$2,200
15in (38cm)	**$4,200-$4,600****

Schieler, 15in (38cm)

at auction	**$3,045**

Disc Eyes,
DRGM 954642 black or white

11-12in (28-31cm)	
	$1,250-$1,500**

Composition face: 1911-1914. Hug Me Kids, Little Bright Eyes, and other trade names. Round all-composition or composition mask face, wig, round glass eyes looking to the side, watermelon mouth; felt body; original clothes; all in very good condition.

10in (25cm)	**$700-$800**
12in (31cm)	**$950**
16in (41cm)	**$1,250**

**Not enough price samples to compute a reliable range.

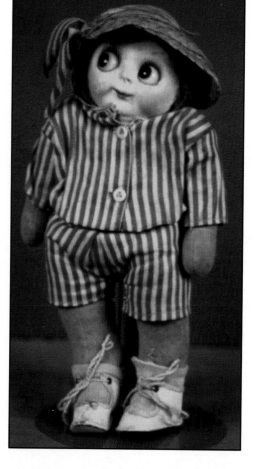

10in (25cm) *Hug Me Kiddie*, all original. *H & J Foulke, Inc.*

GREINER

Marked Greiner: Papier-mâché shoulder head with blonde or black molded hair, painted features; homemade cloth body, leather arms; nice old clothes, entire doll in good condition, some wear acceptable.

'58 label:

15-17in (38-43cm)	**$900-$1,000**
20-23in (51-58cm)	**$1,250-$1,500**
28-30in (71-76cm)	**$1,750-$2,000**
38in (97cm)	**$2,800**
21in (53cm) Excellent,	
all original	**$2,625**

Much worn:

20-23in (51-58cm)	**$650-$750**
28-30in (71-76cm)	**$850-$950**

Glass eyes,
   20-23in (51-58cm) **$2,200-$2,500****

**Not enough price samples to compute reliable average.

'72 label:

19-22in (48-56cm)	**$500-$550**
29-31in (71-79cm)	**$800-$900**
35in (89cm)	**$1,100-$1,200**

FACTS

Ludwig Greiner of Philadelphia, Pa., U.S.A. 1858-1883, but probably as early as 1840s.

Mark: Paper label on back shoulder:

GREINER'S
IMPROVED
PATENTHEADS
Pat. March 30th '58
or
GREINER'S
PATENT DOLL HEADS
No 7
Pat. Mar. 30'58. Ext. '72

32in (81cm) Greiner with '58 label. *H & J Foulke, Inc*

HEINRICH HANDWERCK

Marked Handwerck Child Doll: Ca. 1885-on. Perfect bisque socket head, original or good wig, sleep or set eyes, open mouth, pierced ears; composition ball-jointed body with Handwerck stamp; dressed; entire doll in good condition.

#69, 89, 99 or no mold #:

10-12in (25-31cm), all original	**$550-$650**
14-16in (36-41cm)	**$650-$700***
19-21in (43-53cm)	**$700-$800***
23-25in (58-64cm)	**$800-$900***
28-30in (71-76cm)	**$1,200-$1,400**
32-33in (79-84cm)	**$1,700-$1,800**
36in (91cm)	**$2,200-$2,500**
42in (107cm)	**$3800-$4200**
29in (74cm) totally original with exceptional clothes, at auction	**$2,100**

#79, 109, 119:

14-16in (36-41cm)	**$700-$750**
22-24in (56-61)	**$900-$1,000**
41in (104cm)	**$4,300**

*Allow $100-$150 extra for flirty eyes.

#139 and other shoulder heads, kid body:

16-18in (41-46cm)	**$350-$400**
22-24in (56-61cm)	**$450-$500**

#79, 89 closed mouth:

18-20in (46-51cm)	**$2,300-$2,500**
24in (61cm)	**$2,800-$3,200**

#189, open mouth,

18-20in (46-51cm)	**$900-$950**

Bébé Cosmopolite, 19in (48cm),

all original and boxed	**$1,000**

#160 character child, 22in (56cm)

at auction	**$7,250**

FACTS

Heinrich Handwerck, doll factory, Waltershausen, Thüringia, Germany. Heads by Simon & Halbig. 1855-on. **Trademarks:** Bébé Cosmopolite, Bébé de Réclame, Bébé Superior.

Mark:

Germany   XANDWERCK

HEINRICH HANDWERCK   109-11

SIMON B HALBIG   Germany

23½in (59cm) Handwerk/S&H child with flirty eyes.
Jensen's Antique Dolls.

MAX HANDWERCK

23½in (59cm) Max Handwerck 297 child.
H & J Foulke, Inc.

Marked Max Handwerck Child Doll:
Perfect bisque socket head, original or
good wig, set or sleep eyes, open mouth,
pierced ears; original ball-jointed body;
well dressed; all in good condition.
#283, 297 or 421.

16-18in (41-46cm)	**$375-$400**
22-24in (56-61cm)	**$525-$575**
31-32in (79-81cm)	**$1,000-$1,100**
38-39in (97-99cm)	**$2,000-$2,200**

Bébé Elite Character Baby,

19-21in (48-53cm)	**$550-$650**

FACTS

Max Handwerck, doll factory,
Waltershausen, Thüringia, Germany.
Some heads by Goebel. 1900-on.
Trademarks: Bébé Elite,
Triumph-Bébé.
Mark:

HERTEL, SCHWAB & CO.

Marked Character Baby: Perfect bisque
head; bent limb baby body; dressed; all in
good condition.
#130, 142, 150, 151, 152:

10-12in (25-31cm)	**$425-$500**
15-17in (38-43cm)	**$575-$675**
19-21in (48-53cm)	**$700-$750**
24-25in (61-64cm)	**$900-$1,000**

Toddler

16in (41cm)	**$750**
24in (61cm)	**$1,500**

#150 all bisque,

6in (15cm)	**$400-$450**

#142 all-bisque, painted eyes,

11in (28cm)	**$850-$900**

#159, 2 faces,

10in (25cm) at auction	**$850**

#125 (so-called **Patsy Baby**),

12-13in (30-33cm)	**$950-$1,000**

#126 (so-called **Skippy**),

16in (41cm)	**$1,500**

Child Doll: Ca. 1910. Perfect bisque
head, mohair or human hair wig, sleep
eyes, open mouth with upper teeth; good
quality jointed composition body (some
marked K & W); dressed; all in good condition. Mold **#136.**

14-17in (36-43cm)	**$475-$525**
20-22in (51-56cm)	**$575-$625**
24-25in (61-64cm)	**$700-$750**
33in (84cm) all original and boxed	**$1,350**

Marked Character Child: Perfect
bisque head, painted or sleeping eyes,
closed mouth; jointed composition body;
dressed; all in good condition.

#134, 149, 141:

13in (33cm)	$3,500-$3,800
16-18in (41-46cm)	$6,500-$8,500**

#154 (closed mouth):

14-16in (36-41cm)	$2,300-$2,500
19in (48cm)	$3,100

#154, 166 (open mouth):

16-18in (41-46cm)	$1,200-$1,400

#169 (closed mouth):

19-21in (48-53cm) toddler	
	$3,500-$4,000

#127 (so-called Patsy):

17in (43cm)	$2,100-$2,500

**Not enough price samples to compute a
reliable range.

FACTS

Hertel Schwab & Co., porcelain
factory, Stutzhaus, near Ohrdruf,
Thüringia, Germany. 1910-on.

Marks:

17in (43cm) 127 so-
called *Patsy. H & J
Foulke, Inc.*

24in (61cm) 151
character toddler.
H & J Foulke, Inc.

ERNEST HEUBACH

Heubach Child Doll: Ca. 1888-on. Perfect bisque head; dressed; all in good condition.

#275 or horsehoe, kid or cloth body:
- 19-21in (48-53cm)   **$275-$325**
- 24in (61cm)   **$425-$450**

#250, 251, composition body:
- 8-9in (20-23cm)
  - 5-piece body   **$210-$235**
- 16-18in (41-46cm)   **$350-$400**
- 23-24in (58-61cm)   **$500-$550**

Painted bisque, #250, 407,
- 7-8in (18-20cm)   **$110-$135**

#312 SUR (for Seyfarth & Reinhard):
- 14in (36cm)   **$350-$375***
- 28in (71cm)   **$750-$850***
- 45-46in (113-115cm)   **$3,500**

*Allow $150-$250 extra for a flapper body.

Character Children: 1910-on. Perfect bisque shoulder head with molded hair in various styles, some with hair bows, painted eyes, open/closed mouth; cloth body with composition lower arms,

#261, 262, 271 and others,
- 12in (31cm)
  - **$400-$450****

**Not enough price samples to compute a reliable range.

11in (28cm) 320 character toddler, all original. *H & J Foulke, Inc.*

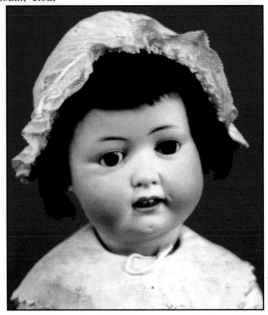

22in (56cm) 267 character baby. *H & J Foulke, Inc.*

Character Baby: 1910-on. Perfect bisque head, good wig, sleep eyes, open mouth (sometimes also wobbly tongue and pierced nostrils): composition bent-limb baby; dressed; all in good condition. #300, 320, 342 and others:

5½-6in (14-15cm)	**$250-$275**
8-10in (20-25cm)	**$250-$275**
14-17in (36-43cm)	**$425-$500**
19-21in (48-53cm)	**$550-$650**
24-25in (61-64cm)	**$850**

Toddler:
9-10in (23-25cm)	
5-piece body	**$375-$450**

Fully jointed body,
15-17in (38-43cm)	**$650-$750**
23-25in (58-64cm)	**$1,250-$1,350**

Painted Bisque Toddler:
11in (28cm) factory original	**$500-$550**

Infant: Ca. 1925. Perfect bisque head; cloth body.

#349, 339, 350,
10½in (26cm)	**$450-$475**
13-16in (33-41cm)	**$575-$675**

#338, 340,
14-16in (36-41cm)	**$725-$825****

**Not enough price samples to compute a reliable range.

FACTS

Ernst Heubach, porcelain factory, Köppelsdorf, Thüringia, Germany. 1887-on.

Mark:

D.E.P. 1902
Heubach · Kopplesdorf.
300 · 14/0
Germany
2/0

9in (23cm) h.c. 349 infant. *H & J Foulke, Inc.*

GEBRÜDER HEUBACH

Heubach Character Child: Ca. 1910. Perfect bisque head; jointed composition or kid body; dressed; all in good condition. (For photographs of Heubach dolls see *Focusing on Dolls*, pages 30-68 and previous *Blue Books*.)

#5636, 7663, laughing child, glass eyes:
12-13in (31-33cm)	**$1,600-$1,900**
15-18in (38-46cm)	**$2,500-$2,800**

#5689 smiling child,
27in (69cm)	**$3,500-$4,000**

#5730 Santa,
19-21in (48-53cm)	**$1,800-$2,200**

#5777 Dolly Dimple:
19-22in (48-567cm)	**$3,000-$3,200**
Shoulder head,	
17-19in (43-48cm)	**$900-$1,100**

#6969, 6970, 7246, 7347, 7407, 8017, pouty child (must have glass eyes):
12-13in (31-33cm)	**$2,000-$2,500**
16-19in (41-48cm)	**$3,500-$4,000**
24in (61cm)	**$5,500-$6,000**
28in (71cm)	**$8,500****

#6692 and other shoulder head pouties,
14-16in (36-41cm)	**$750-$850**

#7054 and other smiling shoulder heads
12-14in (30-36cm)	**$600-$700**
19in (48cm)	**$900-$1,000**

#7407 painted eye, wigged,
16in (41cm)	**$2,350**

#7604, 7820 and other smiling socket heads,
14-16in (36-41cm)	**$800-$1,000**
20in (51cm)	**1,650**

#7602, 6894 and other socket head pouties,
14-16in (36-41cm)	**$750-$950**

#7622 and other socket head pouties (wide lips),
14-17in (36-43cm)	**$1,000-$1,250**

#7661 squinting eyes, crooked mouth,
19in (48cm)	**$6,750**

#7665 Smiling, 16in (41cm) **$1,800**

#7679 Whistler socket head:
10in (25cm)	**$800-$900**
14in (36cm)	**$1,100-$1,300**

**Not enough price samples to compute a reliable average.

FACTS

Gebrüder Heubach, porcelain factory, Licht and Sonneberg, Thüringia, Germany. 1820-on; doll heads, 1910-on.

Mark:

16in (41cm) 7407
pouty character child.
H & J Foulke, Inc.

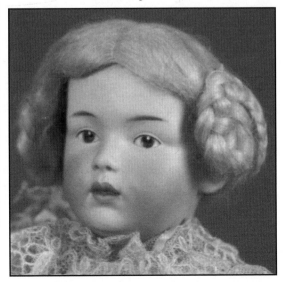

12in (31cm) 7246 pouty character child. *H & J Foulke Inc.*

17in (43cm) pouty shoulder head character. *H & J Foulke, Inc.*

#7684 Screamer,
  16-19in (41-48cm) **$2,500-$3,000****
#7711 12-14in (31-36cm)   **$1,400**
#7743 big ears, 17in (43cm)
                $5,500-$6,000**
#7764 singing girl, 16in (41cm)
                    $10,000**
#7788, 7850 Coquette,
  11in (28cm)   **$950**
  14in (36cm)   **$1,200**
  20in (51cm)   **$1,650**
  Shoulder head, 12in (31cm)**$700-$775**
#7865, 14in (36cm)   **$3,000**
#7852 shoulder head, molded coiled
  braids, 16in (41cm) **$2,200****
#7853 shoulder head, downcast eyes,
  14in (36cm)   **$1,650-$1,850**
#7911, 8191 grinning:
  11in (28cm)   **$850-$900**
  15in (38cm) **$1,200-$1,250**
#7920 18in (46cm)   **$2,700****
#7925, 7926 lady,
  18-19in (46-48cm) **$2,800-$3,100**
#8050 smiling girl with hairbow,
  18in (46cm)   **$12,500****
#8192:
  9-11in (23-28cm)   **$450**
  14-16in (36-41cm)   **$800**
  18-22in (46-56cm) **$1,100**
#8381 Princess Julianna,
  16in (41cm) **$10,000-$12,000**
#8550, molded tongue sticking out:
  13in (33cm) intaglio eyes **$950-$1,050**
  17in (43cm) glass eyes   **$1,500**
#8556, googly-type face **$11,500****
#8420, pouty with glass eyes
  9½in (24cm) twin toddlers **$1,800pr**
  13in (33cm)   **$1,950**
#9102 Cat, 6in (15cm) **$1,000-$1,150****
#9141 Winker:
  7in (18cm) painted eye **$850-$950**
  9in (23cm) glass eye   **$1,500**
**Not enough price samples to compute a reliable average.

#9467 Indian, 14in (36cm) **$2,500**
#10532,
    8½in (21cm) chubby
      5-piece toddler, all original **$900**
    20-22in (51-53cm) **$1,200-$1,300**
#10586, 10633,
    18-20in (46-51cm) **$750-$850**
#11173 Tiss Me,
    8in (20cm) **$1,850-$2,000**
Baby BoKaye, Bonnie Babe,
    7-8in (18-20cm) **$900-$950**
#1907 Jumeau,
    16in (41cm) **$1,800-$2,000**
    20-22in (51-56cm) **$2,400-$2,500**

All-Bisque:
Position Babies and Action Figures,
    5in (13cm) **$400-$500**
Girl with bobbed hair,
    9in (23cm) **$900-$1,000**
Girl with head band,
    6in (15cm) swivel neck **$895**
    9in (23cm) **$1,100**
Girl with three bows,
    9in (23cm) **$1,500**
Boy, 8in (20cm) **$1,200**
Boy or girl,
    4½in (11cm) **$300-$400**
Chin Chin,
    4½in (11cm) **$325-$365**

Heubach Babies: Ca. 1910. Perfect bisque head; composition bent-limb body; dressed; all in nice condition.
#6894, 7602, 6898, 7759 and other pouty babies; #7604 laughing:
    4½in (12cm) **$225-$275**
    6in (15cm) **$275-$300**
    10-12in (25-31cm) **$500-$700**
    14in (36cm) **$750-$800**
#7877, 7977 Baby Stuart:
Painted eyes,
    9in (23cm) **$800-$850**
    13-15in (33-38cm) **$1,300-$1,500**

Glass eyes,
    13in (33cm) **$2,250**
#8420, glass eyes,
    14in (36cm) **$1,250-$1,300**
#7959, molded pink cap,
    14in (36cm) at auction **$4,200**
#8413, open/closed mouth with tongue
    12in (31cm) at auction **$900**

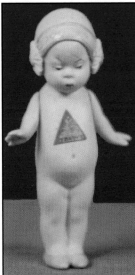

4½in (11cm) *Chin Chin* with chest label. *H & J Foulke, Inc.*

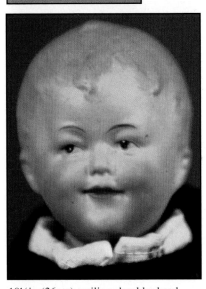

10½in (26cm) smiling shoulder head character. *H & J Foulke, Inc.*

INDIAN DOLLS
BISQUE HEADS

American Indian Doll: Perfect bisque head with light brown or copper tinted complexion sometimes with worry wrinkles between brows and wavy eyebrows, set brown glass eyes, black mohair wig in braids; original clothes, head feathers, moccasins or molded shoes; all in good condition.

7-8in (18-20cm)	$175-$225
12in (30cm)	$375-$425
15in (38cm)	$500-$550
18in (46cm)	$750-$850

Bähr & Pröschild 244, closed mouth:
14-15in (36-38cm)   **$1,800-$2,200**

Gebr. Heubach 8457, 9467 shoulder head on cloth body:
14in (36cm)   **$2,500**

Simon & Halbig 1303,
21in (53cm)   **$17,000****
**Not enough price samples to compute a reliable average.

FACTS

Various German factories, such as Armand Marseille, Bähr & Pröschild and Gebr. Heubach Ca 1895-on.

14in (36cm) Bähr & Pröschild 244, all original. *H & J Foulke, Inc.*

15in (38cm) unmarked Indian, possibly by Armand Marseille, all original. *H & J Foulke, Inc.*

JULLIEN

JUMEAU

19in (48cm) *Jullien Bébé.*
H & J Foulke, Inc.

Marked Jullien Bébé: Perfect bisque head, lovely wig, paperweight eyes, closed mouth, pierced ears; jointed wood and composition body; pretty old clothes; all in good condition.

17-19in (43-48cm)	$3,500-$3,700
24-26in (61-66cm)	$4,200-$4,500

Open mouth:

19-21in (48-53cm)	$1,600-$1,800
29-30in (74-76cm)	$2,600-$2,900

FACTS

Jullien, Jeune of Paris, France. 1875-1904 when joined with S.F.B.J.
Mark: "JULLIEN" with size number

JuLLiEN
1

Poupée Peau Fashion Lady: Late 1860s-on. Perfect bisque swivel head on shoulder plate, old wig, paperweight eyes, closed mouth, pierced ears; all-kid body; appropriate old clothes; all in good condition.
Mark on body: JUMEAU
MEDAILLE D'OR
PARIS

Standard face:

11½-13in (29-33cm)	$2,800-$3,200*
17-18in (43-46cm)	3,600-$3,800*
20in (51cm)	$3,800-$4,200*

FACTS

Maison Jumeau, Paris, France.
1842-on.
Trademark:
Bébé Jumeau (1886)
Bébé Prodige (1886)
Bébé Francais (1896)

14in (36cm) *poupee peau.*
H & J Foulke, Inc

9in (24cm) premiere *Jumeau Bébé*.
H & J Foulke, Inc.

23in (58cm) extreme almond-eyed
Jumeau Bébé. Private Collection.

Poupée Bois, wood body with bisque limbs,

18in (46cm)	**$5,500-$6,500***

Later face with large eyes:

10-12in (25-31cm)	**$1,800-$2,000***
14-15in (36-38cm)	**$2,400-$2,500***

So-called "Portrait Face" (see *11th Blue Book,* page 221):

19-21in (48-53cm)	**$6,000-$7,000***

Wood body (*poupée bois*),

19-21in (48-53cm)	**$9,000-$11,000***

Rare lady face,

21in (53cm)	**$16,000**

Period Clothes for Bébés:

Jumeau shift	**$400-$600**
Jumeau shoes	**$350-$450**
Jumeau dress and hat	**$1,000up**

*Allow extra for original clothes.

Long-Face Triste Bébé: 1879-1886. Designed by Carrier-Belleuse. Marked with size (9-16) number only on head, blue stamp on body. Perfect bisque socket head with beautiful wig, paperweight eyes, closed mouth, applied pierced ears; jointed composition body with straight wrists (separate ball joints on early models); lovely clothes; all in good condition.

20-21in (51-53cm)	**$16,000-$20,000**
28-30in (71-76cm)	**$22,500**

Size	
9	= 21in (53cm)
11	= 24in (61cm)
13, 14	= 29-30in (74-76cm)

Portrait Jumeau: 1877-1883. Usually marked with size number only on head, blue stamp on body; skin or other good wig; spiral threaded enamel paperweight eyes, closed mouth, pierced ears; jointed composition body with straight wrists and separate ball joints; nicely dressed; all in good condition.

Premiere

9in (23cm) all original and boxed,
  at auction **$11,275**
12in (30cm) **$5,500***
14-15in (36-38cm) **$6,000-$7,000**
18-19in (46-48cm) **$7,500-$8,000***
23in (58cm) **$10,000***
*Expect dust specks, uneven eye cuts and uneven eyebrows.

Almond-Eyed

Sizes:
  4/0 = 12in (30cm)
  3/0 = 13½in (34cm)
  2/0 = 14½in (37cm)
  0 = 16in (41cm)
  1 = 17in (43cm)
  2 = 18½in (47cm)
  3 = 20in (51cm)
  4 = 23in (58cm)
  5 = 25in (64cm)

18in (46cm) E 8 J *Jumeau Bébé. Kay & Wayne Jensen Collection.*

12-14½in (30-37cm)
  $13,000-$15,000
16-18½in (41-47cm)
  $18,000-$22,000
20in (51cm)
  $25,000-$30,000
23in (58cm)
  $33,000-$38,000
25in (64cm) **$55,000**
*Allow extra for unusually large eyes.

12½in (31cm) portrait *Jumeau Bébé. Kay & Wayne Jensen Collection.*

Second Series, excellent quality, larger dolls have applied ears. (For photograph see *13th Blue Book*, page 106.)

13-15in (29-38cm) Size 6
$7,000-$8,000
18-20in (46-51cm) Size 8   **$10,000**
22in (56cm) Size 10   **$12,500**
25in (64cm) Size 12 **$16,000-$18,000**

E.J. Bébé: 1881-1886. Perfect bisque socket head with good wig, paperweight eyes, closed mouth, pierced ears; jointed composition body with straight wrists, early models with separate ball joints; lovely clothes; all in good condition.

Early Mark: 8
E.J.

17-18in (43-46cm) size 6   **$10,500**
19-21in (48-53cm) size 8   **$12,500**
23in (58cm) size 9   **$17,500**
E.J.A. 25in (64cm)   **$30,000-$32,000**

Mid to Late Period Mark:
DEPOSÉ

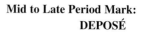

14-16in (36-41cm)   **$6,350-$6,850**
19-21in (48-53cm)   **$7,250-$7,850**
25-26in (64-66cm)   **$9,250-$9,950**
30in (76cm)   **$12,000-$13,000**
Later Tête-style face:
15-16in (38-41cm)   **$5,200-$5,500**
18-19in (46-48cm)   **$5,800-$6,200**
25-26in (64-66cm)   **$8,200-$8,800**

Deposé 9:
21-22in (53-56cm)   **$6,500-$7,500**
9x, bisque lower arms, at auction
21in (53cm)   **$17,050**

Incised "Jumeau Déposé" Bébé: 1886-1889. Head incised as below, blue stamp on body. Perfect bisque socket head with good wig, paperweight eyes, closed mouth, pierced ears; jointed composition body with straight wrists; lovely clothes; all in good condition.

Mark: Incised on head:

DÉPOSÉ
JUMEAU
8

14½in (37cm) incised *Déposé Jumeau Bébé*. *Rhoda Shoemaker Collection.*

14-15in (36-38cm)   **$4,500-$5,000**
18-20in (46-51cm)   **$5,500-$6,000**
24-25in (61-64cm)   **$6,800-$7,500**
19in (48cm) all original lovely clothes
and Jumeau arm band   **$10,340**

Tête Jumeau Bébé: 1885-on, then through S.F.B.J. Red stamp on head as indicated below, blue stamp or "Bebe Jumeau" oval sticker on body. Perfect bisque head, original or good French wig, beautiful stationary eyes, closed mouth, pierced ears; jointed composition body with jointed or straight wrists: original or lovely clothes; all in good condition.

Mark:

DÉPOSÉ
TETE JUMEAU
B^TE SGDG
6

9-10in (23-25cm) #1   **$5,000-$5,500**
12-13in (31-33cm)   **$3,500-$4,000**
15-16in (38-41cm)   **$4,200-$4,600**
18-20in (46-51cm)   **$4,800-$5,200**
21-23in (53-58cm)   **$5,200-$5,500**
25-27in (64-69cm)   **$6,000-$6,500**

30in (76cm)   **$6,800-$7,200**
34-36in (86-91cm)   **$8,000-$8,500**
41in (104cm)   **$12,500***

Lady body, 20in (51cm)   **$5,500***
Open mouth:
14-16in (36-41cm)   **$2,650-$2,950**
20-22in (51-56cm)   **$3,200-$3,500**
24-25in (61-64cm)   **$3,600-$3,800**
27-29in (69-74cm)   **$3,800-$4,000**
32-34in (81-86cm)   **$4,500**
*Allow extra for original clothes.

Bébé Phonographe,
24-25in (61-64cm)   **$6,500-$7,500**
Marked E.D. Bébé: Mark used during the Douillet management, 1892-1899. Perfect bisque head, closed mouth.
17-19in (43-48cm)   **$4,750-$5,000**
Mark:

E.8.D

16½in (42cm)
Tête Jumeau, size 6.
H & J Foulke, Inc.

22in (56cm) 208 Jumeau character. *H Jay Lowe Collection.*

Marked B.L. Bébé: Ca. 1880. For the Louvre department store. Perfect bisque socket head, closed mouth.

Mark:

B. 9 L.

13in (33cm)	**$3,500-$4,000**
18-21in (46-53cm)	**$4,800-$5,200**

Marked R.R. Bébé: Ca. 1880s. Perfect bisque head, closed mouth.

Mark:

R 10 R

21-23in (53-58cm)	**$4,900-$5,300**
26in (66cm) open mouth	**$3,950**

Approximate sizes of E.J.s and Têtes:

1	= 10in (25cm)
2	= 11in (28cm)
3	= 12in (31cm)
4	= 13in (33cm)
5	= 14-15in (36-38cm)
6	= 16in (41cm)
7	= 17in (43cm)
8	= 19in (48cm)
9	= 20in (51cm)
10	= 21-22in (53-56cm)
11	= 24-25in (61-64cm)
12	= 26-27in (66-69cm)
13	= 29-30in (74-76cm)

#230 Character Child: Ca. 1910. Perfect bisque socket head, open mouth, set or sleep eyes, good wig; jointed composition body; dressed; all in good condition.

16in (41cm)	**$1,600**
21-23in (53-58cm)	**$2,000**

#1907 Jumeau Child: Ca. 1907-on. Sometimes red-stamped "Tête Jumeau." Perfect bisque head, open mouth.

16in (40cm)	**$2,500-$2,600**
19-22in (48-56cm)	**$2,900-$3,200**
25-27in (64-69cm)	**$3,600-$3,800**
33in (84cm)	**$4,500**

Papier-mâché face,

22-24in (56-61cm)	**$800-$1,000****

DEP Jumeau: See page 81 for details.
SFBJ Tête Jumeau: See page 174 for details.
Jumeau Characters: Ca. 1900. **Tête Jumeau** mark. Perfect bisque head with glass eyes, character expression.

#203, 208 and others	**$50,000 up**
#221 Great Ladies, 10-11in (25-28cm)	
all original	**$600-$650**
Double-faced laughing and crying,	
18in (46cm) at auction	**$14,500**

Princess Elizabeth Jumeau: 1938 through S.F.B.J. Perfect bisque socket head highly colored, glass flirty eyes.

Mark:

UNIS FRANCE 149
306

Body Incised:

JUMEAU
PARIS
Princess

18-19in (46-48cm)	**$1,600-$1,800**
32-33in (81-84cm)	**$2,700-$3,200****

**Not enough price samples to compute a reliable range.

23in (58cm) 1907 Jumeau. *H & J Foulke, Inc.*

10in (25cm) "Marie Antionette" from the Great Ladies Series, all original. H & J Foulke, Inc

KAMKINS

Marked Kamkins: Molded mask face with painted features, wig; cloth body and limbs; original clothing; all in excellent condition.

18-20in (46-51cm)	**$1,400-$1,600**
Fair to good condition	**$850-$950**
With swivel joints or	
molded derriére,	**$2,000-$2,500**

FACTS

Louise R. Kampes Studios, Atlantic City, N.J. U.S.A.) (1919-1928 and perhaps longer.)

Mark: Red paper heart on left side of chest:

Also sometimes stamped with black on foot or back of head:

KAMKINS
A DOLLY MADE TO LOVE
PATENTED BY L.R. KAMPES
ATLANTIC CITY, N.J.

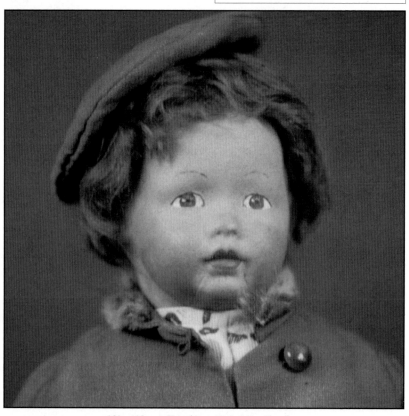

19in (48cm) *Kamkins*. *H & J Foulke, Inc.*

KÄMMER & REINHARDT

Child Doll: 1886-1895. Perfect bisque head; ball-jointed composition body; appropriate clothes; all in good condition.

#192:

Closed mouth:

5in (13cm)	**$550**
6-7in (15-18cm)	**$600-$700***
10in (25cm)	**$900-$1,000**
16-18in (41-46cm)	**$2,800-$3,000**
22-24in (56-61cm)	**$3,200-$3,400**

Open mouth:

7-8in (18-20cm)	**$550-$600***
12in (31cm)	**$700-$800**
14-16in (36-41cm)	**$900-$1,000**
20-22in (51-56cm)	**1,300-$1,500**
26-28in (66-71cm)	**$1,900-$2,100**

*Allow $100-$200 extra for a fully-jointed body.

FACTS

Kämmer & Reinhardt of Waltershausen, Thüringia, Germany. Bisque heads often by Simon & Halbig. 1886-on.
Trademarks: Majestic Doll, Mein Liebling (My Darling), Der Schelm (The Flirt), Die Kokette (The Coquette), My Playmate.
Mark: Size number is height in centimeters.

K ✡ R

SIMON & HALBIG
116/A
50

19½in (50cm) 192 child. *H & J Foulke, Inc.*

18in (46cm) child with walking mechanism. *H & J Foulke, Inc.*

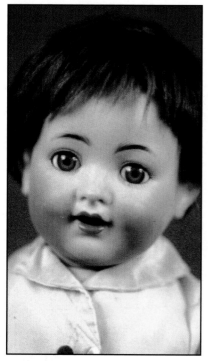

18in (46cm) 22 character toddler. *H & J Foulke, Inc.*

Child Doll: 1895-1930s. Perfect bisque head, open mouth; K & R ball-jointed composition body; appropriate clothes; all in good condition.

#191, 290, 403 or size number only+:
5-piece body,

4½-5in (12-13cm)	**$450-$495**
7-8in (18-20cm)	**$425-$475**
Fully-jointed body,	
8-10in (20-25cm)	**$650-$750**
12-14in (31-36cm)	**$650-$750***
16-17in (41-43cm)	**$750-$800***
19-21in (48-43cm)	**$850-$950***
23-25in (58-64cm)	**$1,050-$1,150***
28in (71cm)	**$1,300-$1,400***
30-31in (76-79cm)	**$1,600-$1,800***
33in (84cm)	**$2,200-$2,300***
36in (91cm)	**$2,500-$2,800***
39-42in (99-107cm)	**$3,600-$4,200***

Closed mouth, 6in (15cm) **$600-$650**

+Numbers 15-100 low on neck are centimeter sizes, not mold numbers.

*Allow $100-$200 additional for flirty eyes; allow $200 extra for flapper body; allow $100 for walking body.

Child Doll: Shoulder head, kid body; all in good condition.

17-18in (41-46cm)	**$450-$500**
22in (56cm)	**$550-$650**

Character Babies or Toddlers: 1909-on. Perfect bisque head; K & R composition body; nicely dressed; all in good condition. (See *Simon & Halbig Dolls, The Artful Aspect* for photographs of mold numbers not pictured here.

#100 Baby, painted eyes:

11-12in (28-31cm)	**$525-$575**
14-15in (36-38cm)	**$700-$750**
18-20in (46-51cm)	**$900-$1,000**
11in (28cm) all original and boxed,	
at auction	**$1,200**
Glass eyes, 16in (41cm)	**$2,000****

#126, 22 baby body:

10-12in (25-31cm)	**$450-$525***
14-16in (36-41cm)	**$550-$600***
18-20in (46-51cm)	**$700-$800***
22-24in (56-61cm)	**$850-$950***
30-33in (76-84cm)	**$1,800-$2,200***

#126 all-bisque baby:

6in (15cm)	**$750-$800**
8½in (21cm)	**$1,000-$1,100****

#126 all-bisque toddler:

7in (18cm)	**$1,400-$1,500****

#126, 22 5-piece toddler body:

6-7in (15-18cm)	**$900+**
9-10in (23-25cm)	**$950+**
15-17in (38-43cm)	**$800-$900+**
23in (58cm)	**$1,050-$1,150***

#126 toddler fully-jointed:

12-13in (31-33cm)	**$750-$850**
15-17in (38-41cm)	**$1,000-$1,200***
23-25in (58-64cm)	**$1,500-$1,700***
28-30in (71-76cm)	**$2,000-$2,200***

*Allow $50-$100 extra for flirty eyes.

#128 baby body:

15-16in (38-41cm)	**$900-$1,000**
20in (51cm)	**$1,500-$1,600***
24in (61cm)	**$2,200****

#128 toddler body:

16-18in (41-46cm)	**$1,500-$1,650****

*Allow $50 additional for flirty eyes.

+With "Star fish" hands.

**Not enough price samples to compute a reliable range.

25in (64cm) 126 flirty-eyed character baby. *H & J Foulke, Inc.*

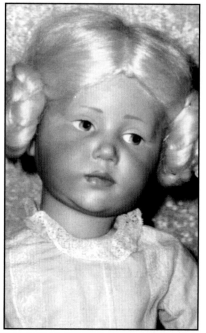

19½in (49cm) 101 pouty character child.
Mary Barnes Kelley Collection.

#121, 122 baby body:	
10-11in (25-28cm)	**$600-$650**
15-16in (38-41cm)	**$800-$1,000**
23-24in (58-61cm)	**$1,300-$1,500**

#121, 122, toddler body:

10in (25cm) 5-piece body	**$1,000+**
13-14in (33-36cm)	**$1,050-$1,200**
20-23in (51-58cm)	**$1,500-$1,700**
26-27in (66-69cm)	**$2,200-$2,400**

#118A baby body,

15in (38cm)	**$2,100****

#119 baby body,

24in (61cm), at auction	**$16,000**

#926, composition head, 5-piece toddler body,

11-12in (28-31cm)	**$400-$500***
17in (43cm)	**$600***

"Puz": composition head baby:

16-17in (41-43cm)	**$400-$450***
25in (64cm)	**$650-$750***

*Allow $50 additional for flirty eyes.

+With "Star fish" hands.

**Not enough price samples to compute a reliable range.

Character Children: 1909-on. Perfect bisque-socket head; K & R composition ball-jointed body; nicely dressed; all in good condition. (See *Simon & Halbig, The Artful Aspect* for photographs of mold numbers not pictured here.)

#101 (Peter or Marie):

8-9in (20-23cm) 5-piece body	**$1,300**
8-9in (20-23cm) jointed body	**$1,800-$2,000**
12in (31cm)	**$2,800-$3,200**
14-15in (36-38cm)	**$3,800-$4,200**
17in (43cm)	**$4,500**
19-20in (48-51cm)	**$5,500**

Glass eyes:

15in (38cm)	**$11,500**
20in (51cm)	**$14,000-$15,000**

13½in (35cm) 112 character child.
Courtesy of Richard W. Withington, Inc.

#102:

12in (31cm)	$20,000**
22in (55cm)	$75,000 up**

#103, 104,

22in (56cm)	$75,000 up**

#105, 22in (56cm) **$170,000**

#106, 22in (56cm) **$145,000**

#107 (Carl):

12in (30cm)	$16,000-$19,000
22in (56cm)	$50,000-$55,000

#108 at auction **$277,095**

#109 (Elise): 7in (18cm) **$2,500-$2800**

9-10in (23-25cm)	$3,000-$3,500
14in (36cm)	$7,500-$8,500
19-21in (48-53cm)	$13,000-$15,000

Glass eyes,

20in (51cm)	$18,000-$20,000

#112, 112x

16-18in (41-46cm)	$16,000

glass eyes

10-11in (25-28cm)	$8,000**

#114 (Hans or Gretchen):

8-9in (20-23cm) jointed body

	$1,800-$2,200
12in (31cm)	$3,200
15-16in (38-41cm)	$4,500
19-20in (48-51cm)	$5,500-$6,000
21-22in (53-56cm)	$6,500-$6,600

Glass eyes:

15in (38cm)	$9,250
24in (61cm)	$18,000

#115,

15-16in (38-41cm)

toddler	$6,000-$6,500**

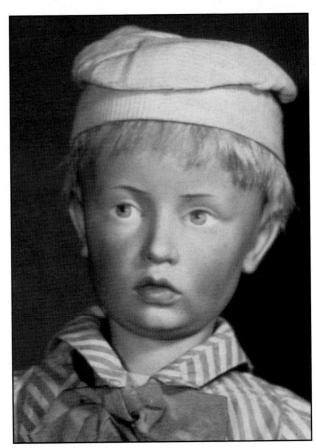

22in (56cm) 107 character child. *H. Jay Lowe Collection.*

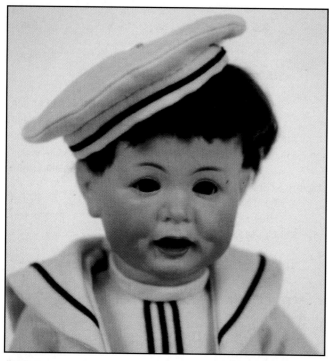

16in (41cm)
116a toddler
character.
*H & J
Foulke, Inc.*

#115A:
Baby, 14-16in (36-41cm)
$3,500-$3,850
Toddler, 15-16in (38-41cm)
$4,500-$5,000
19-20cm (48-51cm) $5,800-$6,200
23in (58cm) $6,600-$7,000
#116,
16in (41cm) toddler $4,500-$5,000**
#116A, open/closed mouth:
Baby,
10-11in (25-28cm) $2,100-$2,300
14-16in (36-41cm) $3,000-$3,500
Toddler,
16-18in (41-46cm) $3,800-$4,300
27in (69cm) $5,500-$5,800
#116A, open mouth:
Baby, 14-16in (36-41cm)
$1,800-$2,200
23in (58cm) $3,800-$4,100**
**Not enough price samples to compute a reliable range.

#117, 117A, closed mouth (may have an
H. Handwerck body):
8in (20cm) $2,400-$2,500
12in (30cm) $3,500-$3,800
14-16in (36-41cm) $4,300-$4,800
18-20in (46-51cm) $5,300-$5,800
22-23in (56-58cm) $6,300-$6,800
30-32in (76-81cm) $7,500-$8,500
#117n, flirty eyes:
14-16in (36-41cm) $1,400-$1,500*
20-22in (51-56cm) $1,900-$2,100*
28-30in (71-76cm) $2,500-$2,600*
#117n, sleep eyes:
14-16in (36-41cm) $1,100-$1,200*
22-24in (56-61cm) $1,500-$1,600*
30-32in (76-81cm) $1,900-$2,100*
28in (71cm) factory original
flapper $2,500
#117x flapper, 14in (36cm)
$3,700-$3,900**
#117, open mouth,
27in (69cm) $4,700-$5,200**
40in (102cm) $6,500-$7,500

#123, 124 (Max & Moritz),
   17in (43cm) each   **$23,000****
#127:
   Baby, 10in (25cm)   **$800-$850**
   14-15in (36-38cm)   **$1,300-$1,400**
   20-22in (51-56cm)   **$1,800-$2,000**
   Toddler or child,
      15-16in (38-41cm)   **$1,750-$1,850**
   Toddler, 25-27in (64-69cm)   **$2,500**
#135 child,
   14-16in (36-41cm)   **$1,500-$1,900****
#201, 13in (33cm)   **$1,500****
#214, 15in (38cm)   **$2,100-$2,500****

Infant: 1924-on. Perfect bisque head; cloth body, composition hands; nicely dressed; all in good condition.
#171, 172,
   14-15in (36-38cm)   **$3,500****
#173, toddler (composition body),
   14in (36cm)   **$1,650****
#175,
   11in (28cm) h.c.
      $1,100-$1,200**
*Allow extra for flapper body.
**Not enough price samples to compute a reliable range.

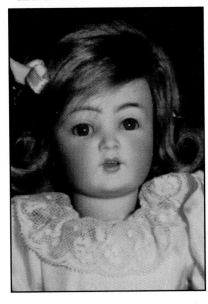

14½in (37cm) 117x flapper, open mouth. *Rhoda Shoemaker Collection.*

18in (46cm) 127 character baby. *H & J Foulke, Inc.*

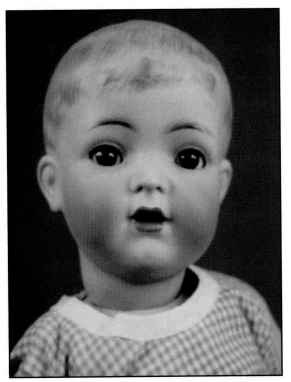

KESTNER

Child doll, early socket head: Ca. 1880. Perfect bisque head, plaster dome; Kestner composition ball-jointed body, some with straight wrists and elbows; well dressed; all in good condition. Many marked with size numbers only.

#169, 128, long-face and round face with no mold number, closed mouth:

10in (25cm)	**$1,500-$1,650**
12in (31cm)	**$1,900-$2,100**
14-16in (36-41cm)	**$2,200-$2,500**
19-21in (48-53cm)	**$2,700-$3,000**
24-25in (61-64cm)	**$3,200-$3,500**
29in (74cm)	**$4,000**
33in (84cm)	**$4,500**

Face with square cheeks, face with white space between lips, no mold number, closed mouth:

11-12in (38-30cm)	**$2,000-$2,200**
14-16in (36-41cm0	**$2,200-$2,500**
19-21in (48-53cm)	**$2,600-$2,800**
24-25in (61-64cm)	**$3,000-$3,200**

Very pouty face:

10-12in (25-31cm)	**$2,800-$3,000**
14-16in (36-41cm)	**$3,200-$3,500**
19-21in (48-53cm)	**$4,000**
24in (61cm)	**$4,200-$4,500**
#XI, 16in (41cm) only	**$3,500-$4,000**
#X, 15in (38cm) only	**$3,500-$4,000**

#103

28-32in (71-78cm)	**$3,500-$4,500**

A.T.-type:

Closed mouth

13in (38cm)	**$7,500-$8,500**
21in (53cm)	**$17,000**

Open mouth, 22in (56cm)

at auction	**$6,720**

Bru-type, molded teeth, jointed ankles:

15in (38cm)	**$3,750**
20in (51cm)	**$5,000**
Kid body, 24in (61cm)	**$3,200**

Open mouth, square cut teeth:

12-14in (31-36cm)	**$1,000-$1,200**
16-18in (41-46cm)	**$1,400-$1,600**
24-25in (61-64cm)	**$1,900-$2,000**
40in (103cm)	**$4,300-$4,600**

FACTS

J.D. Kestner, Jr., doll factory, Waltershausen, Thüringia, Germany. Kestner & Co., porcelain factory, Ohrdruf. 1816-on.

24in (61cm) early pouty Kestner, all original. *H & J Foulke, Inc.*

Child doll, early shoulder head: Ca. 1880s. Perfect bisque head, plaster dome, good wig, set or sleep eyes; sometimes head is slightly turned; kid body with bisque lower arms; marked with size letters or numbers. (No mold numbers.)

Closed mouth:

12in (31cm)	**$650-$675***
14-16in (36-41cm)	**$750-$850***
20-22in (51-56cm)	**$900-$950***
26in (66cm)	**$1,100-$1,300***

A.T.-type, closed mouth,

19in (48cm)	**$10,000**
27in (68cm)	**$17,000**

Open/closed mouth,

16-18in (41-46cm)	**$650-$750**

Open mouth (turned shoulder head):

16-18in (41-46cm)	**$500-$600**
22-24in (56-61cm)	**$700-$750**

Open mouth, square cut teeth,

14-16in (36-41cm)	**$1,000-$1,200**

*Allow $100-$200 extra for a very pouty face or swivel neck.

22in (56cm) early turned shoulder head M, closed mouth. *H & J Foulke, Inc.*

Child doll, bisque shoulder head, open mouth: Ca. 1892. Kid body, some with rivet joints. Plaster dome, good wig, sleep eyes, open mouth; dressed, all in good condition. (See *Kestner, King of Dollmakers* for photographs of mold numbers not pictured here.)

HEAD MARK: 154 8 dep
D made in Germany

BODY MARK:

#145, 154, 147, 148, 166, 195:

12-13in (31-33cm)	**$300-$350***
16-18in (41-46cm)	**$400-$500***
20-22in (51-56cm)	**$550-$600***
26-28in (66-71cm)	**$800-$900***

*Allow additional for a rivet jointed body and/or jointed composition arms.

20in (51cm) 129 child, all original. *H & J Foulke, Inc.*

18in (46cm) 171 *Daisy*. Only this size of the 171 mold is *Daisy*. Other sizes should not be called *Daisy*. *H & J Foulke, Inc.*

19½in (50cm) 164 child, all original. *H & J Foulke, Inc.*

Child doll, open mouth: Bisque socket head on Kestner ball-jointed body; dressed; all in good condition. (See *Kestner, King of Dollmakers* for photographs of mold numbers not pictured here.)

HEAD MARK: *made in Germany. 8. 162.*

BODY MARK:

Germany	or	Excelsior
5-1/2		DRE N. 70686
		Germany

Mold numbers 142, 144, 146, 164, 167, 171, 214:

9in (23cm) all original	**$850**
10-12in (25-31cm)	**$550-$650***
14-16in (36-41cm)	**$750-$850***
18-21in (46-43cm)	**$850-$950***
24-26in (61-66cm)	**$1,000-$1,100***
30in (76cm)	**$1,200-$1,500**
33in (84cm)	**$1,650-$1,850**
36in (91cm)	**$2,200-$2,500**
42in (107cm)	**$3,750-$4,250**

#128, 129, 149, 152, 160, 161, 173, 174:

10-12in (25-31cm)	**$700-$800***
14-16in (36-41cm)	**$900-$1,000***
18-21in (46-53cm)	**$1,100-$1,250***
24-26in (61-66cm)	**$1,300-$1,400***

*Allow 30% additional for all original clothes, wig and shoes.

#133, 5-piece body,
| 6in (15cm) | **$350** |

#155, fully-jointed body:
| 7-8in (18-20cm) | **$800-$900** |
| 10in (25cm) 5-piece body | **$750-$800** |

#171: **Daisy,** blonde mohair wig, blue sleep eyes
| 18in (46cm) only | **$1,250-$1,450** |

#168, 196, 215:
18-21in (46-53cm)	**$700-$750**
26-28in (66-71cm)	**$800-$900**
32in (81cm)	**$1,000-$1,100**

**Not enough price samples to compute a reliable average.

Character Child: 1909-on. Perfect bisque head character face, plaster pate, wig, painted or glass eyes, closed, open or open/closed mouth; Kestner jointed composition body; dressed; all in good condition. (See *Kestner, King of Dollmakers* for photographs of mold numbers not pictured here.)

#143 (Pre 1897):

7in (18cm)	**$750-$800**
9-10in (23-25cm)	**$800-$850**
12-14in (31-36cm)	**$900-$1,000**
18-20in (46-51cm)	**$1,300-$1,700**
24-27in (58-69cm)	**$2,000-$2,500**

#178-190:

Painted eyes:

12in (31cm)	**$2,200-$2,500**
15in (38cm)	**$3,600-$4,000**
18in (46cm)	**$5,000-$5,500**

Glass eyes:

12in (31cm)	**$3,200-$3,500**
15in (38cm)	**$4,800-$5,200**
18in (46cm)	**$6,000-$6,500**

Boxed set, doll with 3 character heads

Painted eyes:

12in (31cm)	**$10,000-$11,000**
15in (38cm)	**$13,000-$14,000**

Glass eyes:

15in (38cm)	**$20,000**

#206:

12in (31cm)	**$10,000****
19in (48cm)	**$25,000****

#208:

Painted eyes:

12in (31cm)	**$10,000****
23-24in (58-61cm)	**$25,000****

#212,

12in (31cm)	**$10,000****

#220 toddler:

11in (28cm)	**$3,700-$4,000**
14-16in (36-41cm)	**$5,000-$6,000**
24in (61cm)	**7,500-$8,000**

#239 toddler:

15-17in (38-43cm)	**$4,000****

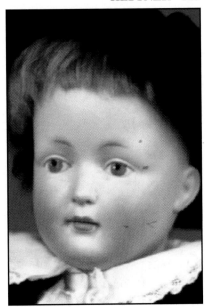

15in (38cm) 182 character boy. *H & J Foulke, Inc.*

26½in (67cm) 241 character child. *Mary Barnes Kelley Collection.*

#241:

17-18in (43-46cm)	**$6,200-$6,400**
21-22in (53-56cm)	**$7,000-$7,500**
27in (68cm)	**$8,500-$9,000**

#249:

13-14in (33-36cm)	**$1,100-$1,200**
20-22in (51-56cm)	**$1,800**
26in (66cm)	**$2,250**

Max & Moritz:

12in (31cm) pair, at auction	**$17,000**

#260:

Toddler: 5-piece body

8-10in (20-25cm)	**$900-$1,100**
19-20in (48-51cm)	**$1,200**

Jointed body:

12-14in (31-36cm)	**$800-$850**
18-20in (46-51cm)	**$900-$1,100**
29in (75cm)	**$1,400-$1,500**
35in (88cm)	**$2,000**
42in (107cm)	**$4,000**

Teenage body:

14in (36cm)	**$900-$1,000**

Character Baby: 1910-on. Perfect bisque head, molded and/or painted hair or good wig, sleep eyes, open or open/closed mouth; Kestner bent-limb body; well dressed; nice condition. (See *Kestner, King of Dollmakers* for photographs of mold numbers not pictured here.)

Mark:

made in
F. Germany. 10
211
J.D.K.

#211, 226, 257:

11-13in (28-33cm)	**$700-$775***
16-18in (41-46cm)	**$900-$1,000***
20-22in (51-56cm)	**$1,150-$1,350***
25in (64cm)	**1,650-$2,250***

#211 Toddler:

14in (36cm)	**$1,650**
26in (66cm)	**$3,500**

#257 Toddler:

8in (20cm)	**$1,100**

*Allow $50-$100 extra for an original skin wig.

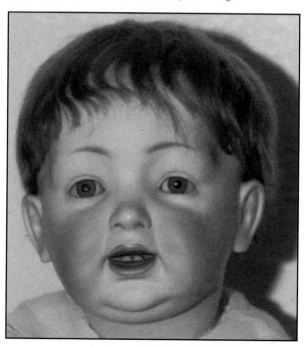

25in (64cm) 211 character baby, size Q 20, the largest size head Kestner made. *Mary Barnes Kelley Collection.*

JDK solid dome:

12-14 (31-36cm)	$600-$700
18in (46cm)	$800
23-25in (58-64cm)	$1,200-$1,500
Painted eyes,	
14in (36cm)	$525-$575

#262, 263: See page 66.

#210, 234, 235, 238 shoulder heads,

11in (28cm)	$1,000-$1,100
14-16in (36-41cm)	$1,300-$1,500

Hilda, #237, 245, and solid dome baby 1070

11-13in (28-33cm)	$2,500-$2,800
16-17in (41-43cm)	$3,200-$3,600
20-22in (51-56cm)	$4,000-$4,500
24in (61cm)	$5,500-$5,800

Toddler:

14in (36cm)	$4,500-$5,000
17-19in (43-48cm)	$5,500
25in (64cm)	$6,000-$7,000

#247:

11in (28cm)	$1,100
14-16in (36-41cm)	$1,800-$2,100

Toddler,

13in (33cm)	$2,200-$2,300
20in (51cm)	$3,200

#267, molded hair:

24in (61cm) at auction	$3,700

JDK solid dome, fat-cheeked (so-called Baby Jean):

12-13in (31-33cm)	$1,200-$1,300
17-18in (43-46cm)	$1,500-$1,650
23-24in (58-61cm)	$2,000-$2,100
15in (38cm) toddler	$1,500-$1,600

All-Bisque Baby:

Painted eyes, stiff neck,

5-6in (13-15cm)	$225-$275

Swivel neck, painted eyes:

7½in (19cm)	$425-$450
9in (23cm)	$600-$650
12in (31cm)	$850

Glass eyes, swivel neck,

5½in (23-25cm)	$900-$1,000
#177 toddler, 8in (20cm)	$1,000
#178 toddler, 8in (20cm)	$1,250

25in (64cm) 260 character child, all original. *H & J Foulke, Inc.*

6in (15cm) 208 all-bisque with yellow boots and swivel neck. *H & J Foulke, Inc.*

All-Bisque Child: Perfect all-bisque child jointed at shoulders and hips. Very good quality.

#130, 150, 160, 184 and 208:

4-5in (10-13cm)	**$225-325***
6in (15cm)	**$350-$375***
7in (18cm)	**$400-$450***
8in (20cm)	**$500-$550***
9in (23cm)	**$700-$800**
11in (28cm)	**$1,100-$1,200**
12in (31cm)	**$1,300-$1,400**

#208, swivel neck, yellow boots

5½-6in (13-15cm)	**$600-$675**
8in (20cm)	**$950**

*Allow 30-40% extra for swivel neck; allow $25-$50 extra for yellow boots.

Early All-Bisque Dolls: see page 25.

Gibson Girl: Ca. 1910. Perfect bisque shoulder head with appropriate wig, closed mouth, up-lifted chin; kid body with bisque lower arms (cloth body with bisque lower limbs on small dolls); beautifully dressed; all in good condition; sometimes marked Gibson Girl on body.

#172:

10in (25cm)	**$950-$1,050**
15in (38cm)	**$2,000-$2,400**
20-21in (51-53cm)	**$3,200-$3,600**

Lady Doll: Perfect bisque socket head, plaster dome, wig with lady hairdo; Kestner jointed composition body with molded breasts, nipped-in waist, slender arms and legs; appropriate lady clothes; all in good condition.

Mark:

made in
D *Germany. 8.*
162.

11in (28cm) fat-cheeked character baby. *H & J Foulke, Inc.*

#162:

16-18in (41-46cm)   **$1,600-$1,900**
Naked, 16-18in (41-46cm)   **$1,200**
All original clothes,
   16-18in (41-46cm)   **$2,300-$2,500**
O.I.C. Baby: Perfect bisque solid dome head, wide open mouth with molded tongue; cloth body, dressed; all in good condition. Mold **#255**.
10in (25cm) h.c.   **$1,000-$1,200****
Siegfried: Perfect bisque head; cloth body with composition hands; dressed; all in good condition. Mold **#272**.
Mark:

Siegfried
made in Germany
9

10in (25cm)   **$1,500****
14in (36cm)   **$2,000****

Marked Century Doll Co. Infant: Ca. 1925. Perfect bisque head; cloth body. Some with smiling face are mold **#277**. Head circumference:
   10-11in (25-28cm)   **$550-$600**
   13-14in (33-36cm)   **$800-$900**
   Double-face   **$2,500****
Mama doll, bisque shoulder head #281,
   21in (53cm)   **$650-$750****
**Not enough price samples to compute a reliable average.

17in (43cm)
162 lady. *H & J Foulke, Inc.*

KEWPIE

All-bisque: 1913-on. Made by J.D. Kestner and other German firms. Often have imperfections in making. Sometimes signed on foot "O'Neill". Standing, legs together, arms jointed, blue wings, painted features, eyes to side.

2½in (5-6cm)	**$110-$125**
4in (10cm)	**$150***
5in (13cm)	**$185***
6in (15cm)	**$235***
7in (18cm)	**$300-$350***
8in (20cm)	**$450-$500***
9in (23cm)	**$600-$700***
10in (25cm)	**$800***
12in (31cm)	**$1,300-$1,500***

Jointed hips:

4in (10cm)	**$500-$550**
6in (15cm)	**$850**
8in (20cm)	**$1,250**

Shoulder head, 3in (8cm)	**$425**
Perfume bottle, 4½in (11cm)	**$550-$600**
Black Hottentot, 5in (13cm)	**$550-$600**
Molded Dress and Hat, 4½in (11cm)	**$1,800**
Button hole, 2in (5cm)	**$165-$175**
Pincushion, 2-3in (5-8cm)	**$250-$300**
Painted shoes and socks:	
5in (13cm)	**$600-$700**
11in (28cm)	**$1,500-$1,800**
With glass eyes and wig,	
6in (15cm) at auction	**$2,400**

*Allow extra for original clothes.

FACTS

Designer: Rose O'Neill, **Mark:** Red and gold paper heart or shield on chest and round label on back.

5in (13cm) *Kewpie* with jointed hips.
H & J Foulke, Inc.

Action Kewpies (sometimes stamped: ©):
Thinker:
  4in (10cm)   **$275-$325**
  7in (18cm)   **$500-$550**
Kewpie with cat,
  3½in (9cm)   **$650**
Kewpie holding pen,
  3in (8cm)   **$450-$475**
Kneeling, with outstretched arms,
  3¾in (9cm)   **$1,100**
Reclining or sitting,
  3-4in (8-10cm)   **$450-$495**
Crawling, 4in (10cm)   **$900**
Tumbling, 3in (8cm)   **$625**
Farmer, Fireman (molded hats),
  4in (10cm)   **$1,000**
Kewpie, 2in (5cm) with rabbit,
  rose, turkey, pumpkin,
  shamrock, etc.   **$500-$550**
Doodledog:
  1½in (4cm)   **1,000**
  3in (9cm)   **$2,500**
  4½in (11cm)   **$3,200**
Huggers, 3½in 9cm)   **$200-$225**
Guitar player, 3½in (9cm)   **$400-$500**
Traveler, 3½in (9cm)   **$325-$350**

Governor or **Mayor**,
  4in (10cm)   **$450-$500**
Kewpie and **Doodledog** on bench,
  3½in (9cm)   **$4,500**
Kewpie sitting on inkwell,
  3½in (9cm)   **$750**
Kewpie Traveler with **Doodledog**,
  3½in (9cm)   **$1,350-$1,650**
Kewpie Soldiers,
  5-6in (13-15cm) standing **$950-$1,250**
  3½in (9cm) sitting   **$1,500**
Kewpie on sled, 2½in (6cm)   **$1,000**
Two **Kewpies** reading book,
  3½in (9cm), standing   **$850-$950**
  5½in (13cm)   **$2,200**
Kewpie at tea table, 4½in (11cm) **$3,200**
Kewpie with basket, 4in (10cm)   **$1,000**
Kewpie Mountain with
  17 figures   **$17,000 up**

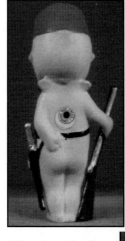

4½in (11cm)
Kewpie soldier,
back view. *H &
J Foulke, Inc.*

4½in (11cm) *Kewpie* soldier, front
view. *H & J Foulke, Inc.*

13in (33cm) composition *Kewpie.*
H & J Foulke, Inc.

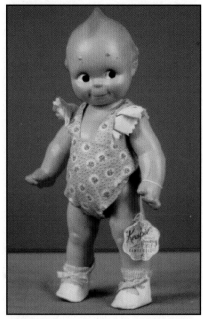

13in (33cm) Cameo composition fully jointed *Kewpie,* all original with tag. *H & J Foulke, Inc.*

Kewpie holding teddy bear,
4in (10cm)   **$850**
Kewpie in bisque swing,
2½in (6cm)   **$4,000**
Glazed Kewpie shaker with animal,
2in (5cm)   **$275-$300**
Kewpie Bellhop in green,
4in (10cm)   **$1,700**
Kewpie in blue felt hat,
5½in (14cm)   **$3,800**
Kewpie with broom & dustpan,
5in (10cm)   **$850**
Kewpie with bunting babies,
3½in (9cm)   **$4,000**
Kewpie riding hobby horse,
4½in (11cm)   **$5,500**
Kewpie riding animal,
4½in (11cm)   **5,000-$5,300**

Bisque head on chubby jointed composition toddler body, glass eyes: Made by J.D. Kestner.
Mark: "Ges.gesch.
                       O'Neill J.D.K."
10in (25cm) 5-piece body   **$5,000**
12-14in (31-36cm)   **$6,500**

Bisque head on cloth body: Mold **#1377** made by Alt, Beck & Gottschalck.
12in (31cm) glass eyes **$2,600-$2,800****
Painted eyes   **$1,600-$2,000****

Celluloid: Made by Karl Standfuss, Saxony, Germany.
2½in (6cm)   **$40-$50**
5in (13cm)   **$90-$110**
8in (20cm)   **$200-$225**
12in (31cm)   **$350**
22in (56cm)   **$550-$600**
Black, 2½in (6cm)   **$125**
5in (13cm)   **$200**
Kewpie/Billiken double face,
2½in (6cm)   **$150**
**Not enough price samples to compute a reliable range.

All-Composition: Made by Cameo Doll Co., Rex Doll Co., and Mutual Doll Co. All-composition, jointed at shoulders, some at hips; good condition.

8in (20cm)	**$200-$250**
11-12in (28-31cm)	**$375-$450**
All original, Boxed	**$550-$600**
Black, 12-13in (31-33cm)	**$400-$450**
Talcum container, 7in (18cm)	**$225-$250**
Composition head, cloth body,	
12in (31cm)	**$250-$275**

All-Cloth: Made by Richard G. Krueger, Inc., or King Innovations, Inc., New York. Patent number 1785800. Mask face with fat-shaped cloth body.

10-12in (25-31cm)	**$225-$250**
18-22in (46-56cm)	**$500-$600**

14in (36cm) *Kewpie* by J.D. Kestner, *H. Jay Lowe Collection.*

Hard Plastic: Ca. 1950s.

Standing Kewpie, 1-piece with jointed arms, 8in (20cm)	**$150-$165**
Boxed	**$225-$250**
Fully-jointed with sleep eyes; all original clothes, 13in (33cm)	**$500**

Vinyl: Ca. 1960s, Cameo Dolls. All original and excellent condition.

12-13in (31-33cm)	**$100-$110***
16in (41cm)	**$135-$165***
Kewpie Baby with hinged body,	
16in (41cm)	**$250**

Kewpie Gal:

8in (20cm)	**$65-$75***
14in (36cm)	**$125***

Ragsy, molded clothes,

8in (20cm)	**$40***

*Allow extra for label and box.

Jesco Dolls, 1980s, Boxed

8in (20cm) Black	**$40-$45**
12in (31cm)	**$60**
18in (46cm)	**$85**
24in (61cm)	**$130-$160**

14in (36cm) Cameo vinyl *Kewpie Gal,* all original and boxed. *H & J Foulke, Inc.*

KLEY & HAHN

Character Baby: Perfect bisque head; bent-limb baby body; nicely dressed; all in good condition.

#138, 158, 160, 167, 176, 458, 525, 531, 680 and others:

11-13in (28-33cm)	**$500-$525**
18-20in (46-51cm)	**$750-$850**
24in (61cm)	**$1,100-$1,200**
28in (71cm)	**$1,600**
Toddler,	
14-16in (36-41cm)	**$1,300-$1,600**
18-20in (46-51cm)	**$1,800-$2,200**

Two-face baby,

13in (33cm)	**$2,000-$2,200**

FACTS

Kley & Hahn, doll factory, Ohrdruf, Thüringia, Germany. Heads by Hertel, Schwab & Co. (100 series), Bähr & Pröschild (500 series) and J.D. Kestner (200 series, 680 and Walküre). 1902-on. **Trademarks:** Walküre, Meine Einzige, Special, Dollar Princess. **Mark:**

19½in (50cm) 160 character toddler. *H & J Foulke, Inc.*

Character Child: Perfect bisque head, closed mouth; jointed composition child or toddler body; fully dressed; all in good condition.

#520, 526:

15-16in (38-41cm)	**$3,500-$3,800**
19-21in (48-53cm)	**$4,500-$5,000**

#536, 546, 549:

15-16in (38-41cm)	**$4,200-$4,500**
19-21in (48-53cm)	**$5,000-$5,500**

#547, 18½in (47cm) at auction   **$6,825**

#548, 568 Toddler

21-23in (53-58cm)	**$2,400**

#154, 166, closed mouth, toddler or jointed body:

16-17in (41-43cm)	**$2,500-$2,650**
19-20in (48-51cm)	**$3,200**

#154, 166, open mouth:

17-18in (43-46cm) jointed body	**$1,400**
25in (64cm)	**$1,850-$1,950**
20in (51cm) baby	**$1,300-$1,400**

#169, closed mouth:

13-14in (33-36cm) toddler	**$2,200-$2,400**
17-19in (43-48cm) toddler	**$3,200-$3,500**

#169, open mouth,

23in (58cm) baby	**$1,500-$1,650****

Child Doll: Perfect bisque head; jointed composition child body; fully dressed; all in good condition.

#250, 282 or **Walküre:**

7½in (19cm)	**$325-$375**
12-13in (31-33cm)	**$425-$450**
16-18in (41-46cm)	**$500-$550***
22-24in (56-61cm)	**$600-$700***
28-30in (71-76cm)	**$900-$1,000**
35-36in (89-91cm)	**$1,500-$1,600**
Head only, 5in (13cm)	**$235**

Special, Dollar Princess.

23-25in (58-64cm)	**$525-$575**

*Allow $100-$150 additional for flapper body.
**Not enough price samples to compute a reliable range.

20in (51cm) 282 child. *H & J Foulke, Inc.*

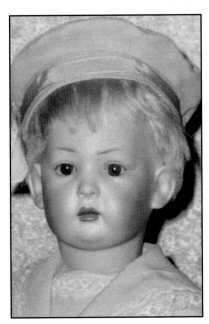

18in (46cm) 169 character toddler with closed mouth. *Mary Barnes Kelley Collection.*

KLING

11½in (30cm) 254 bisque shoulder head with glass eyes. *H & J Foulke, Inc.*

22in (56cm) 189 china shoulder head. *H & J Foulke, Inc.*

Bisque shoulder head: Ca. 1880. Molded hair or mohair wig, painted eyes, closed mouth; cloth body with bisque lower limbs; dressed; in all good condition. Mold numbers in **100** Series.

12-14in (31-36cm)	**$300-$375***
18-20in (46-51cm)	**$500-$550***
23-25in (58-64cm)	**$600-$700***

Glass eyes and molded hair,

15-16in (38-41cm)	**$500-$600***
22in (56cm)	**$900-$950***

Boy styles, such as **131**,

16-18in (41-46cm)	**$900-$1,000**

Girl styles, such as **#186, 176.**

15-17in (38-43cm)	**$900-$1,000**

Lady styles with decorated bodice, such as **#135, 170**,

21-23in (53-58cm)	**$1,500 up**

#116, lady with molded blue bonnet,

16in (41cm) at auction	**$1,600**

#106, lady with molded stand-up collar, glass eyes, 17in (43cm) at auction **$2,100**

*Allow extra for unusual or elaborate hairdo.

China shoulder head: Ca. 1880. Black- or blonde-haired china head with bangs, sometimes with a pink tint; cloth body with china limbs; dressed; all in good condition.

#188, 189, 200 and others:

13-15in (33-38cm)	**$275-$325**
18-20in (46-51cm)	**$400-$450**
24-25in (61-64cm)	**$525-$575**

FACTS
Kling & Co., porcelain factory, Ohrdruf, Thüringia, Germany. 1870-on.
Mark:

Bisque head: Ca. 1890. Perfect bisque head, glass eyes, appropriate body; dressed; all in good condition.

#123, closed mouth shoulder head:

6½in (17cm)	**$250-$275**
10-12in (25-31cm)	
Original costume	**$500-$700**
Redressed	**$250-$300**
15in (38cm)	**$500-$600**

#166 or **167,** closed mouth shoulder head,

16-18in (41-46cm)	**$750-$850**

#182 socket head, closed mouth, composition body

14in (36cm)	**$1,600-$1,800**

#373 or **377** shoulder head, open mouth:

13-15in (33-38cm)	**$375-$425****
19-22in (48-56cm)	**$475-$525****

#370, 372, 182 socket head, open mouth:

14-16in (36-41cm)	**$450-$500**
22-24in (56-61cm)	**$600-$700**
27in (69cm)	**$900-$1,000**

**Not enough price samples to compute a reliable range.

All Bisque: Glass eyes, wig, shirred pink or blue hose **#61, #71,**

5-6in (11-15cm)	**$290-$325**

black boots **#36, #69**

5-6in (11-15cm)	**$350-$400**

KÖNIG & WERNICKE

K & W Character: Perfect bisque head; composition baby or 5-piece toddler body; appropriate clothes; all in good condition.

#98, 99, 100, 1070:

8½in (21cm)	**$350-$375**
10-11in (25-28cm)	**$450-$475**
14-16in (36-41cm)	**$600-$650***
19-21in (48-53cm)	**$750-$850***
24-25in (61-64cm)	**$1,100-$1,250**

Toddler, fully-jointed body:

13-15in (33-38cm)	**$800-$1,000**
19-20in (48-51cm)	**$1,450-$1,650**

All-Composition Toddler,

22in (56cm)	**$700**

*Allow extra for flirty eyes.

Child #4711, Mein Stolz (My Pride),

37in (94cm)	**$1,800-$2,000**

FACTS
König & Wernicke, doll factory, Waltershausen, Thüringia, Germany. Heads by Hertel Schwab & Co. and Bähr & Pröschild. 1912-on.
Trademarks: Mein Stolz, My Playmate

Mark:

K & W
1070

20in (51cm) K & W toddler.

KÄTHE KRUSE

Cloth Käthe Kruse: Molded muslin head, hand-painted; jointed at shoulders and hips:

Doll I (1910-1929), 16in (41cm), Early model, wide hips:

Mint, all original	**$4,500-$5,200**
Very good	**$3,200-$3,800**
Fair	**$1,800-$2,200**
Jointed knees, Very good	**$6,500 up****
"Frog" hands, good	**$5,000**

Doll I (1929-on), 17in (43cm), Later model, slim hips:

Molded hair, mint	**$3,300-$3,800**
Very good	**$2,200-$2,600**

Doll 1H (wigged):

Mint, all original	**$3,200-$3,600**
Very good	**$2,000-$2,500**
Boxed with tag at auction	**$5,400**

U.S. Zone, all original excellent,

18in (46cm)	**$2,500-$3,000**

Doll II "Schlenkerchen" Smiling Baby (1922-1936), 13in (33cm)

Excellent	**$10,000**
Very worn	**$4,500**

Doll V & VI Babies "Traumerchen" (5-pound weighted **Sand Baby**) and **Du Mein** (unweighted):

Cloth head,	
19½-23½in (50-60cm)	**$5,000-$6,000**
Magnesit head,	
21in (53cm)	**$1,600**

Doll VII (1927-1952) and **Doll X** (1935-1952), 14in (35cm):

All original	**$1,800-$2,000**

With **Du Mein** head (1928-1930).

14in (36cm):

Showing wear	**$1,800-$2,200**
Mint	**$2,900**

**Not enough price samples to compute a reliable average.

FACTS

Käthe Kruse, Bad Kösen, Germany; after World War II, Donauworth. 1910-on.

Mark: On cloth: "Käthe Kruse" on sole of foot, sometimes also "Germany" and a number.

Käthe Kruse
82971

Made in
Germany

Hard plastic on back: Turtle mark and "Käthe Kruse."

17in (43cm) *Doll I.* H & J Foulke, Inc.

Hampelchen: tab-jointed hips
  17-18in (43-46cm)   **$2,400-$2,800**
Doll VIII "German Child" (1929-on),
20½in (52cm) wigged, turning head:
  Mint, all original   **$2,200-$2,800**
  Good condition, suitably
    dressed   **$1,500-$1,800**
Doll IX "Little German Child" (1929-
on), wigged, turning head, 14in (36cm):
  All original, mint   **$1,350-$1,650**
U.S. Zone Germany: Dolls IX or X with
cloth or Magnesit heads, very thick paint
finish; all original, very good condition
(1945-1951), 14in (35cm)
  Cloth head, mint   **$1,100-$1,300**
  Magnesit, mint   **$750-$850**
  Hard plastic, mint   **$600-$700**

17½in (44cm) *Doll IH* "Martin," all original U.S. Zone, cloth face. *H & J Foulke, Inc.*

Hard Plastic (Synthetic) Head: Ca.
1948-on. Hard plastic head with human
hair wig, painted eyes; pink muslin body;
original clothes; all in excellent condition.
US. Zone, 21in (53cm)   **$950**
Ca. 1952-1975:
  14in (35cm)   **$375-$425**
  19-21in (48-53cm)   **$500-$575**
1975-on:
  14in (36cm)   **$300-$350***
  19-21in (48-53cm)   **$400-$450***
  20in (51cm) Du Mein   **$600-$700**
  18in (46cm) Slim Grandchild   **$900**

Hanna Kruse Dolls:
10in (25cm) Däumlinchen with foam
rubber stuffing (1957-on)   **$200-$225***
13in (33cm) Rumpumpel Baby or
  Toddler, 1959-on.   **$350-$400**
10in (25cm) Doggi, (vinyl head),
  1964-1967   **$225-$250****
  14in (36cm) all hard plastic baby
      $100-$125
*Retail store price may be higher.

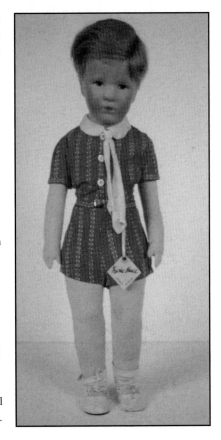

20½in (52cm) *Doll VIII* "Friedebald," all original, cloth face. *H & J Foulke, Inc.*

All-Hard Plastic (Celluloid) Käthe Kruse: Wig or molded hair and sleep or painted eyes; jointed neck, shoulders and hips; original clothes; all in excellent condition. Turtle mark. 1955-1961.

16in (41cm)	**$450-$500**
Redressed	**$225-$275**
Vinyl head, 16in (41cm)	**$350-$450****

**Not enough price samples to compute a reliable range.

Mannikin, Ca. 1950

46-52in (116-132cm) **$2,200-$2,500**

KRUSE-TYPE

Bing Art Dolls: Nurnberg, Germany. 1921-1932. Cloth head, molded face, hand-painted features; cloth body with jointed shoulders and hips (some with pinned joints), mitten hands; all original clothing; very good condition. "Bing" stamped or impressed on sole of shoe.

Cloth head, painted hair:

10-12in (25-30cm)	**$425-$475**
14in (35cm)	**$850-$950**

Cloth head, wigged 10in (25cm)

$300-$350

Composition head, wigged

7in (18cm) **$100-$120**

Heine & Schneider Art Doll: Bad-Kösen, Germany. 1920-1922. All cloth or head of pressed cardboard covered with cloth, molded hair; cloth body with jointed shoulders and hips (some with cloth covered composition arms and hands.) Appropriate or original clothes; all in good condition. Mark stamped on foot.

17-19in (43-48cm) **$1,300-$1,500****

Unmarked Child Dolls: Ca. 1920s.

15-17in (38-43cm) **$375 up***

*Depending upon quality.

**Not enough price samples to compute a reliable range.

20½in (52cm) "Ilsebill," all original, 1986, Model 52H. *H & J Foulke, Inc.*

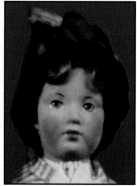

8in (20cm) Bing child, all original. *H & J Foulke, Inc.*

GEBRÜDER KUHNLENZ

G.K. doll with closed mouth: Ca. 1885-on. Perfect bisque socket head (some with closed Belton-type crown), inset glass eyes, closed mouth, round cheeks; jointed composition body; dressed; all in good condition.

#28, 31, 32:

8-10in (20-25cm	$850-$1,100*
15-16in (38-41cm)	$1,600-$1,700*
21-23in (53-58cm)	$2,400-$2,600*

#34, Bru-type, French body:

15in (38cm)	$3,500-$4,000**
18in (46cm)	$5,200-$5,600**

#38 shoulder head, kid body:

14-16in (36-41cm)	$675-$750*
22-23in (56-58cm)	$1,000-$1,100**

*Allow more for a very pretty doll.

**Not enough price samples to compute a reliable range.

19in (48cm) 38.27.5 turned shoulder head child. *Jensen's Antique Dolls.*

FACTS

Gebrüder Kuhnlenz, porcelain factory, Kronach, Bavaria. 1884-on.

Mark:

G^br 165 K
9
Germany 44-31

G^br K

and/or numbers, such as:

41-28   56-18   44-15

The first two digits are mold numbers; second two are size number.

15in (38cm) 34.26 socket head child. *Courtesy of Richard W. Withington, Inc.*

G.K. child doll: Ca. 1890-on. Perfect bisque socket head, sleep or paperweight-type eyes, open mouth, molded teeth; jointed composition body, sometimes French; dressed; all in good condition.

#41, 44, 56 (character-type face):

9-10in (23-25cm)	**$700**
16-19in (41-48cm)	**$900-$1,000**
24-26in (61-66cm)	**$1,300-$1,500**

#165:

18in (46cm)	**$425-$450**
22-24in (56-61cm)	**$525-$575**
34in (86cm)	**$1,200-$1,300**
#61, 47 shoulder head,	
19-22in (48-56cm)	**$650-$750**

G.K. Tiny Dolls: Perfect bisque socket head, wig, stationary glass eyes, open mouth with molded teeth; 5-piece composition body with molded shoes and socks; all in good condition. Usually mold #44 7-8in (18-20cm):

Crude body	**$185-$210**
Better body	**$250-$300**

All-Bisque: Swivel neck, usually mold #31, #41, or #44.

Bootines,	
7-8in (18-20cm)	**$900-$1,200**
9½in (24cm) at auction	**$2,800**
Mary Janes:	
5in (13cm)	**$500-$600**
8in (20cm)	**$1,000-$1,200**

24in (61cm) 165 child. *H & J Foulke, Inc.*

LANTERNIER

Marked Lanternier Child: Ca. 1915. Perfect bisque head, good or original wig, large stationary eyes, open mouth, pierced ears; papier-mâché jointed body; pretty clothes; all in good condition.

Cherie, Favorite or La Gerogienne:
16-18in (41-46cm)	$675-$775*
22-24in (56-61cm)	$900-$1,000*
28in (71cm)	$1,400-$1,600*

*Allow extra for lovely face and bisque.

Lanternier Lady: Ca. 1915. Perfect bisque head with adult look, good wig, stationary glass eyes, open/closed mouth with molded teeth; composition lady body; dressed; all in good condition.
Lorraine,
16-18in (41-46cm)	$850-$1,250*

Characters, "Toto" and others: Ca. 1915. Perfect bisque smiling character face, good wig, glass eyes, open/closed mouth with molded teeth, pierced ears; jointed French composition body; dressed; all in good condition.
17-19in (43-48cm)	$900-$1,100

*Depending upon costume and quality.

FACTS
A Lanternier & Cie. Porcelain factory of Limoges, France. 1915-1924.
Mark:

LIMOGES

FABRICATION FRANÇAISE

AL & Cⁱᵉ
LIMOGES

A   1

LEATHER, MORROCAN

Morrocan? Leather Baby: Tan leather, beautifully molded face, detailed painted eyes with real upper eyelashes, original short human hair wig, open/closed mouth with painted teeth, one pierced ear with earring; original Morrocan outfit; all in very good condition.

16½in (42cm)	$800-$1,000**

**Not enough samples to compute a reliable average.

FACTS
Possibly Morrocan

16½in (42cm) Morrocan Leather Baby, all original. *H & J Foulke, Inc.*

LEATHER
FRENCH

LENCI

Leather Doll: Baby or child doll with molded or painted hair, painted features, jointed shoulders and hips; original clothes; excellent condition.

Baby, 5in (13cm)	**$2,250**
Child, 6in (15cm)	**$3,000****

**Not enough price samples to compute a reliable average.

FACTS
Unknown French maker. Ca. 1920.
All leather.
Mark: None on doll; may have "Made in France" label.

5in (13cm) French leather baby and 6in (15cm) leather child, all original. *H & J Foulke, Inc.*

Lenci: All-felt (sometimes cloth torso); pressed felt head; jointed shoulders and hips; painted features, eyes ususally side-glancing; orignal clothes, often of felt or organdy; in excellent condition.

Miniatures and Mascottes:

8-9in (20-23cm) Regionals	**$350-$400**
Children or unusual costumes	**$450-$600**
Chinese Boy, boxed	**$550**

FACTS
Enrico & Elena di Scavini,
Turin, Italy. 1920-on
Mark: "LENCI" on cloth and various paper tags; sometimes stamped on bottom of foot.

Lenci & E. SCAVINI
TURIN (Italy)
Made in ITALY
N. 159G

34in (86cm) child, all original. *H & J Foulke, Inc.*

Children #300, 109, 149, 159, 111:

13in (33cm)	**$850 up**
16-18in (41-46cm)	**$1,000 up**
20-22in (51-56cm)	**$1,300 up**

#300 children, 17in (43cm):

Girl in yellow organdy gown, boxed	**$1,800**
Fascist Boy	**$1,800**
Boy in coat and hat, boxed	**$2,100**
Sports Series, Baseball	**$4,000**

#1500, scowling face,

17-19in (43-48cm)	**$1,700-$2,000**
Baby, 18-21in (46-53cm)	**$2,000-$2,500**

Googly, watermelon mouth,

22in (56cm)	**$1,600-$2,000**

1930s Children:

"Benedetta" face, 19in (48cm)	**$1,300 up**
"Mariuccia" face, 17in (43cm)	**$1,100 up**
"Henriette" face, 25in (63cm)	**$1,700 up**
"Laura" face, 16in (41cm)	**$1,000 up**

"Lucia" face, 14in (36cm):

Child clothes	**$800-$1,200**
Regional outfits	**$700-$900**

Ladies and long-limbed novelty dolls.

24-28in (61-71cm)	**$1,500 up**
40in (102cm), Faded color	**$1,000-$1,250**

Glass Eyes, 20in (51cm),

Valentine, Widow Allegra	**$2,200-$2,600**
Beccacine-type	**$3,000**

"Surprised Eye" (round painted eyes), fancy clothes,

20in (51cm)	**$2,200-$2,600**

Butterfly, Japanese lady,

17in (43cm)	**$2,000-$2,200**

Brown South Seas,

16in (41cm)	**$1,800-$2,000**

9in (23cm) Mascotte "Red Riding Hood," all original. *H & J Foulke, Inc.*

26in (66cm) lady with long limbs, all original. *H & J Foulke, Inc.*

Teenager, long legs,	
17in (43cm)	**$1,200 up**
Winkers,	
12in (31cm)	**$750-$950**
1935 Round face,	
11in (28cm)	**$450-$500**
20in (51cm)	**$800-$1,000**
1950 Characters	**$300 up**
Catalogs	**$900-$1,200**
Purse	**$300**
Wood head, 6in (15cm)	**$60-$90**
Mask face, disc eyes,	
23in (58cm)	**$600-$700**
Hand Puppet	**$400-$500**
Flocked hard plastic,	
11in (28cm)	**$200-$250**
Celluloid-type, 6in (15cm)	**$60-$75**

Collector's Note: Mint examples of rare dolls will bring higher prices. To bring the prices quoted, Lenci dolls must be clean and have good color. Faded and dirty dolls bring only about one-third to one-half of these prices.

Modern Series: 1979 on.

13in (28cm)	**$110-$135**
22-21in (51-53cm)	**$225-$275**
22in (56cm) surprised eyes	**$300-$330**
26in (66cm) lady	**$275-$375**
27-28in (69-71cm)	
long gown	**$325-$425**

11in (28cm) flocked hard plastic doll, all original. *H & J Foulke, Inc.*

8in (20cm) novelty doll of the 1950s, all original. *H & J Foulke, Inc.*

LENCI-TYPE

Felt or Cloth Doll: Mohair wig, painted features; stuffed cloth body; original clothes or costume; excellent condition.

Child dolls,

16-18in (41-46cm)
  depending upon quality up to **$750**
7½in (18cm) excellent quality
  child   **$250-$350**
Regional costume, very good quality:
7½-8½in (19-22cm)   **$40-$50**
12in (31cm)   **$90-$110**
Alma, Turin, Italy,
16in (41cm)   **$400-$500**
18in (46cm) Boy, detailed outfit **$800**

Dean's Rag Book Company,
England:
14-16in (36-41cm)   **$500-$600**
Composition face,
18in (46cm)   **$600-$700**

Farnell's Alpha Toys, London, England,
  Alpha Imp, 10in (25cm)   **$250**
  King George VI, 1937
  16in (41cm)   **$400-$450**
Allwin Nightdress Case,
  20in (51cm)   **$400**

Eugenie Poir, Gre-Poir French Doll Makers, Paris and New York.
  Cloth face, very good
    condition   **$300-$350**
  Felt face:
    Mint condition   **$550-$650**
    Good condition   **$300-$400**
Raynal, Venus, Marina, Clelia, Paris, France.
  17-18in (43-46cm) mint **$550-$750**
Poupeés Nicette, 14in (36cm)
  Regional costumes   **$250-$300**

FACTS

Various Italian, French and English firms. 1920-1940.
Mark: Various paper labels, if any.

20in (51cm) Allwin nightdress case, all original. *H & J Foulke, Inc.*

19in (48cm) unmarked felt child, exceptional quality, all original. *H & J Foulke, Inc.*

LIBERTY OF LONDON

British Coronation Dolls: 1939. All-cloth with painted and needle-sculpted faces; original clothes; excellent condition. The **Royal Family** and **Coronation Participants.**

9-9½in (23-24cm)	**$165-$175**
6in (15cm),	
Princess Margaret	**$400-$425**
7in (17cm),	
Princess Elizabeth	**$400-$425**

Other English Historical and Ceremonial Characters: All cloth with painted and needle-sculpted faces; original clothes; excellent condition.

9-10in (23-25cm)	**$135-$165**
Beefeater (Tower Guard)	**$85**

FACTS

Liberty & Co. of London, England.
1906-on.
Mark: Cloth label or paper tag
"Liberty of London."

Winston Churchill,
all original. *H & J*
Foulke, Inc.

ARMAND MARSEILLE
(A.M.)

Child Doll: 1890-on. Perfect bisque head, nice wig, sleep eyes, open mouth; composition ball-jointed body; pretty clothes; all in good condition.

#390 (larger sizes marked only "A. [size] M."), *Florodora, 1894:*

9-10in (23-25cm)	**$235-$265***
12-14in (31-36cm)	**$225-$275***
16-18in (41-46cm)	**$325-$375***
20in (51cm)	**$400-$425***
23-24in (58-61cm)	**$450-$500***
28-29in (71-74cm)	**$650-$700**
30-32in (76-81cm)	**$750-$850**
35-36in (89-91cm)	**$1,000-$1,200+**
38in (96cm)	**$1,500-$1,800+**
40-42in (102-107cm)	**$2,000+**

Head only with sleeping eyes,
6in (15cm) **$85**

*Add $100-$200 for factory original clothes.
+Allow more for an exceptionally pretty doll.

FACTS

Armand Marseille of Köppelsdorf, Thüringia, Germany (porcelain and doll factory). 1885-on.

Marks:

A.M.-DEP
No. 3600.
3.
Made in Germany

A0½M
Florodora
Armand Marseille
Made in Germany

1894
A M 5/0 DEP
Germany

18 Made in Germany
A (Baby 2½ Betty) M
D R G M.

23in (58cm) 390 child.
H & J Foulke, Inc.

26in (66cm) *Queen Louise,*
H & J Foulke, Inc.

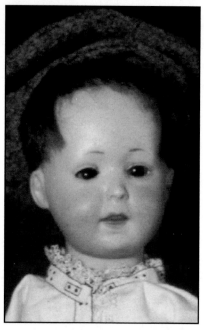

13in (33cm) 590 character boy with open/closed mouth. *H & J Foulke, Inc.*

11in (28cm) 251/248 character baby with open/closed mouth and molded tongue. *H & J Foulke, Inc.*

5-piece composition body, (excellent quality body):

6-7in (15-18cm)	**$200-$225**
9-10in (23-25cm)	**$260-$285**
Closed mouth,	
5-5½in (12-14cm)	**$250-$275**

Cardboard and stick leg body:

9-10in (23-25cm)	**$125**
12-14in (31-36cm)	**$135-$165**
16-18in (41-46cm)	**$210-$260**

#1894 (composition body; early pale bisque):

14-16in (36-41cm)	**$500-$600**
21-23in (53-58cm)	**$750-$850**
26in (66cm)	**$950**

#370, 3200, 1894, Florodora, Anchor 2015, Rosebud, Lily, Alma, Mabel, Darling, Beauty, Princess shoulder heads on kid or cloth bodies

11-12in (28-31cm)	**$125-$150**
14-16in (36-41cm)	**$175-$225**
22-24in (56-61cm)	**$375-$425**
25-26in (64-66cm)	**$450-$500**

#2000: 14in (36cm)   **$900****

Queen Louise, Rosebud (composition body):

12in (31cm)	**$340-$365**
23-25in (58-64cm)	**$550-$600**
28-29in (71-74cm)	**$700-$800**

Baby Betty:

14-16in (36-41cm) composition body	**$550-$600**
19-21in (48-53cm) kid body	**$525-$575**

#1894, 1892, 1896, 1897 shoulder heads (excellent quality),

19-22in (48-56cm)   **$475-$525**

Character Children: 1910-on. Perfect bisque head, molded hair or wig, glass or painted eyes, open or closed mouth; composition body; dressed; all in good condition. (For photographs of dolls not shown here, see previous *Blue Books*.)

#230 Fany (molded hair):

15-16in (38-41cm)   **$6,000-$6,500**

#231 Fany (wigged):
  14-15in (36-38cm) **$5,500-$6,000**
#250, 11-13in (28-33cm) **$750**
#251/248 (open/closed mouth):
  12in (31cm) **$1,650**
  16-18in (41-46cm) **$2,600-$3,000**
#340, 13in (33cm) **$2,600****
#372 Kiddiejoy shoulder head, "mama" body,
  19in (48cm) **$650****
#400 (child body):
  13in (33cm) **$1,600-$1,800****
  17in (43cm) **$2,600-$2,800****
#500, 600, 13-15in (33-38cm)**$700-$800**
#550 (glass eyes):
  12in (31cm) **$2,200-$2,500**
  18-20in (46-51cm) **$3,400-$3,600***
#560, 11-13in (28-33cm) **$750-$850**
#590, (open/closed mouth),
  15-16in (38-41cm) **$1,300-$1,400**
#620 shoulder head,
  16in (41cm) **$1,250****
#640 shoulder head (same face as 550 socket), 20in (51cm) **$1,500-$1,650****
#700:
  11in (28cm) painted eyes **$2,100****
  14in (36cm) glass eyes **$4,000-$4,500****
A.M. (intaglio eyes),
  16-17in (41-43cm) **$6,000 up**
  23in (58cm) **$15,000 up**
**Not enough price samples to compute a reliable range.

Character Babies and Toddlers: 1910-on. Perfect bisque head, good wig, sleep eyes, open mouth some with teeth; composition bent-limb body; suitably dressed; all in nice condition.

Marks:

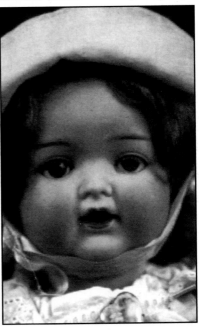

18in (46cm) 1330 character toddler, 5-piece body. *H & J Foulke, Inc.*

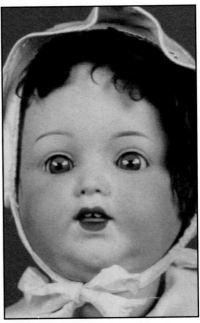

23in (58cm) 996 character baby. *H & J Foulke, Inc.*

9in (23cm) 560a character toddler. *H & J Foulke, Inc.*

Mold #990, 985, 971, 996, 1330, 326 (solid dome), 980, 991, 327, 329, 259 and others:

10-11in (25-28cm)	**$275-$300**
13-15in (33-38cm)	**$325-$375**
18-20in (46-51cm)	**$400-$500**
22in (56cm)	**$625-$650**
24-25in (61-64cm)	**$750**

#233:

13-15in (33-38cm)	**$500-$550**
20in (51cm)	**$700-$800**

#250,

11in (28cm)	**$400-$500**

#251/248 (open/closed mouth),

11-12in (28-31cm)	**$800-$900**

#251/248 (open mouth),

12-14in (31-36cm)	**$650-$750**

#410 (two rows of teeth),

15-16in (38-41cm)	**$1,200-$1,500****

#518:

16-18in (41-46cm)	**$600-$700**
25in (64cm)	**1,000-$1,200**

14in (36cm) h.c., 14in (36cm) long 341 infant. *H & J Foulke, Inc.*

#560A:
10-12in (25-31cm)	**$525-$550**
15-17in (38-43cm)	**$650-$700**

#580, 590 (open/closed mouth):
9in (23cm)	**$650-$750**
15-16in (38-41cm)	**$1,200-$1,500**

#590 (open mouth):
12in (31cm)	**$600**
16-18in (41-46cm)	**$850-$950**

#920 shoulder head, "mama" body,
21in (53cm)   **$650****

Melitta, 19in (48cm) toddler
   $1,100-$1,250

#995, painted bisque toddler,
18in (46cm)   **$500-$600**

**Not enough price samples to
compute a reliable range.

Infant: 1924-on. Solid-dome
bisque head with molded and/or
painted hair, sleep eyes; composition body or hard-stuffed jointed cloth body or soft-stuffed
cloth body; dressed; all in good
condition.

7½in (19cm) painted
bisque *Just Me* 310. *H & J
Foulke, Inc.*

Mark:

A. M.
Germany.
351.14K

#351, 341, Kiddiejoy and **Our Pet:**
Head circumference:
8-9in (20-23cm)	**$225-$250***
10in (25cm)	**$275-$300***
12-13in (31-33cm)	**$350-$425***
15in (38cm)	**$600***

**Allow $25-$75 extra for composition body.

7in (18cm) long all original in basket
with label **$395**
6in (15cm) compo body **$225-$250**
24in (61cm) wigged toddler
$1,000-$1,100
Hand Puppet **$200-$225**
#352,
17-20in (43-51cm) long **$575-$625**
#347, head circumference,
12-13in (31-33cm) **$475-$525**
Baby Phyllis:
Head circumference:
9in (23cm) black **500**
12-13in (31-33cm) **$425-$475**
Baby Gloria, RBL, New York,
15-16in (38-41cm) **$700-$800**
Kiddiejoy, open mouth with tongue,
13½in (34cm) h.c. **$650**

Marked "Just Me' Character: Ca.
1925. Perfect bisque socket head, curly
wig, glass eyes to side, closed mouth;
composition body; dressed; all in good
condition. Some of these dolls, particularly the painted bisque ones, were used by
Vogue Doll Company in the 1930s and
will be found with original Vogue labeled
clothes.
Mark:

Just ME
Registered
Germany
A 310/5/0 M

7½-8in (19-20cm) **$1,250-$1,500**
9in (23cm) **$1,750-$2,000**
11in (28cm) **$2,500**
13in (33cm) **$3,000**

Painted bisque:
7-8in (18-20cm)
all original **$900-$1,000**
10in (25cm)
all original **$1,200-$1,400**

Lady: 1910-1930. Bisque head with
mature face, mohair wig, sleep eyes,
open or closed mouth; composition lady
body with molded bust, long slender
arms and legs; appropriate clothes; all in
good condition.
#401 and **400** (slim body),
14in (36cm):
Open mouth **$1,250-$1,450**
Closed mouth **$2,250-$2,500**
Painted bisque **$900-$1,000**
#300: (M.H.):
9in (23cm) **$1,400-$1,500****
All original **$1,650***
#400: flapper body,
16-19in (41-48cm) **$2,500-$3,000**
**Not enough price samples to compute a
reliable range.

14in (36cm) 401 lady, boxed and all
original. *H. Jay Lowe Collection.*

METAL DOLLS
(AMERICAN)

Metal Child: All metal, body fully jointed at neck, shoulders, elbows, wrists, hips, knees and ankles; sleep eyes, open/closed mouth with painted teeth; dressed; all in good condition. (Body may be jointed composition with metal hands and feet.)

16-20in (41-51cm) **$325-$425**

Babies: All metal baby.
11-13in (28-33cm) **$100-$125**
Metal head/cloth baby,
18-20in (46-51cm) **$165-$185**

FACTS
Various U.S. companies, such as Atlas Doll & Toy Co. and Giebeler-Falk, N.Y., U.S.A. Ca. 1917-on.

METAL HEADS
(GERMAN)

Marked Metal Head Child: Metal shoulder head on cloth or kid body, bisque or composition hands; dressed; very good condition, not repainted.
Molded hair, painted eyes:
12-14in (31-36cm) **$125-$150**
23in (58cm) **$210-$235**
Molded hair, glass eyes:
12-14in (31-36cm) **$150-$175**
20-22in (51-56cm) **$225-$250**
Wig and glass eyes:
14-16in (36-41cm) **$225-$250**
20-22in (51-56cm) **$275-$325**

FACTS
Buschow & Beck, Germany (Minerva): Karl Standfuss, Germany (Juno); Alfred Heller, Germany (Diana). Ca. 1888-on.
Mark:

Mark may often be found on front of shoulder plate.

22in (56cm) German metal head child.
H & J Foulke, Inc.

MISSIONARY RAGBABIES

MULTI-FACED DOLLS

Beecher Baby: Handmade stuffed stockinette doll with looped wool hair, painted eyes and mouth, needle sculpted face; appropriately dressed; all in good condition.

20-23in (51-59cm)   **$3,500-$4,000**

Fair condition,
    18in (46cm)   **$1,800-$2,200**

FACTS

Julia Beecher, Elmira, N.Y., U.S.A.
1893-1910. All cloth. 16-23in (41-58cm)
Designer: Julia Jones Beecher
Mark: None

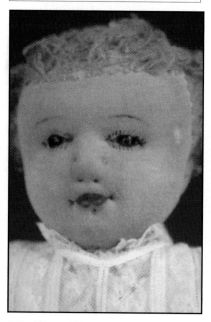

21in (53cm) *Missionary Rag Baby. H & J Foulke, Inc.*

Marked C.B. Doll: Carl Bergner, Sonneberg, Germany. Perfect bisque head with two or three different faces, usually sleeping, laughing and crying, papier-mâché hood hides the unwanted face(s); a ring through the top of the hood attached to a dowel turns the faces; cloth torso, composition limbs or jointed composition body; dressed; all in good condition.

13in (33cm) 2 or
    3 faces   **$1,500-$1,800**
13in (33cm) two-faced black and white
202 dep   **$1,800-$2,200**
    13in (33cm) **Red Riding Hood,**
    Grandmother and **Wolf** **$6,000****
14in (31cm) two-faced, frowning
    and hint of a smile
Simon & Halbig-type   **$3,500****

Character Babies: German. Ca. 1910. Perfect bisque head with two faces, usually crying, sleeping or smiling; swivel neck; composition or cloth body; dressed; all in good condition. Some have papier-

14in (36cm) unusual mold double-face doll. *Kay & Wayne Jensen Collection.*

mâché hoods to cover unwanted faces, while some use cloth bonnets.

17in (43cm) HvB (von Berg)
  two-faced baby   **$1,200-$1,400**

13in (33cm) Gebr. Heubach
  three-faced baby   **$1,800-$2,000**

13in (33cm) Kley & Hahn
  two-faced baby   **2,000-$2,200**

9in (23cm) Max Schelhorn
  two-faced baby   **$650-$750**

French Dolls:
Jumeau, laughing and crying character faces (#211 & 203).

18in (46cm)   **$14,500**

American Composition Dolls:
Trudy. 3-in-1 Doll Corp., New York.
  Sleeping, crying, smiling, all original,
  14in (36cm)   **$250-$295**

Johnny Tu-Face. Effanbee,
New York.
  Crying and smiling,
  16in (41cm)   **$400****

**Not enough price samples to compute a reliable average.

FACTS
Various German, French and American companies. 1888 and perhaps earlier.

14in (36cm) unusual mold double-face doll. *Kay & Wayne Jensen Collection.*

MUNICH ART DOLLS

Munich Art Dolls: Molded composition character heads with hand-painted features; fully-jointed composition bodies; appropriate regional or "country style" clothes; all in good condition.

13-14in (33-36cm)   **$2,400-$3,000**
18-19in (46-48cm)   **3,500-$5,000**

FACTS
Marion Kaulitz. 1908-1912. All-composition, fully-jointed bodies.
Designer: Paul Vogelsanger and others.
Mark: Sometimes signed on doll's neck.

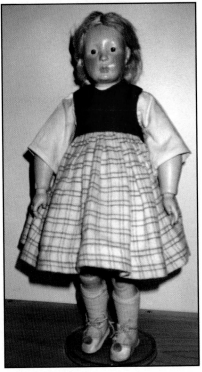

Munich Art Doll. *Courtesy of Dorothy Hunt, Sweetbriar.*

OHLHAVER

13in (33cm) character girls, all original.
H & J Foulke, Inc.

Revalo Character Baby or Toddler:
Perfect bisque socket head, good wig,
sleep eyes, hair eyelashes, painted lower
eyelashes, open mouth; baby bent-limb
body; dressed; all in good condition.
#22:

15-17in (38-41cm)	**$550-$600**
22in (56cm)	**$800-$850**
Toddler,	
17-19in (41-48cm)	**$1,000-$1,200**

Revalo Child Doll: Bisque socket head,
good wig, sleep eyes, hair eyelashes,
painted lower eyelashes, open mouth;
ball-jointed composition body; dressed;
all in good condition. Mold **#150** or
#10727.

14-15in (36-38cm)	**$500-$600**
18-20in (46-51cm)	**$700-$750**
24-25in (61-64cm)	**$850-$950**
Shoulder head, 22in (56cm)	**$650-$675**

Revalo Character Doll: Bisque head
with molded hair, painted eyes,
open/closed mouth; composition body;
dressed; all in good condition.

Coquette, 12-13in (31-33cm)	**$850**
Coquette with hairbows,	
13-14in (33-36cm)	**$1,000-$1,100**

22in (56cm) *Revalo* shoulder head child.
H & J Foulke, Inc.

FACTS

Gebrüder Ohlhaver, doll factory,
Sonneberg, Thüringia, Germany. Heads
made by Gebrüder Heubach, Ernst
Heubach and Porzellanfabrik
Mengersgereuth. 1912-on.
Trademarks: Revalo.

Mark:

Revalo
Germany
3

ORIENTAL DOLLS

Japanese Traditional Dolls:
Ichimatsu (play doll): 1868-on. Papier-mâché swivel head on shoulder plate, hips, lower legs and feet (early ones have jointed wrists and ankles); cloth midsection, cloth (floating) upper arms and legs; hair wig, dark glass eyes, pierced ears and nostrils; original clothes; all in very good condition.

Meiji Era (1868-1912):

3-5in (8-13cm)	**$200-$250**
12-14in (31-36cm)	**$350-$450***
18-20in (46-51cm)	**$600-$700***
24-26in)61-66cm)	**$1,200-$1,400***

Early three-bend body **(Mitsuore)**:

14-16in (36-41cm)	**$1,500 up**

Fully jointed lady, all original and boxed with additional wigs,

20in (51cm)	**$2,300**

*Allow extra for a sexed boy.

Ca. 1920s:

13-15in (33-38cm)	**$175-$225**
17-18in (43-46cm)	**$275-$325**
Ca. 1940s, 12-14in (31-36cm)	**$85-$95**

Traditional Lady (**Kyoto** or **Fashion Doll**):

Ca. 1900, 12in (31cm)	**$500 up**
1920s:	
10-12in (25-31cm)	**$150-$175**
16in (41cm)	**$235-$265**
1940s, 12-14in (31-36cm)	**$85-$95**
6½in (16cm) Geisha with 6 wigs, boxed	**$95**

Traditional Warrior:

1880s, 16-18in (41-46cm)	**$800 up**
1920s, 11-12in (28-31cm)	**$250 up**

Royal Personages:

Ca. 1890, 10in (25cm)	**$800 up**
1920s-1930s:	
4-6in (10-15cm)	**$100-$125**
12in (31cm)	**$350 up**

Baby with bent limbs:

Ca. 1910, 11in (28cm)	**$250 up**
Ca. 1930s, souvenir dolls:	
8-10in (20-25cm)	**$65-$85**

Carved Ivory, Ca. 1890:

2-3in (5-8cm) fully jointed, exquisite carving	**$350**
lesser quality	**$225**

Chinese Papier-Mâché: Ca 1930-1940. All original, so-called "Opera" dolls.

8in (20cm)	**$40-$45**
26in (66cm)	**$500**

20in (51cm) Ichimatsu, all original with box. *H & J Foulke, Inc.*

17in (43cm) Simon & Halbig 1199
Oriental, all original. *H & J Foulke, Inc.*

12in (31cm) **Emperor**, all original, Ca.
1850. *Betty Lunz Collection.*

Oriental Bisque Dolls: Ca. 1900-on. Made by French and German firms. Bisque head tinted yellow; matching ball-jointed or baby body; original or appropriate clothes; all in excellent condition. (See previous *Blue Books* for photographs of dolls not pictured here.)

B.P. #220:

16-17in (41-43cm) **$3,200-$3,500****

Belton-type:

12in (31cm) 127 **$1,700**

BSW #500

11in (28cm) **$1,100-$1,300**
14-15in (36-38cm) **$1,800-$2,200***

Bru Jne, 20in (51cm) **$26,000****
Tête Jumeau, closed mouth,
19-20in (48-51cm)**$48,000-$62,000****
Jumeau, open mouth,
18in (46cm) **$4,500****

JDK 243:

13-14in (33-36cm) **$4,800-$5,800**
16-18in (41-46cm) **$6,200-$6,800**

A.M. 353:

12-14in (31-36cm) **$1,000-$1,150**
10in (25cm) cloth body **$700**

A.M. Girl: 8-9in (20-23cm) **$650**

S&H 1329:

11in (28cm) **$1,200**
14-15in (36-38cm) **$1,800-$2,200***
18-19in (46-48cm) **$2,700-$2,800***

S&H 1099, 1129, and **1199:**

8in (20cm) **$1,200**
15in (38cm) **$2,700-$2,800***
19-20in (48-51cm) **$3,200-$3,500***

*Allow extra for elaborate original outfits.
**Not enough price samples to compute a reliable range.

S PB H, 9in (23cm) **$650**
   19in (48cm) **$2,000***
#164, 16-17in (41-43cm)**$2,300-$2,500***
Unmarked:
   4½in (12cm) painted eyes **$175-$195**
   4¾in (12cm) glass eyes **$400-$500**
   11-12in (28-31cm)
      glass eyes **$850-$950**

All-Bisque Dolls:
JDK Baby,
   5½in (14cm) **$1,650****

Heubach **Chin Chin,**
   4in (10cm) **$325-$365**

S&H Child,
   4½in (11cm) **$625-$675**
   5½in (14cm) **$750-$775**
   7in (18cm) **$850-$950**
   Man with molded hat and mustache
      2½in (6cm) **275-$300**

Bisque Heads of Unknown Origin:
Lady with molded hair or hat, wood jointed body, 13in (33cm) **$750-$850**
Character man with molded mustache, jointed body, 11in (28cm) **$1,100****

German Papier Mâché: Ca. 1925
August Moller,
   14in (36cm) all original and boxed
      at auction **$650**

American Cloth: Oil painted stockinette in the Chase manner. Original clothes.
   16in (41cm) **$1,050**
**Not enough price samples to compute a reliable range.

5½in (14cm) J.D. Kestner all-bisque Oriental baby with chest label. *H & J Foulke, Inc.*

17in (43cm) J.D. Kestner 243 Oriental baby. *H & J Foulke, Inc.*

PAPIER-MÂCHÉ
(SO-CALLED FRENCH-TYPE)

French-type Papier-mâché: Shoulder head with painted black pate, brush marks around face, nailed on human hair wig (often missing), set-in glass eyes, closed or open mouth with bamboo teeth, pierced nose; pink kid body with stiff arms and legs; appropriate old clothes; all in good condition, showing some wear.

12-14in (31-36cm)	**$1,100-$1,300**
18-20in (46-51cm)	**$1,800-$2,000**
24-26in (61-66cm)	**$2,200-$2,500**
32in (81cm)	**$2,800-$3,100**

20in (51cm) lady with trunk, additional original outfit, a few accessories,

at auction	**$3,990**

Painted eyes:

6-8in (15-20cm)	**$375-$475**
14-16in (36-41cm)	**$1,000-$1,200**

Wood-jointed body:

6in (15cm)	**$750-$800**

Shell decoration:

4½in (12cm)	**$500-$600**
8in (20cm) pair	**$1,000-$1,200**
18in (46cm) pair	**$2,200**

Poupard, molded bonnet and clothes,

18in (46cm)	**$400-$500**

FACTS

Heads by German firms such as Johann Müller of Sonneberg and Andreas Voit of Hildburghausen, were sold to French and other doll makers. 1835-1850.

Mark: None.

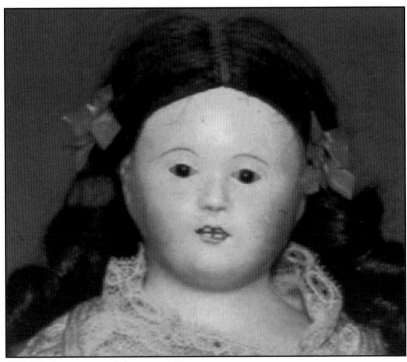

17in (43cm) French papier-mâché, all original. *Sweetbriar.*

PAPIER-MÂCHÉ
(GERMAN)

Papier-mâché Shoulder Head: Ca. 1840s to 1860s. Unretouched shoulder head, molded hair, painted eyes; some wear and crazing; cloth or kid body; original or appropriate old clothing; entire doll in fair condition.

16-18in (41-46cm)	**$900-$1,000***
22-24in (56-61cm)	**$1,100-$1,300***
32in (81cm)	**$1,900-$2,200***
18½in (47cm) all original, exceptional model and condition	
at auction	**$5,000**

Glass eyes, short hair:

19in (48cm)	**$1,650-$1,850**
24in (61cm)	**$2,400**
21in (53cm) all original provincal costume	**$2,600**

Glass eyes, long hair,

22in (56cm)	**$1,700-$2,000**

Flirty eyes, long hair,

23in (58cm)	**$2,700-$3,000**
Long curls, 19in (48cm)	**$2,300**

*Allow extra for an unusual model.

Molded Hair Papier-mâché: (so-called "milliners' models") 1820s-1860s. Unretouched shoulder head, various molded hairdos, eyes blue, black or brown, painted features; original kid body, wooden arms and legs; original or very old handmade clothing; entire doll in fair condition.

Long curls:

9in (23cm)	**$550**
13in (33cm)	**$675-$725**
23in (58cm)	**$1,400-$1,500**
13in (33cm) all original, at auction	**$1,900**

Covered wagon hairdo:

7in (18cm)	**$275-$325**
11in (28cm)	**$450-$500**
15in (38cm)	**$675-$775**

Side curls with braided bun:

9-10in (23-25cm)	**$750-$850**
13-15in (31-38cm)	**$1,300-$1,500**

Center part with molded bun:

7in (18cm)	**$525**
11in (28cm)	**$950-$1,000**
Wood-jointed body	**$1,200-$1,350**

Side curls with high beehive (Apollo knot):

11in (28cm)	**$950-$1,000**
18in (46cm)	**$1,900-$2,100**

17½ (45cm) papier-mâché boy, all original. *H. Jaye Lowe Collection.*

FACTS
Various German firms of Sonneberg such as Johann Müller, Müller & Strasburger, F.M. Schilling, Heinrich Stier, A. Wislizenus, and Cuno & Otto Dressel. 1816 on.

14½in (37cm) molded hair papier-mâché original. *H. Jay Lowe Collection*

Coiled braids at ears, braided bun:
10-11in (25-28cm)	**$1,000-$1,100**
20in (51cm)	**$2,000-$2,200**

Braided coronet,
11in(28cm)	**$1,250-$1,450**

Molded bonnet and red snood,
13in (33cm)	**$1,250-$1,500**

Patent Washable Dolls: 1880-1915. Composition shoulder head with mohair or skin wig, glass eyes, closed or open mouth; cloth body with composition arms and lower legs, sometimes with molded boots; appropriately dressed; all in good condition.

Superior Quality:
12-14in (31-36cm)	**$500-$600**
16-18in (41-46cm)	**$700-$750**
22-24in (56-61cm)	**$850-$900**
30in (76cm)	**$1,200-$1,400**

13in (33cm) papier-mâché with molded hat, all original. *H. Jay Lowe Collection.*

Standard Quality:

11-12in (28-31cm)	**$150-$175**
14-16in (36-41cm)	**$225-$250**
22-24in (56-61cm)	**$325-$375**
30-33in (76-84cm)	**$450-$500**
38in (97cm)	**$600-$700**
Lady, 13-16in (33-41cm)	**$750-$850**
Oriental, 12in (31cm)	**$225-$250**

Sonneberg-type Papier-mâché: Ca. 1880-1910. Shoulder head with molded and painted black or blonde hair, painted eyes, closed mouth; cloth body sometimes with leather arms; old or appropriate clothes; all in good condition, showing some wear.

Mark: Usually unmarked. Some marked:

M & S
Superior
2015

13-15in (33-38cm)	**$275-$325***
18-19in (46-48cm)	**$400-$450***
23-25in (58-64cm)	**$550-$650***
Peddlar, 13in (33cm) all original with tray of antique wears	**$1,450**
Glass eyes, 18in (46cm)	**$550-$600**
Topsy Turvy, 7½in (19cm) all original	**$300**

*Allow extra for an unusual hairdo.

Papier-mâché Child: Ca. 1920-on. Papier-mâché head, hard stuffed body, good wig, painted features; original clothes, all in good condition.

10-12in (25-31cm)	**$90-$110**

11½in (30cm) patent washable, all original dressed as a baby. *H & J Foulke, Inc.*

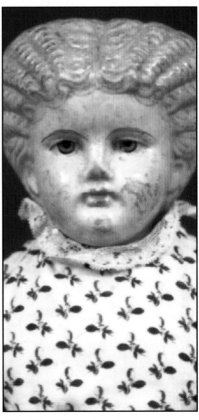

20in (51cm) Sonneberg-type papier-mâché, all original. *H & J Foulke, Inc.*

PARIAN-TYPE
(UNTINTED BISQUE)

17in (43cm) parian lady with decorated shoulder plate. *Private Collection.*

20in (51cm) so-called *Empress Eugenie* with lustre head piece and green snood. *Private Collection.*

Unmarked Parian: Pale or untinted shoulder head, sometimes with molded blouse, beautifully molded hairdo (may have ribbons, beads, comb or other decoration), painted eyes, closed mouth; cloth body; lovely clothes; entire doll in fine condition.

Common, plain style:

8-10in (20-25cm)	**$135-$185**
16in (41cm)	**$300-$350***
24in (61cm)	**$475-$525***

Swivel neck, 17½in(45cm) **$525-$575**

Molded white blouse, blue scarf

22in (56cm)	**$500-$550**

Very fancy hairdo and/or elaborately decorated blouse **$800-$2,500**

Very fancy with glass eyes **$1,500-$3,250**

Pretty hairdo, may have simple ribbon or comb:

14-15in (36-38cm)	**$475-$525**
18-20in (46-51cm)	**$750-$850**

Simple hairdo with applied flowers,

20in (51cm)	**$850**

Man, molded collar and tie,

16-17in (41-43cm)	**$750**

Child, glass eyes, molded blonde curls,

14-16in (36-41cm)	**$1,150-$1,250**

"Augusta Victoria,"

17in (43cm)	**$1,200-$1,300**

*Allow $100 for glass eyes.

FACTS
Various German firms. Ca. 1860s through 1870s.
Mark: Ususally none, sometimes numbers.

Molded plate, blonde curls, ribbon, glass eyes,

    16-18in (41-46cm)   **$1,300-$1,500**

Alice hairdo, 21in (53cm)   **$850-$950**

    14in (36cm)   **$425-$450**

"Countess Dagmar,"

    19in (48cm)   **$850-$950**

"Irish Queen," Limbach 8552,

    16in (41cm)   **$600-$700**

"Dolley Madison," glass eyes, swivel neck,

    20in (51cm)   **$1,600**

Pink lustre hat or snood,

    17in (43cm)   **$1,700-$1,800**

Pink lustre tiara, gold earrings,

    14-16in (36-41cm)   **$1,500**

Molded straw bonnet, fancy shoulder plate,

    16in (41cm)   **$2,500**

Blue bows and snood,

    24in (61cm)   **$1,200**

Molded flowers and gold coronet, all original

    14½in (37cm)   **$1,650**

Light brown hair waving past shoulders, applied Dresden flowers,

    21in (53cm)   **$1,700**

Fancy blonde hair, molded black bow and holes for attaching beads,

    19in (48cm)   **$1,000**

Molded yellow bonnet with flowers,

    10in (25cm)   **$1,650**

Molded necklace, fancy hair, glass eyes,

    18in (46cm)   **$1,800**

All-Parian, pink lustre boots,

    5½in (14cm)   **$225-$250**

    3¾in (8cm) boy with

        molded hat   **$350**

Head only, decorated shoulder plate, painted eyes

    5in (13cm)   **$450**

Head only, molded blouse with black bow, pierced ears, blonde hair

    3½in (8cm)   **$325**

14½in (27cm) parian lady with molded flowers in her hair, all original. *H & J Foulke, Inc.*

11in (28cm) parian child with glass eyes and long curls. *H & J Foulke, Inc.*

P.D.

PHILADELPHIA BABY

P.D. Bébé: Perfect bisque head with paperweight eyes, closed mouth, pierced ears, good wig; jointed composition body (some have metal hands); appropriate clothes; all in good condtion.

19-23in (48-58cm) **$14,000-$16,000**

FACTS
Probably Petit & Dumontier, Paris, France. Some heads made by François Gaultier. 1878-1890.
Mark:

P.2.D

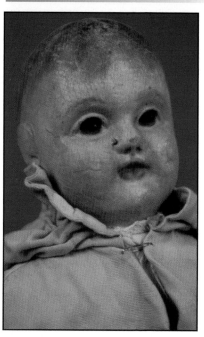

Philadelphia Baby. H & J Foulke, Inc.

Philadelphia Baby: All-cloth with treated shoulder-type head, lower arms and legs; painted hair, well-molded facial features, ears; stocking body; very good condition.

18-22in (46-56cm)	**$4,200**
Mint condition	**$5,000-$5,500**
Fair, showing wear	**$2,500**
Very worn	**$1,600-$1,800**

Rare style face (See *6th Blue Book*, page 302 for exact doll.), at auction **$9,350**

18½in (47cm) P 2 D. *Private Collection.*

FACTS
J.B. Sheppard & Co., Philadelphia, Pa., U.S.A. Ca. 1900. All-cloth.
Mark: None

PRE-GREINER (SO-CALLED)

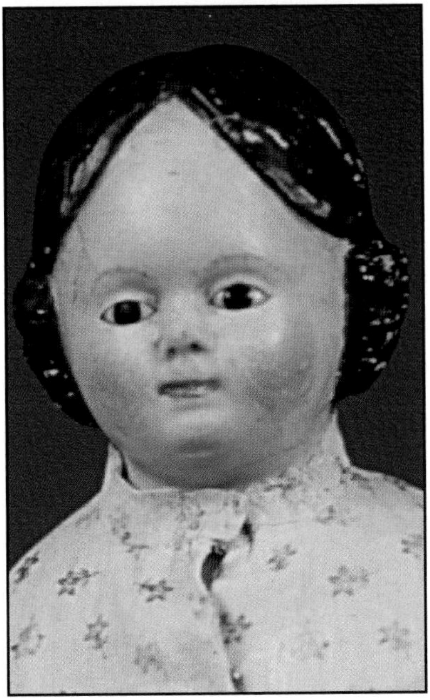

23in (58cm) pre-Greiner, some touch up.
H & J Foulke, Inc.

Unmarked Pre-Greiner: Papier-mâché shoulder head; molded and painted black hair, pupil-less black glass eyes; stuffed cloth body, mostly homemade, wood, leather or cloth extremities; dressed in good old or original clothes, all in good condition.

18-22in (46-56cm)	**$1,000-$1,350**
28-32in (71-81cm)	**$2,000-$2,300**
Fair condition, much wear,	
20-24in (51-61cm)	**$700-$800**
Flirty eye, 30in (76cm)	**$3,000**

FACTS

Unknown and various, Ca. 1850.
Mark: None.

RABERY & DELPHIEU

Marked R.D. Bébé: Ca. 1880s. Perfect bisque head, lovely wig, paperweight eyes, closed mouth; jointed composition body; beautifully dressed; entire doll in good condition. Very good quality bisque, very pretty.

12-14in (31-36cm)	**$2,500-$3,000**
18-19in (46-48cm)	**$3,600-$3,800**
24-25in (61-64cm)	**$4,000-$4,500**
28in (71cm)	**$4,800-$5,200**
Lesser quality bisque (uneven coloring or much speckling), not as pretty,	
16-18in (41-46cm)	**$2,250-$2,350**
Open mouth:	
19-22in (48-56cm)	**$1,900-$2,200**
26-28in (66-71cm)	**$2,800-$3,000**

FACTS

Rabery & Delphieu of Paris, France. 1856 (founded)-1899, then with S.F.B.J.

Mark:
On back of head: R 5/0 D

Body mark: BÉBÉ RABERY
S^{e} ——
(Please note last two lines illegible)

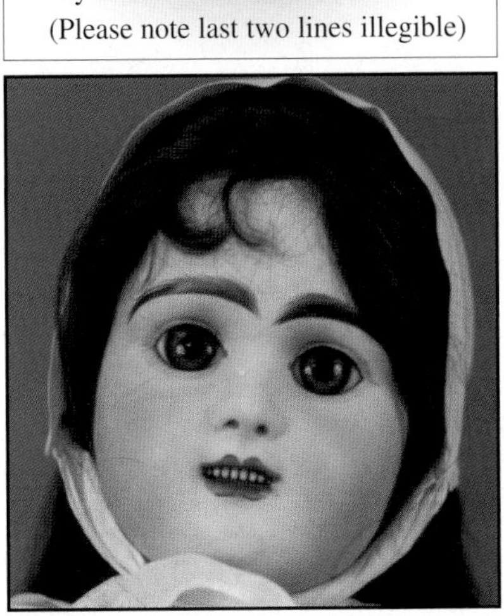

25in (64cm) R.D. with open mouth.
Private Collection.

RAGGEDY ANN AND ANDY

Early Raggedy Ann or **Andy:** Volland. All-cloth with movable arms and legs; brown yarn hair, button eyes, painted features; legs of striped fabric for hose and black for shoes; original clothes; all in good condition.
Mark: "PATENTED SEPT. 7, 1915"

Early hand painted
face Ann	**$1,500-$2,000**
Printed face	**$1,300-$1,500**
Wear, stains, not original	
clothes	**$800-$900**

Molly'es Raggedy Ann or **Andy:** 1935-1938, manufactured by Molly'es Doll Outfitters. Red hair and printed features; original clothes; all in good condition.
Mark:
"Raggedy Ann and Raggedy Andy Dolls, Manufactured by Molly'es Doll Outfitters" (printed writing in black on front torso)

16in (41cm) Volland *Raggedy Ann*, all original.

18-22in (46-56cm)	**$1,400-$1,800 each**

Babies
14in (36cm) pair	**$4,000-$5,000**

Georgene Raggedy Ann or **Andy:** 1938-1963, manufactured by Georgene Novelties, Inc. Red hair, black button eyes; original clothes; all in good condition, light wear and fading acceptable.
Mark: Various cloth labels sewn in side seam of body.

Black Outline Nose, Ca. 1938-1944
19-20in (48-51cm)	**$1,200-$1,500**
32in (81cm)	**$2,500-$2,800**

Asleep/Awake, Black Outline Nose
13in (33cm)	**$800**
Pair	**$1,800**

Asleep/Awake, plain nose
12in (30cm)	**$650**

Face #2, long nose, Ca. 1944-1946
19in (48cm)	**$1,000-$1,200**

Silsby Label, 1946
15in (38cm)	**$400-500**
20in (51cm) pair	**$1,500-$1,800**
20in (51cm) pair, blue stockings,	
no clothes, at auction	**$3,151**

Small nose, curved sides, bright color, excellent condition
15in (38cm)	**$275-$300**
boxed pair	**$825-$875**
19-20in (48-51cm)	**$325-$375**
boxed	**$450-$500**
23in (58cm)	**$375-$425**

FACTS
Various makers. 1915 to present.
All-cloth
Creator: Johnny B. Gruelle.

Small nose, worn faded, all original

15in (38cm)	**$150-$175**
19in (48cm)	**$175-$200**
23in (58cm)	**$200-$250**

Beloved Belindy,

19in (48cm)	**$1,500-$2,000**

Knickerbocker Toy Co. Raggedy Ann or **Andy:** 1963-1982. Bright color, excellent condition.

Early, 1964

15in (38cm) boxed with clouds	**$250**

Various print dresses

15in (38cm)	**$135-$150**
19in (48cm)	**$165-$185**

Common print dress

15in (38cm)	**$65-$85**
19in (48cm)	**$85-$95**
32-35in (81-86cm)	**$750-$850**
Beloved Belindy, 15in (38cm)	**$750-$850**

Camel with Wrinkled Knees,

15in (38cm)	**$285-$325**

Musical, 1966.

15in (38cm) boxed	**$225**

Teach N Play, 1971.

18in (46cm)	**$100-$125**

Embraceables, 1973.

7in (18cm) Boxed	**$100-$125**

Talking, 1973

18in (46cm) boxed	**$225**

Hand Puppets, 1973

9½in (24cm)	**$27 pair**

Applause, 1981-

Embroidered eyes

12in (31cm)	**$10**
17in (43cm)	**$15**

Classic model, button eyes

17-20in (43-51cm)	**$20**
25in (63cm)	**$30**
Black, 12in (30cm) pair	**$40-$45**
Asleep/Awake, pair	**$65-$75**

1992 75th Anniversary

19in (48cm) Ann or Andy, boxed	**$75-$100**

1993 Molly-E Baby Raggedy Ann

13in (33cm)	**$80-$100**

1994 Raggedy Ann or Andy

13in (33cm) boxed	**$80-$100**
Camel with Wrinkled Knees	**$75-$80**

15in (38cm) 1951 Georgene Novelties pair, all original and boxed. *H & J Foulke, Inc.*

15in (38cm) Knickerbocker *Raggedy Ann,* all original and boxed. *H & J Foulke, Inc.*

11in (28cm)
1996
Anniversary
Pair, boxed.
*H & J
Foulke, Inc.*

15in (38cm) Knickerbocker *Beloved
Belindy* all original with tag. *H & J
Foulke, Inc.*

1995 Raggedy Ann, U.S. Patent,
    17in (43cm)   **$80-$100**
1997 Stamp Doll,
    17in (43cm) boxed   **$50-$65**
1998 Stars & Stripes,
    17in (43cm) boxed   **$85**

Hasbro, Inc. 1983-
    12in (31cm), boxed   **$10**
    18in (46cm), boxed   **$17**
    24in (61cm)   **$35**
    1996 Anniversary pair,
      11in (28cm) boxed   **$55-$65**

Playskool, 1989-
    1991 Dress Me Raggedy Ann
      14in (35cm) boxed   **$25-$35**

Alexander
    1993 Mop Top Wendy &
      Billy, pair   **$90-$100**

RECKNAGEL

R.A. Child: Ca. 1890s-World War I. Perfect marked bisque head, jointed composition or wooden body; good wig, set or sleep eyes, open mouth; some dolls with molded painted shoes and socks; all in good condition.

1907, 1909, 1914:

  8-9in (20-23cm)

    5-piece body   **$140-$165**

    16-18in (41-46cm)   **$325-$375***

    24in (61cm)   **500-$550***

*Fine quality bisque only.

R.A. Character Baby: 1909-World War I. Perfect bisque head; cloth baby body or composition bent-limb baby body; painted or glass eyes; nicely dressed; all in good condition.

#121, 126, 127, 1924 infants,

  8-9in (20-23cm) long   **$235-$285**

#23 character babies,

  7-8in (18-20cm)   **$300-$350**

#22, 28, and 44 bonnet babies,

  8-9in (20-23cm)   **$550-$600**

  11in (28cm)   **$800**

Character children:

  6-8in (15-20cm) composition

    body   **$300-$350**

  18in (46cm) smiling face,

    at auction   **$1,700**

#31 Max and #32 Moritz,

  molded hair, painted features,

  8in (20cm)   **$650-$700**

#45 and 46, googlies,

  7in (18cm)   **$500-$550**

#43, 44 googlies with molded hats,

  7in (18cm)   **600**

FACTS

Th. Recknagel, porcelain factory, Alexandrienthal, Thüringia, Germany. 1886-on.

Mark: 1907
R/A DEP
I 9/0

8in (20cm) 32 *Moritz* character. *Courtesy of Mimi Hiscox.*

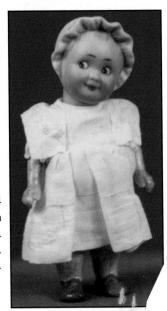

7in (18cm) 44 googly with molded hat. *H & J Foulke, Inc.*

ROLLINSON DOLL

Marked Rollinson Doll: All molded cloth with painted head and limbs; painted hair or human hair wig, painted features (sometimes teeth also); dressed; all in good condition.

Chase-type with painted hair,
18-22in (46-51cm)	**$800-$1,200**

Child with wig:
16in (41cm)	**$800-$1,200**
26in (66cm)	**$1,500-$2,000**

FACTS

Utley Doll Co., Holyoke, Mass.,
U.S.A. 1916-on.
Designer: Gertrude F. Rollinson
Mark: Stamp in shape of a diamond with a doll in center, around border: "Rollinson Doll Holyoke, Mass."

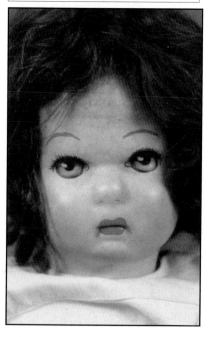

Rollinson child with wig. *Nancy A. Smith Collection.*

S.F.B.J.

Child Doll: 1899-on. Perfect bisque head, good French wig, set or sleep eyes, open mouth pierced ears; jointed composition body; nicely dressed; all in good condition.

Jumeau-type, paperweight eyes (no mold number), 1899-1910:
14-16in (36-41cm)	**$1,100-$1,250**
21-23in (53-58cm)	**$1,700-$1,900**
25-27in (64-69cm)	**$2,200-$2,500**
20in (51cm) boxed, all original with Jumeau shift & shoes	**$3,100**

#301 (some stamped "Tête Jumeau" on labeled Jumeau body):
10in (25cm)	**$650**
12-14in (31-36cm)	**$700-$800**
20-23in (51-58cm)	**$1,050-$1,150**
28-30in (71-76cm)	**$1,500-$1,700**
37in (94cm)	**$2,500-$2,800**
14in (36cm) boxed, all original with Jumeau shift and shoes	**$1,700**
22in (56cm), lady body	**$1,200-$1,400**

#60, end of World War I on:
7½in (19cm) with Jumeau tag	**$425-$450**
12-14in (31-36cm)	**$650-$700**
19-21in (48-53cm)	**$800-$850**
28in (71cm)	**$1,100-$1,200**

Bluette #301,
10½-11in (27-29cm)	**$900-$1,100**
with trunk, wardrobe, and catalog, at auction	**$3,500**

Walking, kissing and flirting:
22in (56cm)	**$1,700-$1,800**

FACTS

Société Française de Fabrication de
Bébés & Jouets, Paris, France.
1899-on.
Mark:

DÉPOSÉ
S.F.B.J.

S.F.B.J
307
PARIS

All original $2,400
Papier-mâché head #60, fully-jointed body:
17in (43cm) $300-$325
22in (56cm) $400-$500
18in (46cm) child in original sailor outfit, like new $1,400

Character Dolls: 1910-on. Perfect bisque head, wig, molded, sometimes flocked hair on mold numbers 237, 266, 227, and 235, sleep eyes, composition body; nicely dressed; all in good condition.

Mark:

#226, 20in (51cm) $2,100-$2,300
#227, 17in (43cm) $1,850-$1,900
#229, 16in (41cm) $2,000-$2,200**
#230 (sometimes Jumeau).
12-14in (30-36cm) $1,200-$1,400
19-22in (48-56cm) $1,900-$2,100
#233, 18in (46cm) $5,100**
#234, 18in (45cm) toddler $3,200**
#235, 16in (41cm) child $1,850-$1,900
15in (38cm) baby, all original
Au Nain Bleu outfit $2,200
**Not enough price samples to compute a reliable average.

#236 baby:
12-13in (31-33cm) $700-$800
15-17in (38-43cm) $900-$1,100
20-22in (51-56cm) $1,400-$1,500
25in (64cm) $1,700-$1,800
Toddler:
15-16in (38-41cm) $1,400-$1,500
24in (61cm) $1,950-$2,000
#237, 15-16in (38-41cm) $2,000-$2,200
#238 child,
15-16in (38-41cm) $2,200

Lady, 18-19in (46-48cm) $3,000
#239, 13in (33cm) Poulbot
all original $5,500-$6,500**
#242 nursing baby,
13-14in (33-35cm) 3,250**
#245 Googly, (See page 96.)
#246, 16½in (42cm) at auction $3,100
#247 Toddler
18-21in (46-53cm) $2,100-$2,600
#248,
10-12in (25-30cm) $7,500-$8,500**
#250, 25in (51cm) at auction $2,530
#251 toddler:
14-15in (36-38cm) $1,300-$1,500
24in (61cm) $2,200-$2,400

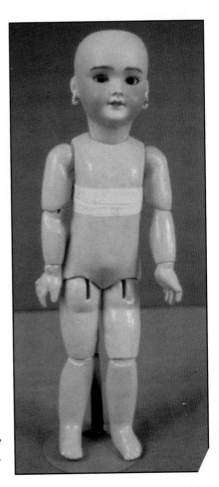

18½in (47cm) SFBJ 301 *Tête Jumeau. H & J Foulke, Inc.*

#252 baby: 10in (25cm) **$2,500-$3,000**

15in (38cm) **$4,000-$4,200**

Toddler:

10in (25cm) **$3,200-$3,600**

13in (33cm) **$4,800**

20in (51cm) **$6,500**

27-28cm (69-71cm) **$9,000-$11,000**

Boxed set, 12in (30cm) baby with

3 character heads (233, 235, 237)

$7,500-$8,500**

**Not enough price samples to compute a reliable range.

25in (64cm) SFBJ child.
Jensen's Antique Dolls.

16½in (42cm) 246 character girl.
Courtesy of McMasters Doll Auction.

19in (48cm) 252 pouty character toddler. *Private Collection.*

14in (36cm) 238 character girl. *Private Collection.*

BRUNO SCHMIDT

Marked B.S.W. Child Doll: Ca. 1898-on. Bisque head, good wig, sleep eyes, open mouth; jointed composition child body; dressed; all in good condition.

18-20in (46-51cm)	**$500-$600**
24-26in (61-66cm)	**$750-$850**
22in (56cm) flirty eyes	**$825-$850**

Marked B.S.W. Character Dolls: Bisque socket head, glass eyes; jointed composition body; dressed; all in good condition.

#2048, 2094, 2096 (so-called "Tommy Tucker"), molded hair, open mouth:

13-14in (33-36cm)	**$900-$1,100**
19-21in (48-53cm)	**$1,350-$1,450**
25-26in (64-66cm)	**$1,700-$1,900**

18in (46cm) 2048 so-called *"Tommy Tucker"*. H & J Foulke, Inc.

21in (53cm) 2025 (529) character child. *Jensen's Antique Dolls.*

FRANZ SCHMIDT

#2048 (closed mouth):

16-18in (41-46cm)   **$2,500****

#2072:

23in (58cm) toddler **$4,500-$5,000****

17in (43cm)   **$3,000-$3,500****

#2033 (so-called "Wendy") (537):

12-13in (30-33cm)   **$14,000**

15-17in (38-43cm)   **$18,000-$22,000**

20in (51cm)   **$30,000**

#2023 (539):

24in (61cm) at auction   **$3,000**

#2025 (529), closed mouth, wigged:

22in (56cm)   **$6,500-$7,000**

#2097, #692, character baby, open mouth:

13-14in (33-36cm)   **$500-$550**

18in (46cm)   **$750-$850**

24in (61cm)   **$1,200**

#2097 toddler, 17in (43cm)   **$1,250**

#425 all-bisque baby,

5½-6in (13-15cm)   **$250-$300**

#426 all-bisque toddler,

9½in (24cm)   **$1200****

**Not enough price samples to compute a reliable average.

Marked S & C Child Doll: Ca. 1890-on. Perfect bisque socket head, good wig, sleep eyes, open mouth; jointed composition child body; dressed; all in good condition. Some are Mold **#293** or **269**.

6in (15cm)   **$275-$325**

16-18in (41-46cm)   **$500-$550**

22-24in (56-61cm)   **$650-$750**

29-30in (74-76cm)   **$1,050-$1,200**

FACTS

Franz Schmidt & Co., doll factory, Georgenthal near Waltershausen, Thüringia, Germany. Heads by Simon & Halbig, Gräfenhain, Thüringia, Germany. 1890-on.

14in (36cm) 1272 toddler. *H & J Foulke, Inc.*

FACTS

Bruno Schmidt, doll factory, Waltershausen, Thüringia, Germany. Heads by Bähr & Pröschild, Ohrdruf, Thüringia, Germany. 1898-on.

Mark:

42in (107cm)   **$3,200-$3,600**

Shoulder head, kid body,

26in (66cm)   *S & C*   **$650**

Mark: *SIMON & HALBIG*

28

Marked F.S. & Co. Character Baby:
Ca. 1910. Perfect bisque character head,
good wig, sleep eyes, open mouth, may
have open nostrils; jointed bent-limb
composition body; suitably dressed; all in
good condition.

#1271, 1272, 1295, 1296, 1297, 1310:
Baby:

12-14in (31-36cm)	**$575-$675**
20-21in (51-53cm)	**$900-$950**
26-27in (66-69cm)	**$1,500-$1,650**

Toddler:

7in (18cm), 5-piece body	**$850**
10in (25cm),	
5-piece body	**$1,100-$1,250**
13-15in (33-38cm)	**$1,150-$1,350**
19-21in (48-53cm)	**$1,500-$1,700**
26-27in (66-69cm)	**$1,950-$2,150**

#1266, bald head, painted eyes, closed
mouth

16-17in (41-43cm)   **$3,500-$3,900**

#1267, open/closed mouth, painted eyes

24in (61cm) at auction   **$2,800**

#1286, molded hair with blue ribbon,
glass eyes, open smiling mouth,

16in (41cm) toddler   **$4,000****

Mark: *1295*
F. S. & Co
Made in
Germany
30

**Not enough price samples to compute a
reliable average.

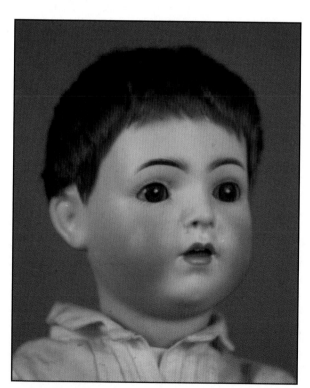

19in (48cm) 1295
toddler. *H & J
Foulke, Inc.*

SCHMITT

Marked Schmitt Bébé: Ca. 1879. Perfect bisque socket head with skin or good wig, large paperweight eyes, closed mouth, pierced ears; Schmitt-jointed composition body; appropriate clothes; all in good condition.

Long face: (For photograph see *13th Blue Book*, page 179.)

16-18in (41-46cm)	**$16,000-$18,000**
23-25in (58-64cm)	**$25,000**
30in (76cm)	**$30,000-$32,000**

Short face (parted lips)

14-16in (36-41cm)	**$12,500-$13,500**
22in (56cm)	**$17,000-$19,000**

Oval/round face: (For photograph see *11th Blue Book,* page 321.)

11-13in (28-33cm)	**$9,000-$10,000****
15-17in (38-43cm)	**$12,000-$14,000****

Cup and saucer neck,

17in (43cm) at auction	**$17,050**

Open/closed mouth, two rows of teeth,

24in (61cm)	**$25,000****

Papier-mâché head,

16in (41cm)	**$2,200-$2,600**

Body only, signed,

15in (38cm) at auction	**$1,400**

*Allow one-third less for dolls that do not have strongly molded faces.

**Not enough price samples to compute a reliable average.

FACTS
Schmitt & Fils, Paris, France, 1854-1891.
Mark: On both head and body:

14in (36cm) Schmitt with short face, signed head and body. *H & J Foulke, Inc.*

SCHOENAU & HOFFMEISTER

Child Doll: Perfect bisque head; original or good wig, sleep eyes, open mouth; ball-jointed body; original or good clothes; all in nice condition.

#1906, 1909, 5700, 5800:

14-16in (36-41cm)	**$350-$400**
21-23in (53-58cm)	**$550-$600***
28-30in (71-76cm)	**$850-$950**
33in (84cm)	**$1,200-$1,300**
39in (99cm)	**$2,400-$2,500**

*Allow $10-$200 extra for a flapper body.

#4000, 4600, 5000, 5500:

15-17in (38-43cm)	**$450-$500**
22in (56cm)	**$600-$650**
26in (66cm)	**$850-$900**

Künstlerkopf,

24-26in (61-66cm)	**$850-$950**

Shoulderhead, kid body,

18-20in (46-51cm)	**$275-$350**
13-15in (33-38cm) hinged pink kid body	**$425-$475**

FACTS

Schoenau & Hoffmeister, Porzellan-fabrick Burggrub, Burggrub, Bavaria, Germany, porcelain factory, 1901-on. Arthur Schoenau also owned a doll factory. 1884-on.
Trademarks: Hanna, Burggrub Baby, Bébé Carmencita, Viola, Kunstlerkopf, Das Lachende Baby.
Mark: ﹕

A S ⛧ *S⭐PB H*
4600
Germany

26in (66cm) 4000 child. *H & J Foulke, Inc.*

Character Baby: 1910-on. Perfect bisque socket head, good wig, sleep eyes, open mouth; composition bent-limb baby body; all in good condition. #169, 769 "Burggrub Baby" or "Porzellanfabrik Burggrub."

13-15in (33-38cm)	**$375-$475**
18-20in (46-51cm)	**$550-$650**
23-24in (58-61cm)	**$750-$800**
28in (71cm)	**$1,000-$1,100**
Painted bisque,	
14in (36cm) toddler, factory	
original	**$325-$350**

Princess Elizabeth, 1929, Chubby 5-piece body:

17in (43cm)	**$1,700-$1,900**
20-23in (51-58cm)	**$2,000-$2,200**

Pouty Baby: Ca. 1925. Perfect bisque solid dome head with painted hair, tiny sleep eyes, closed pouty mouth; cloth body with composition arms and legs; dressed; all in good condition.

11-12in (28-31cm)	**$650-$750**

Hanna:
Baby:

14-16in (36-41cm)	**$750-$800**
20-22in (51-56cm)	**$1,000-$1,200**
26in (66cm)	**$1,400-$1,500**
Toddler,	
14-16in (36-41cm)	**$1,100-$1,250**

Brown, See page 58.

OX: 15in (38cm) toddler
$1,400-$1,500**

Das Lachende Baby, 1930.
23-24in (58-61cm)   **$2,200-$2,500****

**Not enough price samples to compute a reliable range.

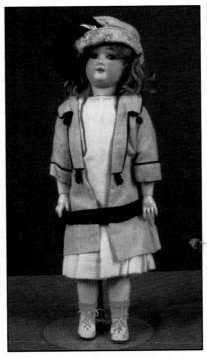

13½in (34cm) shoulder head child with hinged pink kid body. *H & J Foulke, Inc.*

20in (51cm) 1909 child, all original and boxed. *H & J Foulke, Inc.*

SCHOENHUT

Salesman's Cutaway Sample:
$800-$1,000

Shoes, very good condition **$200-$250**
Character: 1911-1930. Wooden head and spring-jointed body, marked head and/or body; original or appropriate wig, brown or blue intaglio eyes, open/closed mouth with painted teeth or closed mouth; original or suitable clothing; original paint may have a few scuffs.
14-21in (36-53cm)

Excellent condition	**$1,700-$2,100***
Good, some wear	**$1,150-$1,350***

*Allow extra for rare faces and exceptional original condition.

Character with carved hair: Ca. 1911-1930. Wooden head with carved hair, comb marks, possibly a ribbon or bow, intaglio eyes, mouth usually closed; spring-jointed wooden body; original or suitable clothes; original paint may have a few scuffs.
14-21in (36-53cm):

Excellent condition	**$2,200-$2,500**
Good, some wear	**$1,600-$1,800**
Early style	**3,500-$4,000**
20in (51cm) man	**$2,200**

Tootsie Wootsie,
15in (38cm)	**$3,000****

Snickelfritz, 15in (38cm),
wear	**$2,500****

Carved hat, restored **$2,500****
**Not enough price samples to compute a reliable average.

Baby Face: Ca. 1913-1930. Wooden head and fully-jointed toddler or bent-limb baby body, marked head and/or body; painted hair or mohair wig, painted eyes, open or closed mouth; suitably

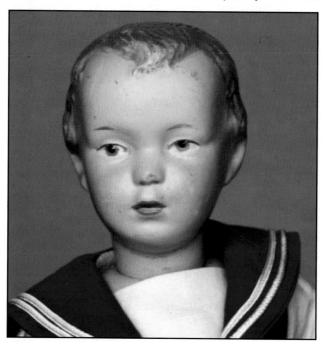

16in (41cm)
16/200 character
boy in replica of
outfit 604.
*Private
Collection.
Photograph by
Carol Corson.*

dressed; original paint; all in good condition, with some wear.

Mark:

Baby:

12in (31cm)	**$550-$600**
15-16in (38-41cm)	**$700-$800**

Toddler:

11in (28cm)	**$800-$900**
14in (36cm)	**$800-$850***
16-17in (41-43cm)	**$850-$950***

*Allow more for mint condition.

Mama Doll: 1924-1927. Wood head and hands, cloth body.

14-17in (36-43cm) **$1,100-$1,200****

Walker: Ca. 1919-1930. All-wood with "baby face," mohair wig, painted eyes; curved arms, straight legs with "walker" joint at hip; no holes in bottom of feet; original or appropriate clothes; all in good condition; original mint.

13-17in (33-43cm) **$700-$900***

*Allow $100 additional for original shoes with "wedge" sole.

**Not enough price samples to compute a reliable average.

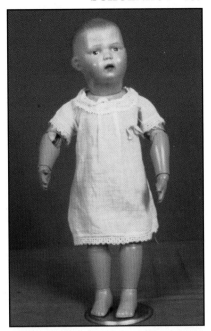

14in (36cm) 107 toddler, original factory shift. *Private Collection.*

FACTS

Albert Schoenhut & Co., Philadelphia, Pa., U.S.A. 1872-on. Wood, spring-jointed, holes in bottom of feet to fit metal stand. 11-21in (28-53cm).

Designer: Early: Adolph Graziana and Mr. Leslie; later: Harry E. Schoenhut.

Mark: Paper label:

Incised:
SCHOENHUT DOLL
PAT. JAN. 17, '11, U.S.A.
& FOREIGN COUNTRIES

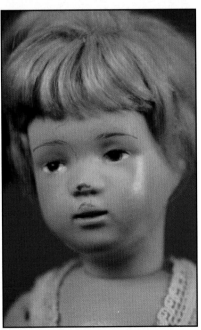

15in (38cm) 312 character child, all original. *H & J Foulke, Inc.*

Miss Dolly: Ca. 1915-1930. Wooden head and spring-jointed wooden body; original or appropriate mohair wig, decal eyes, open/closed mouth with painted teeth; original paint; original or suitable clothes.

14-21in (36-53cm):

Excellent condition	**$750-$850**
Good condition,	
some wear	**$550-$650**

Sleep Eyes: Ca. 1920-1930. Used with "baby face" or "dolly face" heads. Mouths on this type were open with teeth or barely open with carved teeth. Original paint.

14-21in (36-53cm):

Excellent condition	**$900-$1,100**
Good condition	**$750-$850**

All-Composition: Ca. 1924. Molded blonde curly hair, painted eyes, tiny closed mouth; original or appropriate clothing; in good condition.

Paper label on back:

13in (33cm)	**$500-$600****

**Not enough price samples to compute a reliable range.

17in (43cm) *Miss Dolly,* replaced wig. *H & J Foulke, Inc.*

SIMON & HALBIG

Shoulder head with molded hair: Ca. 1870s. Perfect bisque shoulder head, painted or glass eyes, closed mouth, molded hair; cloth body, bisque lower arms; appropriately dressed; all in good condition.

Mark:

$$S \ 7 \ H$$

on front shoulder plate

18-20in (46-51cm)   **$1,500-$2,000**
9in (23cm) painted eyes,
   swivel neck   **$1,250**

12in (31cm) glass eyes,
   swivel neck   **$1,500**

FACTS

Simon & Halbig, porcelain factory, Gräfenhain, Thüringia, Germany, purchased by Kämmer & Reinhardt in 1920. 1869-on.

Mark:

$$S \ 13 \ H$$
$$949$$
$$1079-2$$
$$DEP$$
$$S \ H$$
$$Germany$$

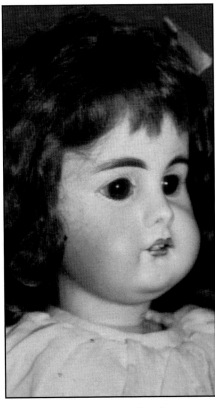

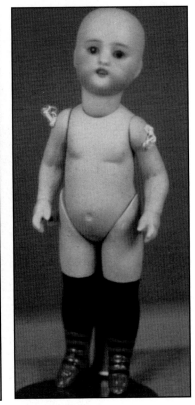

21in (53cm) 949, open mouth with square teeth. *Jensen's Antique Dolls.*

7¾in (19cm) 886 all-bisque child. *H & J Foulke, Inc.*

12½in (32cm) 905, kid over composition body. *Kay & Wayne Jensen Collection.*

24in (61cm) 740 turned shoulder head. *H & J Foulke, Inc.*

Fashion Doll (Poupée): Ca. 1870s. Perfect bisque socket head on bisque shoulder plate, glass eyes, closed mouth, good mohair wig or molded blonde hair; gusseted kid lady body; appropriately dressed; all in good condition. No marks. (For face see *12th Blue Book* page 330.)

15-16in (38-41cm)	**$2,800-$3,000**
Twill over wood body:	
9-10in (23-25cm)	**$3,300-$3,800**
15-16in (38-41cm)	**$5,200-$5,700**
Cloth body, 15in (38cm)	**$2,100**

Child doll with closed mouth: Ca. 1879. Perfect bisque socket head on ball-jointed wood and composition body; good wig, glass set or sleep eyes, closed mouth, pierced ears, dressed; all in good condition. (See *Simon & Halbig Dolls, The Artful Aspect* for photographs of mold numbers not shown here.)

#719, 19-21in (48-53cm)	**$3,800-$4,200**
24in (61cm)	**$5,000**
#749, 20-22in (51-56cm)	**$3,800****
#905, 908,	
14-17in (36-43cm)	**$2,750-$3,250**
#929, 14in (36cm)	**$2,750**
18-21in (46-53cm)	**$3,500-$4,500****
#939, 14-15in (36-38cm)	**$2,500-$2,700**
19-22in (48-56cm)	**$3,100-$3,600**
27in (69cm)	**$4,700**
#949:	
15-16in (38-41cm)	**$2,100-$2,500**
22-23in (56-58cm)	**$2,900-$3,100**
27-28in (69-71cm)	**$3,800-$4,200**
#979, 15-16in (38-41cm)	**$3,000****

All-Bisque Child: 1880-on. All-bisque child with swivel neck, pegged shoulders and hips; appropriate mohair wig, glass eyes, open or closed mouth; molded stockings and shoes.

#886 and **890:**
Over-the-knee black or blue stockings:

4½in (11cm)	**$500-$550**
5½-6in (14-15cm)	**$750-$800***
7-7½ (18-19cm)	**$900-$1,000***
8½-9in (22-23cm)	**$1,200-$1,500***

Early model with 5-strap bootines, closed mouth:

7in (18cm)	**$1,800-$2,000***
9in (23cm)	**$2,650-$2,850***

Open mouth with square cut teeth:

6in (15cm)	**$1,350-$1,500***
8in (20cm)	**$1,800-$2,200***

Kid or Cloth Body:
#720, 740, 940, 950:

9-10in (23-25cm)	**$550-$650**
16-18in (41-46cm)	**$1,200-$1,400**
22in (56cm)	**$1,600-$1,800**
#949, 18-21in (46-53cm)	**$1,800-$2,200**
#920, 16-20in (41-51cm)	
	$2,000-$2,500**
#905, 12in (31cm)	**$1,200-$1,300**
20in (51cm)	**$2,000-$2,200**

*Allow extra for original clothes and multi-strap shoes.

**Not enough price samples to compute a reliable range.

Child doll with open mouth and composition body: Ca. 1889 to 1930s. Perfect bisque head, good wig, sleep or paperweight eyes, open mouth, pierced ears; original ball-jointed composition body; very pretty clothes; all in nice condition. (See *Simon & Halbig Dolls, The Artful Aspect* for photographs of mold numbers not shown here.)

#719, 739, 749, 759, 769, 939, 949, 979:

12-14in (31-36cm)	**$1,150-$1,450***
19-22in (48-56cm)	**$2,000-$2,300***
29-30in (74-76cm)	**$2,800-$3,000***
23in (58cm) Edison, operating	**$4,800**

*Allow $200-$300 extra for square cut teeth.

#929, 23in (58cm) at auction	**$3,800**
#905, 908,	
12-14in (31-36cm)	**$1,500-$1,800**

17in (43cm) 739, fully jointed composition body, totally original baby outfit. *H & J Foulke, Inc.*

#1009:

15-16in (38-41cm)	**$800-$900**
19-21in (48-53cm)	**$1,100-$1,300**
24-25in (61-64cm)	**$1,500-$1,800**

#1039:

16-18in (41-46cm)	**$800-$1,000***
23-25in (58-64cm)	**$1,150-$1,350***

*Allow $100 extra for flirty eyes.

#1139, 13in (33cm)	**$1,100-$1,200****

#1039, key-wind walking body, (R.D.):

16-22in (41-56cm)	**$1,700-$1,800**

#1039, walking, kissing,

20-22in (51-56cm)	**$1,050-$1,250**

#1078, 1079:

7-8in (18-20cm)	
5-piece body	**$425-$475**
8in (20cm)	**$500-$550**
10-12in (25-31cm)	**$500-$600**
14-15in (36-38cm)	**$650-$675**
17-19in (43-48cm)	**$775-$850**
22-24in (56-61cm)	**$900-$1,000**
28-30in (71-76cm)	**$1,200-$1,400**
34-35in (86-89cm)	**$2,000-$2,200**

42in (107cm) **$3,800-$4,200**
#1109,
  14in (36cm) **$850**
  18in (46cm) **$1,100**
#1248, 1249, Santa:
  13-15in (33-38cm) **$900-$1,000**
  21-24in (53-61cm) **$1,300-$1,500**
  26-28in (66-71cm) **$1,700-$1,900**
  32in (81cm) **$2,200-$2,300**
  38in (96cm) **$3,200**
  Head only, 5in (13cm) **$715**
#540, 550, 570, Baby Blanche:
  22-24in (56-61cm) **$825-$875**
#176, (A. Hülss):
  Flapper, 18in (46cm) **$850**

Child doll with open mouth and kid body: Ca. 1889 to 1930s. Perfect bisque swivel head on shoulder plate or shoulder head with stationary neck, sleep eyes; well costumed; all in good condition.
#1010, 1040, 1080, 1260:
  14-16in (36-41cm) **$500-$600**
  21-23in (53-58cm) **$700-$800**

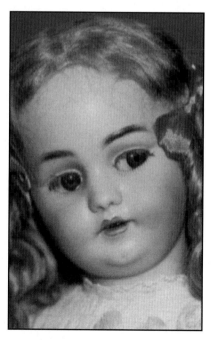

#1009, 17-19in (43-48cm) **$850-$950**
#1250 with pink kid body and composition arms:
  14-16in (36-41cm) **$550-$650**
  22-24in (56-61cm) **$800-$900**
  29in (74cm) **$1,000-$1,100**
#949, 19-21in (48-53cm) **$1,200-$1,400**

So-called "Little Women" type: Ca. 1900. Mold number 1160. Shoulder head with fancy mohair wig, glass set eyes, closed mouth: cloth body with bisque limbs, molded boots; dressed; all in good condition.
  5½-7in (14-18cm) **$350-$400**
  10-11in (25-28cm) **$425-$475**
  14in (36cm) **$650-$750**

Character Child: Ca. 1909. Perfect bisque socket head with wig or molded hair, painted or glass eyes, open or closed mouth, character face, jointed composition body; dressed; all in good condition. (See *Simon & Halbig Dolls, The Artful Aspect* for photographs of mold numbers not shown here.)
#120, 18-19in (46-48cm) **$3,200-$3,400**
#150:
  14in (36cm) **$12,000****
  20in (51cm) **23,000****
#151:
  14-15in (36-38cm) **$5,000-$5,500**
  18in (46cm) **$7,500**
  24in (61cm) **$13,000**
#153:
  14in (36cm) **$18,000**
  17in (43cm) **$30,000**
#160 for H. Handwerck
  22in (56cm) at auction **$7,250**
#174, 28in (71cm) at auction **$2,700**
  19in (48cm) toddler **$1,650**

19in (48cm) 1039 child with flirty eyes. *Jensen's Antique Dolls.*

#1279:

14-17in (36-43cm)	**$2,000-$2,400**
19-21in (48-53cm)	**$2,700-$3,200**
27in (69cm)	**$5,500-$6,000**
33in (84cm)	**$6,500**

#1299, 14-17in (36-43cm)**$1,200-$1,600**

#1339:

18in (46cm)	**$1,000-$1,100****
28-32 (71-81cm)	**$1,900-$2,100****
29in (73cm) repaired neck,	
at auction	**$1200**

#1388, 23in (58cm) **$30,000****

#1398, 23in (58cm) **$20,000****

IV, #1448:

13-14in (33-36cm)	**$16,000-$18,000****
17-18in (43-46cm)	**$24,000****
25in (63cm) at auction	**$33,000**

**Not enough price samples to compute a reliable range.

14in (36cm) 1279 character child. *H & J Foulke, Inc.*

Character Baby: Ca. 1909 to 1930s. Perfect bisque head, molded hair or wig, sleep or painted eyes, open or open/closed mouth composition bent-limb baby or toddler body; nicely dressed; all in good condition. (See *Simon & Halbig Dolls, The Artful Aspect* for photographs of mold numbers not shown here.)

#156 (A. Hülss):

Baby, 15-17in (38-43cm)	**$650-$750**
23in (58cm)	**$1,250-$1,350**
Toddler,	
10-11in (25-28cm)	**$850-$950**
18-20in (46-51cm)	**$1,300-$1,500**

#1294:

Baby, 17-19in (43-48cm)	**$750-$850**
23-25in (58-64cm)	**$1,100-$1,300**
Toddler, 20in (51cm)	**$1,500-$1,600**
28in (71cm) with	
clockwork eyes	**$2,500****

#1428:

10-11in (25-28cm)	**$1,000-$1,200**
Baby,	
13-14in (33-36cm)	**$1,500-$1,800**
21in (53cm)	**$2,700-$3,000**

Toddler,	
15-18in (38-46cm)	**$2,400-$2,600**
24in (61cm)	**$3,750-$4,250**

#1488:

15in (38cm)	**$4,000-$4,200**
Baby, 20in (51cm)	**5,500**
Toddler,	
16-18in (41-46cm)	**$4,500-$5,000**

#1489 Erika, baby:

21-22in (53-56cm)	**$3,700-$4,200****

#1498:

Baby, 16in (41cm)	**$2,500****
Toddler, 22in (56cm)	**$4,600****

#172, baby **$3,500****

Lady doll: Ca. 1910. Perfect bisque socket head, good wig, sleep eyes, pierced ears; lady body, molded bust, slim arms and legs; dressed; all in good condition.

#1159 (may have an H. Handwerck body):

12in (31cm)	**$1,100-$1,200**

19½in (50cm) 1305 character doll.
Ralph's Antique Dolls.

16-18in (41-45cm)	**$1,800-$2,000**
24in (61cm)	**$2,500-$2,700**
27-28in (69-71cm)	**$3,000**
#1468, 1469:	
13-15in (33-38cm)	
naked	**$2,200-$2,400**
Original clothes	**$3,000-$4,200**
#1303 lady,	
20in (51cm)	**$18,000-$20,0000******
#152 lady:	
18in (46cm)	**$15,000 up****
25in (64cm)	**$25,000****
#1308 man,	
13in (33cm)	**$13,000****
#1307, 21in (53cm)	**$12,500**
#1303 Indian, 21in (53cm)	**$17,000****
#1305, 18in (46cm)	**$12,500**
Mary Pickford,	
40in (102cm) at auction	**$34,000**

**Not enough price samples to compute a reliable range.

18in (46cm) 1159 lady, all original shift and label. *H & J Foulke, Inc.*

20in (51cm) 1498 baby. *Mary Barnes Kelley Collection.*

SNOW BABIES & SANTAS

Snow Babies: All-bisque immobile figures with snowsuits and caps of pebbly-
textured bisque; painted features; various
positions.

Standing,	
1½in (4cm)	**$55-$65**
2½in (6cm)	**$150-$160**
4¾in (12cm)	**$400-$450**
Sitting,	
1½in (4cm)	**$50-$60**
3-3½in (8-9cm)	**$250-$300**
Jointed arms and legs,	
3½in (9cm)	**$350-$400**
5¼in (13cm)	**$450-$500**
Shoulder head on cloth body,	
4½in (11cm)	**$185-$210**
10in (25cm)	**$300-$350**
Fine early quality with high hood,	
2in (5cm)	**$185-$210**
With musical instrument,	
2in (5cm)	**$125-$150**
Twins, 2in (5cm)	**$150-$160**
Snowman, 2½in (6cm)	**$100-$125**
Snow bear, 1½in (4cm)	**$60-$75**

Snow baby riding snow bear,	
3in (9cm)	**$350**
Tumbling snow baby,	
2½in (6cm)	**$175-$185**
Snow baby on sled, 1½in (4cm)	**$125**
3in (8cm)	**$225**
Three snow babies on sled	**$225**
Santa on snow bear	**$400-$450**
Snow babies sliding on cellar door,	
2½in (6cm)	**$275-$325**
Snow dog and snowman on sled,	
2in (5cm)	**$275-$325**
Santa going down chimney	**$375**
Santa on train	**$425**
Snow Children	
Seated girl, 1½in (4cm)	**$135**
Boy or girl on sled	**$185-$210**

"No Snows":

Boy and girl on sled,	
2in (5cm)	**$165-$185**
Skiing boy, 2½in (6cm)	**$110**
Santa, 3in (9cm)	**$125-$135**
2in (5cm)	**$95**

Action Figures:

Huskies pulling sled with snow baby,	
3in (9cm)	**$325**
Reindeer pulling sled with snow baby,	
2in (5cm)	**$275**
Snow baby riding reindeer,	
2½in (6cm)	**$325**

4¾in (12cm)
snow babies.
H & J Foulke, Inc.

SONNEBERG TÄUFLING
(SO-CALLED MOTSCHMANN BABY)

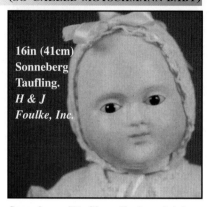

16in (41cm)
Sonneberg
Taufling.
H & J
Foulke, Inc.

Sonneberg Täufling: Papier-mâché or wax-over-composition head with painted hair, dark pupil-less glass eyes; composition lower torso; composition and wood arms and legs jointed at ankles and wrists, cloth covered midsection with voice box, upper arms and legs cloth covered, called floating joints; dressed in shift and bonnet. (For body photograph see *11th Blue Book*, page 336.)

Very good condition:

6in (15cm)	**$650-$750**
12-14in (31-36cm)	**$1,000-$1,200**
18-20in (46-51cm)	**$1,600-$2,000**
24in (61cm)	**$2,800-$3,000**

Fair condition, with wear:

12-14in (31-36cm)	**$600-$750**
18-20in (46-51cm)	**$950-$1,150**

Note: Some are found stamped Ch. Motschmann, but he was the holder of the patent for the voice boxes, not the manufacturer of the dolls.

FACTS
Various Sonneberg factories such as Heinrich Stier; many handled by exporter Louis Lindner & Söhn, Sonneberg, Thüringia, Germany. 1851-1880s.
Mark: None.

STEIFF

Steiff Doll: Felt, plush or velvet, jointed; seam down middle of face, button eyes, painted features; original clothes; most are character dolls, many have large shoes to enable them to stand; all in excellent condition.

Children (Character Dolls):

11-12in (28-31cm)	**$1,000-$1,250**
16-17in (41-43cm)	**$1,500-$1,650**
Black child, 17in (43cm)	**$2,100**
Adults,*	**$1,500 up**
Gnome, 12in (31cm)	**$700-$900**

*Fewer women are available than men.

U.S. Zone Germany:

12in (31cm) child with glass eyes	**$500-$600**

Collector's Note: To bring the prices quoted, Steiff dolls must be clean and have good color. Faded and dirty dolls bring only one-third to one-half of these prices.

FACTS
Fräulein Margarete Steiff, Würtemberg, Germany. 1894-on.
Mark: Metal button in ear.

14in (36cm) probably *Schneid the Tailor*, 1913. *Nancy A. Smith Collection.*

JULES STEINER

Round face: Ca. 1870s. Perfect very pale bisque socket head, appropriate wig, bulgy paperweight eyes, round face, pierced ears; jointed composition body; dressed; all in good condition.
Mark: None, but sometimes body has a label.
Two rows of pointed teeth,
16-19in (41-48cm)	**$6,000-$7,000**

Closed mouth,
18-22in (46-56cm)	**$10,000-$12,000**

Gigoteur: Kicking, crying bébé, mechanical key-wind body with composition arms and lower legs.
17-18in (43-46cm)	**$2,100-$2,300**
23in (58cm)	**$2,600-$2,750**
21in(53cm) all original and boxed at auction	**$4,800**

Täufling-type body: Bisque shoulders, hips and lower arms and legs.
18-21in (46-53cm)	**$6,500**
Swivel neck	**$7,500**

Marked C or A Series Steiner Bébé: 1880s. Perfect socket head, cardboard pate, appropriate wig, sleep eyes with wire mechanism or bulgy paperweight eyes with tinting on upper eyelids, closed mouth, round face, pierced ears with tinted tips; jointed composition body with straight wrists and stubby fingers (sometimes with bisque hands); appropriately dressed; all in good condition. Sizes 4/0 (8in) to 8 (38in). Series "C" more easily found than "A."
Mark: (incised)   S ᴵᴱ A O

(red script)
~ ℒᵍ⁺ Sℊ ℬℊ ℐ ℒₐᵤₚₑₙ ᴰᵗ

(incised)   S ᴵᴱ C 4

(red stamp)   J. STEINER B. S.

8-10in (20-25cm)	**$6,000-$7,000**
15-16in (38-41cm)	**$6,500-$7,000**
21-24in (53-61cm)	**$8,000-$9,000**
28in (71cm)	**$12,000**
12in (31cm) Au Nain Bleu label, at auction	**$7,700**

Wax pate with inset hair,
15½in (39cm)	**$25,000****

Series G:
18in (46cm)	**$21,000****
28in (71cm)	**$32,000****

FACTS

Jules Nicolas Steiner and successors, Paris, France. 1855-1908.

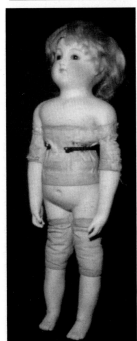

Early Steiner with täufling-type body. *Frances Walker Collection. Courtesy of Richard W. Withington, Inc.*

9in (23cm) Figure A *Le Petit Parisien,* all original. *H & J Foulke, Inc.*

19in (48cm) Series G Bourgoin Steiner. *Private Collection.*

Figure A Steiner Bébé: Ca. 1887-on. Perfect bisque socket head, cardboard pate, appropriate wig, paperweight eyes, closed mouth, pierced ears; jointed composition body; appropriately dressed; all in good condition. Figure "A" more easily found than "C."

Mark: (incised)

> J. STEINER
> B^TE S.G D.G.
> PARIS
> F^RE A 15

Body and/or head may be stamped:
"Le Petit Parisien
BEBE STEINER
MEDAILLE d'OR
PARIS 1889"
or paper label of doll carrying flag
Mark: head (incised):
1892 on

> A-19
> PARIS

(red stamp):
"LE PARISIEN"
body (purple stamp):
"BEBE 'LE PARISIEN'
MEDAILLE D'OR
PARIS"

8-10in (20-25cm) 5-piece body	**$3,000-$3,500***
8-10in (20-25cm) fully jointed	**$4,000-$5,000***
15-16in (38-41cm)	**$5,000-$5,600***
22-24in (56-61cm)	**$6,000-$6,800***
28-30in (71-76cm)	**$7,500-$8,000***
38in (96cm)	**$11,000-$12,000**

*Must have beautiful and excellent quality decoration.

Open mouth:

17in (43cm)	**$2,500**
22in (56cm)	**$2,900**
33in (84cm) with wire eyes	**$4,500**

22in (56cm) Figure A *Le Petit Parisien.*
Private Collection.

Figure B: Open mouth with two rows of teeth.

23-25in (58-64cm)	**$5,000 -$6,000**
32in (81cm) at auction	**$7,000**

Figure C: closed mouth,

19-23in (48-58cm)	**$6,000-$7,500**

Figure D: closed mouth,

25in (64cm) at auction	**$38,000**

**Not enough price samples to compute a reliable average.

SWAINE & CO.

Swaine Character Babies: Ca. 1910-on. Perfect bisque head; composition baby body with bent limbs; dressed; all in good condition. (See previous *Blue Books* for photographs of specific models.)

Incised Lori, molded hair, glass eyes, open/closed mouth,

22-24in (56-61cm)	**$2,500-$2,700**

#232, (open-mouth **Lori**):

8½in (21cm)	**$750-$800**
12-14in (31-36cm)	**$1,100-$1,350**
20-22in (51-56cm)	**$1,700-$1,800**

17in (43cm) DIP toddler. *Mary Barnes Kelley Collection.*

DIP (wig, glass eyes, closed mouth):

8½–9½in (21-24cm)	**$750-$800**
11in (28cm)	**$900-$950**
14-16in (36-41cm)	**$1,400-$1,600**
14in (36cm) toddler	**$1,950**

DV (molded hair, glass eyes, open/closed mouth):

13in (33cm)	**$1,450**
16in (41cm)	**$1,650**

DI (molded hair, intaglio eyes, open/closed mouth):

12-13in (31-33cm)	$**850-$900**

B.P., B.O. (smiling character):

16-18in (41-46cm)	**$5,000-$5,500****

F.P.,

8-9in (20-23cm)	**$1,050-$1,250****

A.P., (wig, painted eyes, closed mouth)

15in (38cm) atu auction	**$5,200**

**Not enough price samples to compute a reliable range.

FACTS

Swaine & Co., porcelain factory, Hüttensteinach, Sonneberg, Thüringia, Germany. Ca. 1910-on for doll heads.
Mark: Stamped in green:

THULLIER

Marked A.T. Child: Perfect bisque head, cork pate, good wig, paperweight eyes, pierced ears, closed mouth; body of wood, kid or composition; appropriate old wig and clothes, excellent quality; in good condition.

Early face, soft features and decoration.

12-13in (31-33cm)	**$30,000-$35,000**
16-18in (41-46cm)	**$40,000-$45,000**
24in (61cm)	**$55,000-$60,000**

18in (46cm) A 9 T. *Private Collection.*

Later face, heavier features and decoration.

16-18in (41-46cm)	**$23,000-$25,000**
26in (66cm)	**$32,000-$35,000**

Open mouth, two rows of teeth:

20-22in (51-56cm)	**$9,000-$12,000**
36in (91cm)	**$25,000**

Approximate size chart:

1 =	9in (23cm)
3 =	12in (31cm)
7 =	15½in (39cm)
9 =	18in (46cm)
12 =	22-23in (56-58cm)
15 =	36-37in (91-93cm)

FACTS

A. Thuillier, Paris, France. Some heads by F. Gaultier. 1875-1893.

Mark: A. 8 . T.

UNIS

Unis Child Doll: Perfect bisque head, wood and composition jointed body; good wig, sleep eyes, open mouth; pretty clothes; all in nice condition.

#301 or 60 (fully-jointed body):

8-10in (20-25cm)	**$425-$475**
15-17in (38-43cm)	**$675-$725**
23-25in (58-64cm)	**$1,000**
28in (71cm)	**$1,200-$1,300**

5-piece body:

5in (13cm) painted eyes	**$160-$185**
6½in (17cm) glass eyes	**$275-$300**
11-13in (28-33cm)	**$350-$375**

Black or brown bisque,

11-13in (28-33cm)	**$375-$425**

Bleuette,

11in (28cm)	**$750-$950***

Princess (See page 113.)

16in (41cm) all original with wicker trunk, wardrobe and accessories	**$1,000**

*Depending upon quality of bisque.

#251 character toddler:

14-15in (36-38cm)	**$1,400-$1,500**
28in (71cm)	**$2,200-$2,400**

Composition head 301 or 60:

11-13in (28-33cm)	**$150-$175**
20in (51cm)	**$350-$400**

Composition head #251 or #247 toddler,

22in (56cm)	**$650-$750**

FACTS

Société Française de Fabrication de Bébés et Jouets. (S.F.B.J.) of Paris and Montreuil-sous-Bois, France. 1922 on.

Mark:

IZANNAH WALKER

Izannah Walker Doll: Stockinette, pressed head, features and hair painted with oils, applied ears, treated limbs; muslin body; appropriate clothes; in good condition.

Pre-patent dolls:

17-19in (43-48cm)	**$16,000-$18,000**
Fair condition	**$8,500-$9,500**
Very worn	**$3,000-$4,000**

1873 patent dolls, molded ears,

18in (46cm)	**$4,000-$6,000**

FACTS

Izannah Walker, Central Falls, R.I., U.S.A. 1873, but probably made as early as 1840s.

Mark: Later dolls are marked:

Patented Nov. 4th 1873

19in (48cm) Unis 60 child. *H & J Foulke, Inc.*

20in (51cm) Izannah Walker. *Private Collection.*

WAX DOLL
(POURED)

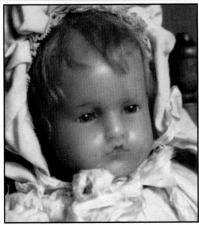

17in (43cm) English poured wax, signed Pierotti, all original. *Joanna Ott Collection.*

English Poured Wax Doll: Various firms in London, England, such as Montanari, Pierotti, Peck, Meech, Marsh, Morrell, Cremer and Edwards. 1850s through the early 1900s. Head, lower arms and legs of wax; cloth body; set-in hair, glass eyes; lovely elaborate original clothes or very well dressed; all in good condition.

Baby:

17-19in (43-48cm)	**$1,500-$1,750***
23-24in (58-61cm)	**$1,900-$2,200***
Child, 17-18in (43-46cm)	**$1,500-$1,800***

Baby or child, lackluster ordinary face,

20-22in (51-56cm)	**$800-$1,000**
Lady, 22-24in (56-61cm)	**$2,500-$3,500**

*Varies greatly depending upon appeal of face.

Mark: Sometimes stamped on body with maker or store.

French Fashion Lady: Ca. 1930. Wax head, couturier outfit.

13in (33cm)	**$400-$600**

Mechanical Baby in Satin Lined Wood Box, musical, 12in (31cm) **$350-$450**

WAX
(REINFORCED)

Reinforced Poured Wax Doll: Poured wax shoulder head lined on the inside with plaster composition, glass eyes (may sleep), closed mouth, open crown, pate, curly mohair or human hair wig nailed on (may be partially inset into the wax around the face); muslin body with wax-over-composition lower limbs (feet may have molded boots); appropriate clothes; all in good condition, but showing some nicks and scrapes.

Child or baby,

11in (28cm)	**$250-$275**
14-16in (36-41cm)	**$375-$425**
19-21in (48-53cm)	**$500-$550**
Lady, 23in (58cm)	**$800-$1,000**
with molded shoulder plate	**$2,500****

with molded gloves,

all original	**$2,500****

Socket head on ball-jointed composition body (Kestner-type):

13in (33cm)	**$700-$800**
19in (48cm)	**$1,200-$1,300**

**Not enough price samples to compute a reliable average.

FACTS

Various firms in Germany. 1860-1890.
Mark: None.

16in (41cm) Reinforced German wax. *H & J Foulke, Inc.*

WAX-OVER COMPOSITION

English Slit-head Wax: Ca. 1830-1860. Round face, human hair wig, glass eyes (may open and close by a wire), faintly smiling; all in fair condition, showing wear.

18-22in (46-56cm) **$900-$1,100**
26-28in (66-71cm **$1,300-$1,500**

Molded Hair Doll: Ca. 1860-on. German wax-over-composition shoulder head; nice old clothes; all in good condition, good quality.

14-16in (36-41cm) **$275-$325**
22-25in (56-64cm) **$450-$550**
Alice hairdo, 16in (41cm), early model, squeaker torso **$550-$650**

Wax-over Doll with Wig: Ca. 1860s to 1900. German. Original clothing or suitably dressed; entire doll in nice condition. Standard quality:

16-18in (41-46cm) **$250-$300**
22-24in (56-61cm) **$350-$400**
Superior quality (heavily waxed):
16-18in (41-46cm) **$375-$425**
22-24in (56-61cm) **$550-$650**
30in (76cm) **$750**
"Blinking" eye doll, eyes open and close with bellows in torso,
16in (41cm) all original **$1,000**

Molded Bonnet Wax-over Doll: Ca. 1860-1880. Nice old clothes; all in good condition.
16-17in (41-43cm),
common model **$375-$425**
20in (51cm) boy with cap **$550-$600**
20-24in (51-61cm) lady with
unusual hat **$2,000-$3,000**

Double-Faced Doll: 1880-on. Fritz Bartenstein. One face crying, one laughing, rotating on a vertical axis by pulling a string, one face hidden by a hood. Body stamped "Bartenstein."
15-16in (38-41cm) **$850**

FACTS
Numerous firms in England, Germany or France. During the 1800s.
Mark: None.

23in (58cm) wax-over composition with molded hair, all original. *H & J Foulke, Inc.*

NORAH WELLINGS

Wellings Doll: All-fabric, stitch-jointed shoulders and hips; molded fabric face (also of papier-mâché, sometimes stockinette covered), painted features; all in excellent condition. Most commonly found are sailors, Canadian Mounties, Scots and Black Islanders.

Characters (floppy limbs):

8-10in (20-25cm)	**$75-$100**
13-14in (33-36cm)	**$150-$200**
Glass eyes,	
14in (36cm) black	**$250-$300**

Children:

12-13in (31-33cm)	**$400-$500**
16-18in (41-46cm)	**$600-$700**
23in (58cm)	**$900-$1,000**
11½in (29cm) chubby toddler	**$350**
Glass eyes,	
16-18in (41-46cm)	**$700-$800**

Boudoir Doll,	
22-24in (56-61cm)	**$300-$400**
Old Couple,	
26in (66cm)	**$1,200-$1,500 pair**
Bobby,	
16in (41cm) glass eyes	**$800-$1,000**
Harry the Hawk, 10in (25cm)	**$200**
Nightdress Case	**$400**
Baby, 11in (28cm)	**$350-$400**
Rabbit, 9in (23cm)	**$350**

FACTS

Victoria Toy Works, Wellington, Shropshire, England, for Norah Wellings.
1926-Ca. 1960.
Designer: Norah Wellings
Mark: On tag on foot: "Made in England by Norah Wellings."

11½in (29cm) chubby toddler, all original. *H & J Foulke, Inc.*

12in (31cm) native girl, all original. *H & J Foulke, Inc.*

WOOD, ENGLISH

William & Mary Period: Ca. 1690. Carved wooden face, painted eyes, tiny lines comprising eyebrows and eyelashes, rouged cheeks, flax or hair wig; wood body, cloth arms, carved wood hands (fork shaped), wood-jointed legs. Appropriate clothes; all in fair condition.

12-17in (31-43cm)	**$40,000**

Queen Anne Period: Ca. early 1700s. Carved wooden face, dark glass eyes (sometimes painted), dotted eyebrows and eyelashes; jointed wood body, cloth upper arms; appropriate clothes; all in fair condition.

18in (46cm)	**$18,500**
24in (61cm)	**$25,000**

Georgian Period: Mid to late 1700s. Round wooden head with gesso covering, inset glass eyes (later sometimes blue), dotted eyelashes and eyebrows, flax or hair wig; jointed wood body with pointed torso; appropriate clothes; all in fair condition.

12-13in (31-33cm)	**$2,500-$3,200**
16-18in (41-46cm)	**$4,500**
24in (61cm)	**$6,000**

Early 19th Century: Wooden head, gessoed, painted eyes, pointed torso, flax or hair wig; old clothes (dress usually longer than legs); all in fair condition.

13in (33cm)	**$1,300-$1,600**
16-21in (41-53cm)	**$2,000-$3,000**

FACTS

English craftsmen. Late 17th to mid 19th century. **Mark:** None.

22in (56cm) Queen Anne, all wood doll, redressed in old fabrics. *Private Collection.*

WOOD, GERMAN
(PEG WOODENS)

Early to Mid 19th Century: Delicately carved head, varnished, carved and painted hair and features, with a yellow tuck comb in hair, painted spit curls, sometimes earrings; mortise and tenon peg joints; old clothes; all in fair condition.

4in (10cm)	**$450-$550**
6-7in (15-18cm)	**$650-$750**
12-13in (31-33cm)	**$1,350-$1,450**
17-18in (43-46cm)	**$1,800-$2,000**
28in (71cm) exceptional carving, naked, at auction	**$16,200**
Fortune tellers, 17-20in (43-51cm)	**$2,500-$3,000**
Shell dolls, 8½in (28cm)	**$1,200-$1,300 pair**
Peddler with lovely old wares, 8in (20cm)	**$2,400**

Late 19th Century: Wooden head with painted hair, carving not so elaborate as previously, sometimes earrings, spit curls; dressed; all in good condition.

4in (10cm)	**$125-$135**
7-8in (18-20cm)	**$175-$225**
12in (31cm)	**$350-$400**
19in (48cm)	**$600-$700**

Turned red torso,

10in (25cm)	**$150-$200**

Wood shoulder head, carved bun hairdo, cloth body, wood limbs:

9in (23cm) all original	**$350-$400**
17in (43cm)	**$500-$550**
24in (61cm)	**$800-$900**

Early 20th Century: Turned wood head, carved nose, painted hair, peg-jointed, painted white lower legs, painted black shoes.

11-12in (28-31cm)	**$60-$80**

FACTS

Craftsmen of the Grodner Tal, Austria, and Sonneberg, Germany, such as Insam & Prinoth (1820-1830) Gorden Tirol and Nürnberg verlagers of peg-wood dolls and wood doll heads. Late 18th to 20th century.
Mark: None.

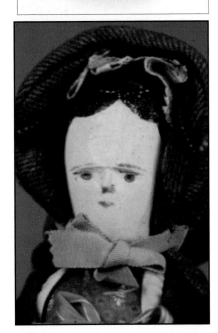

19in (48cm) German peg-wood, Ca. 1875. *H & J Foulke, Inc.*

WOOD, GERMAN
(20TH CENTURY)

"Bébé Tout en Bois" (Doll All of Wood): All of wood, fully jointed; wig, inset glass eyes, open mouth with teeth; appropriate clothes; all in fair to good condition.

Child:

13in (33cm)	**$425-$475**
17-19in (43-48cm)	**$650-$750**
22-24in (56-61cm)	**$950**
18in (46cm) mint, all original	**$1,100**
Baby, 16½in (42cm)	**$400-$500**

FACTS
Various companies, such as Rudolf Schneider and Schilling, Sonneberg, Thüringia, Germany. 1901-1914.
For French trade.
Mark: Usually none; sometimes Schilling "winged angel" trademark.

10in (25cm) *Tout en Bois* child. *H & J Foulke, Inc.*

WOOD, SWISS

15in (38cm) Swiss wood lady, all original. *H & J Foulke, Inc.*

Swiss Linden Wood Doll: Wooden head with hand-carved features and hair with good detail (males sometimes have carved hats); all carved wood jointed body; original, regional attire; excellent condition.

9-10in (23-25cm)	**$275-$375**
12in (31cm)	**$450-$550**
15in (38cm)	**$750-$850**
17-18in (43-46cm)	**$1,000-$1,200**
12in (31cm) boy with carved hat	**$600-$650**
13in (33cm) wood and cloth babies	**$450**
14in (36cm) wood, cloth papier-mâché lady	**$400-$450**

FACTS
Various craftsmen, Brienz, Switzerland. 20th century.
Mark: Usually a paper label on wrist or clothes.

MODERN & COLLECTIBLE DOLLS

Unless otherwise indicated, values given in this section are retail prices for clean dolls in excellent overall condition, with good complexion color, perfect hair in original set, and original unfaded clothing, including underwear, shoes and socks. Dirty and faded dolls that have been heavily played with are worth 10-30% of these values.

16in (41cm) Horsman 1917 Uncle Sam's Kid, all original. *H & J Foulke, Inc.* See page 278 for more information.

MADAME ALEXANDER

Cloth Dolls. Original tagged clothing.
Characters: Ca. 1933-1940. All-cloth with molded felt or flocked mask face, painted eyes to the side. **Little Women, David Copperfield, Oliver Twist, Edith, Babbie,** and others.

16in (41cm) only:

Fair	$200-$300
Good	$350-$450
Excellent	$650-$750

Alice,
19-20in (48-51cm)

Fair	$200-$300
Good	$350-$450
Excellent	$650-$750

Playmates, 1940s. 28in (71cm)

Fair to good	$400

Dressed Rabbit, 16in (41cm) $850**

FACTS

Alexander Doll Co. Inc., New York, N.Y., U.S.A. 1923 - on, but as early as 1912 the Alexander sisters were designing doll clothes and dressing dolls commercially.

Mark: Dolls themselves marked in various ways, usually "ALEXANDER." Clothing has a white cloth label with blue lettering sewn into a seam which says "MADAME ALEXANDER" and usually the name of the specific doll. Cloth and other early dolls are unmarked and identifiable only by the clothing label.

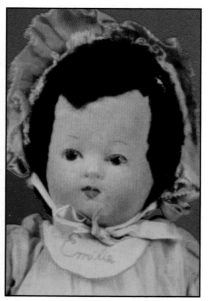

15in (38cm) cloth *Dionne Quintuplet,* all original. *H & J Foulke, Inc.*

12in (31cm) *Little Shaver,* all original. *H & J Foulke, Inc.*

7in (18cm) *Little Women,* all original boxed set. *H & J Foulke, Inc.*

Cloth Baby: Ca. 1936.

13in (33cm) very good	**$300-$350**
17in (43cm) very good	**$475-$525**
24in (61cm)	**$625**

Cloth Dionne Quintuplet: Ca. 1935.

17in (43cm) very good	**$850-$900****
24in (61cm)very good	
	$1,200-$1,300**

Susie Q. & Bobby Q.: Ca. 1938.

12in (31cm) excellent with purse or book strap	**$900-$1,050**
15in (38cm)	**$1,300**

Little Shaver: 1942. Yarn hair. Very good condition.

7in (18cm)	**$475-$500**
10-12in (25-31cm)	**$450-$500**
20in (51cm)	**$750**

Kamkins-type (hard felt face). Very good condition.

20in (51cm)	**$650-$750****
Funny, 18in (46cm) 1963-1977	**$65**
Muffin, 14in (36cm) 1963-1977	**$95**

**Not enough samples to compute a reliable average.

20in (51cm) *Dionne Quintuplet* *"Cecile,"* all original. *H & J Foulke, Inc.*

COMPOSITION DOLLS. All in original tagged clothing; excellent condition, with bright color and perfect hair, faint crazing acceptable.

Dionne Quintuplets: 1935.

7-8in (18-20cm)	**$275-$325**
Matched set	**$2,000-$2,200**
in basket with extra outfits	**$2,400-$2,600**
with 5 pieces of wood Dionne furniture, at auction	**$3,300**
10-11in (25-28cm) baby	**$350-$375**
11-12in (28-31cm) toddler	**$400-$450**
14in (36cm) toddler	**$500-$550**
16in (41cm) baby with cloth body	**$450**
20in (51cm) toddler	**$700-$750**

23-24in (58-61cm) baby

with cloth body	**$650-$750**
Pins, each	**$90-$100**

Each Quint has her own color for clothing:

Yvonne - pink; **Annette** - yellow; **Cecile** - green; **Emelie** - lavender; **Marie** - blue.

Small dolls, 1935-1945. 7-9in (18-23cm).

Foreign Countries	**$175-$225**
Storybook Characters	**$200-$300**
Special Outfits	**$400-$500**
Birthday Dolls	**$325-$375**
Bride and Bridesmaids	**$225-$250 each**
Little Women	**$275 each**

Little Colonel: 1935.

8½in (22cm)	**$600-$700****
13in (33cm)	**$650-$700**

Unnamed Girl: Dimples, sleep eyes. Ca. 1935. 13in (33cm) **$400-$450**
Nurse: Ca. 1935. 13in (33cm) **$800-$900**
Betty: Ca. 1935. Painted or sleep eyes, wigged or molded hair.

13in (33cm)	**$425-$475**
19in (48cm)	**$700-$750**

Baby Jane, 1935.

16in (41cm)	**$900-$1,000**

Topsy Turvy: Ca. 1936.

7½in (19cm)	**$185-$210**

Dr. DaFoe, 1936.

14in (36cm)	**$1,500-$1,600**

Three Little Pigs, 1938-1939.

12-13in (31-33cm)	**$750-$800 each**

**Not enough price samples to compute a reliable average.

8½in (22cm) *Little Colonel,* all original. *H & J Foulke, Inc.*

Marionettes: 1935. Character faces.

10-12in (25-30cm)

Tony Sarg	$250-$275
Disney	$350-$400

Babies: 1936-on. "Little Genius", "Baby McGuffey," "Precious," "Butch," "Bitsey." Composition head, hands and legs, cloth bodies.

11-12in (28-31cm)	$250-$300
16-18in (41-46cm)	$400-$450
24in (61cm)	$550
Pinky, 16-18in (41-46cm)	$450-$550

Princess Elizabeth Face: Original tagged clothes; all in excellent condition.

Princess Elizabeth, 1937.

13in (33cm) closed mouth	$400-$500
16-18in (41-46cm)	$550-$650
22-24in (56-61cm)	$750-$850
27in (69cm)	$950-$1,000
8in (20cm) Dionne head, missing crown	
at auction	$735

McGuffey Ana, 1937, braids.

9in (23cm) painted eyes	$400-$425
11in (28cm) closed mouth	$475-$525
15-16in (38-41cm)	$525-$625
20-22in (51-56cm)	$750-$850

Snow White, 1937, closed mouth, black hair.

13in (33cm)	$500-$550
16-18in (41-46cm)	$700-$750

Flora McFlimsey, 1938.

13in (33cm)	$550-$650
15in (38cm)	$700-$800
22in (56cm)	$1,000-$1,100

Kate Greenaway, 1938.

13in (33cm)	$600-$650
16-18in (41-46cm)	$800-$850

Wendy Ann Face. Original tagged clothes; all in excellent condition.

Wendy Ann, 1936.

9in (23cm) painted eyes	$350-$375
14in (36cm) swivel waist	$450-$550
21in (53cm)	$800-$900
14in (36cm) molded hair	$600-$650**

13in (33cm) *Betty,* all original.
H & J Foulke, Inc.

17in (43cm) *Baby McGuffey,* all original. *H & J Foulke, Inc.*

15in (38cm) *Princess Elizabeth,* all original. *H & J Foulke, Inc.*

Scarlett O'Hara, 1937, black hair, blue or green eyes.

11in (28cm)	**$850**
14in (36cm)	**$950-$1,000**
18in (46cm)	**$1,450**
21in (53cm)	**$1,850**

Madelaine du Bain, 1938.

14in (36cm)	**$550-$650**

Miss America, 1939.

14in (36cm)	**$850****

Bride & Bridesmaids, 1940.

14in (36cm)	**$400-$450**
18in (46cm)	**$600-$650**
21in (53cm)	**$750-$850**

Portraits, 1940s.

21in (53cm)	**$2,000 up**
Judy, boxed at auction	**$4,000**

Sleeping Beauty, Cinderella. Ca. 1941.

14in (36cm)	**$550-$650**

Carmen (Miranda), 1942 (black hair).

9in (23cm) painted eyes	**$350-$375**
14-15in (36-38cm)	**$550-$650**
21in (53cm)	**$1,200-$1,400****

Fairy Princess or Fairy Queen, 1942.

14in (36cm)	**$650-$700**
18in (46cm)	**$750-$800**

Armed Forces Dolls, 1942.
WAAC, WAVE, WAAF, Soldier, Marine

14in (36cm)	**$1,000**

**Not enough price samples to compute a reliable average.

Special Faces. Original tagged clothes; all in excellent condition.
Jane Withers, 1937.

13in (33cm) closed mouth	
	$1,000-$1,100

15-16in (38-41cm)	**$1,250-$1,350**
21in (53cm)	**$1,650-$1,850**

Sonja Henie, 1939.
14in (36cm), swivel waist
$750-$800
15in (38cm), gift set, boxed $3,200
18in (46cm) $900-$1,000
21in (53cm) $1,200-$1,400

Jeannie Walker, 1941.
13-14in (33-36cm) $750-$800
18in (46cm) $1,100**
13in (33cm) boxed,
at auction $1,732.50
14in (36cm) Nonwalker $550-$650

Special Girl, 1942, cloth body.
22in (56cm $550-$650**

Margaret Face: Original tagged clothes; all in excellent condition with perfect hair and pretty coloring.

Margaret O'Brien, 1946,
with dark braided wig:
14in (36cm) $950-$1,050
18in (46cm) $1,350-$1,500

Karen Ballerina, 1946,
with blonde wig in coiled braids:
14in (36cm) $850-$950
18in (46cm) $1,250
21in (53cm) $1,650-$1,850

Alice-in-Wonderland, 1947.
14in (36cm) $525-$575
18in (46cm) $650-$750
21in (53cm) $850-$950

**Not enough price samples to compute reliable average.

21in (53cm) **Bride,** all original. *H & J Foulke, Inc.*

14in (36cm) **Scarlett O'Hara,** original red taffeta coat and hat. *H & J Foulke, Inc.*

15in (38cm) *Jane Withers*, all original.
H & J Foulke, Inc.

13in (33cm) *Jeannie Walker*, all original. *H & J Foulke, Inc.*

HARD PLASTIC DOLLS. 1948-on. Original tagged clothes; excellent condition with bright color and perfect hair.

Margaret face: 1948 -1956.
Alice in Wonderland, 1949-1952. See Maggie face.
Babs, 1948-1949.

14in (36cm)	**$1,000**
18in (46cm)	**$1,200**

Bride, 1948

14in (36cm)	**$650-$700**
20in (51cm)	**$1,200-$1,400**
21in (53cm) 1951 Victorian, at auction	**$4,600**

Bride, Pink gown, 1950.

14in (36cm)	**$1,000**
18in (46cm)	**$1,200**

Cinderella, 1950.
Ball gown,

14in (36cm)	**$850**
18in (46cm)	**$1,250**

"Poor" dress

14in (36cm)	**$650**

Cynthia (black), 1952-1953.

14in (36cm)	**$850**
18in (46cm)	**$1,150**

Fairy Queen, 1947-1948.

14in (36cm)	**$750**
18in (46cm)	$950

Fashions of the Century, 1954.

18in (46cm) at auction	**$3,400**

Glamour Girls, 1953.

18in (46cm)	**$1,450-$1,650**

Godey Ladies, 1950.

14in (36cm)	**$1,400-$1,600**

Groom, 18in (46cm) **$650-$850**
Margaret O'Brien, 1948.

14in (36cm)	**$800-$900**
18in (46cm)	**$1,000-$1,200**

Margaret Rose, 1948-1953.

14in (36cm)	**$750-$800**
18in (46cm)	**$850-$900**
18in (46cm) Beaux Arts Series, 1953	**$1,650**

Mary Martin, 1950. Sailor suit,
14in (36cm)	**$850**
18in (46cm)	**$1,000**

McGuffey Ana, 1949.
14in (36cm)	**$900-$1,000**
17in (43cm)	**$1,200**

Nina Ballerina, 1949-1951, blonde:
14in (36cm)	**$850**
18in (46cm)	**$1,100**
21in (53cm)	**$1,600**

Peggy Bride, Ca. 1950.
20in (51cm)	**$1,200**

Prince Charming, 1950.
14in (36cm)	**$775**
18in (46cm)	**$875**

Prince Philip, Ca. 1950.
18in (46cm)	**$800-$850**

Queen Elizabeth II, 1953.
18in (46cm) with long	
velvet cape	**$1,600**
no cape	**$800-$1,000**

Snow White, 1952.
14in (36cm)	**$750-$800**
18in (46cm)	**$1,100**

Story Princess, 1954-1956.
14in (36cm)	**$650-$700**
18in (46cm)	**$750-$800**

Wendy-Ann, 1947-1948.
14in (36cm)	**$750-$800**
18in (46cm)	**$850-$950**

Wendy Bride, 1950.
14in (36cm)	**$600-$650**
18in (46cm)	**$850**

Wendy (from **Peter Pan** set), 1953.
14in (36cm)	**$550-$600**

Maggie Face: 1948-1956.
Alice in Wonderland, 1949-1952.
14in (36cm)	**$600-$650**
18in (46cm)	**$750-$800**

Annabelle, 1952.
15in (38cm)	**$650-$750**
18in (46cm)	**$850-$900**

Glamour Girls, 1953.
18in (46cm)	**$1,450-$1,650**

Godey Man, 1950.
14in (36cm)	**$1,200**

John Powers Models,
14in (36cm)	**$1,500-$1,600**

Kathy, 1951.
14in (36cm)	**$725**
18in (46cm)	**$875**

Margot Ballerina, 1953.
14in (36cm)	**$600-$650**
18in (46cm)	**$750-$800**

Maggie, 1948-1953.
14in (36cm)	**$525-$550**
17in (43cm)	**$700**
20in (51cm) Bridesmaid	**$850**

Me and My Shadow, 1954.
18in (46cm)	**$1,600-$2,000**

Peter Pan, 1953.
15in (38cm)	**$700-$800**

Polly Pigtails, 1949.
14in (36cm)	**$525-$550**
17in (43cm)	**$700**

18in (46cm) hard plastic Margaret-face *Alice in Wonderland*, all original except apron. *H & J Foulke, Inc.*

15in (38cm) *Margot Ballerina*, all original. *H & J Foulke, Inc.*

18in (46cm) *Cinderella*, all original. *H & J Foulke, Inc.*

Rosamund Bridesmaid, 1953.

15in (38cm)	**$650-$700**
18in (46cm)	**$800-$850**

Little Women: 1948-1956.
Floss hair, 1948 - 1950.

14-15in (36-38cm)	**$450-$500 each**
Amy, loop curls	**$525**
Dynel hair	**$375-$425 each**
Little Men, 1952.	**$900-$1,100**

(Nat, Stuffy, Tommy Bangs.)

Babies: 1948-1951. Cloth body, hard plastic or vinyl limbs. **Baby Genius, Bitsey, Butch.**

12in (31cm)	**$325-$375**
16-18in (41-46cm)	**$525-$550**

Winnie and Binnie: 1953-1955.

15in (38cm)	**$350-$400**
18in (46cm)	**$500-$550**
25in (64cm)	**$650**
Mary Ellen, 31in (79cm)	**$550-$600**

Sweet Violet, fully jointed body,

18in (46cm)	**$1,000 up**

Victoria, black, green-and-white dress,

15in (38cm) at auction	**$3,200**
Flower Girl, 15in (38cm)	**$650**
18in (46cm)	**$1,050**
Skating outfit, 15in (38cm)	**$700-$750**

Cissy: 1955-1959.

21in (53cm) street clothes	**$375-$475**
Cocktail dresses	**$550-$750**
Ball gowns	**$800-$1,200**
Queen	**$1,000-$1,200**
Bride	**$800-$1,100**
Satin brocade #2101, 1955,	
at auction	**$2,600**
Bridesmaid	**$850**

Cissy at auction:

Lady in Red, #2285, 1958	**$3,100**
Lissy, #2245, 1961	**$2,800**
Lady Hamilton, #2175, 1957	**$2,100**
Renoir, gold, 1961	**$3,000**

White tulle gown with
hat #2282, 1958. **$2,800**
Gainsborough, #2176, 1957 **$3,100**
Melanie, #2235, 1961 **$2,100**

Alexander-Kins: 1953-to present. All
hard plastic; original tagged clothes; all in
excellent condition with perfect hair and
rosy cheeks. A played-with doll having
partial or faded costume will bring 25% of
quoted prices.

Wendy: 7½-8in (19-20cm).
1953. Straight-leg nonwalker **$450 up**
nude **$300**
1954-55. Straight-leg walker **$400 up**
nude **$275**
1956-1964. Bent-knee walker **$350 up**
nude **$185**
1965-1972. Bent-knee nonwalker **$275**
nude **$90**
Wendy, basic (panties, shoes and socks),
boxed **$325-$375**
Quizkin, 1953 **$450-$550**
Wendy in Special Outfits:
Agatha, 1953 **$900-$1,000**
American Girl, 1962-1963 **$350**
Amish Boy or Amish Girl,
1966-1969 **$350**
Aunt Pitty Pat, 1957 **$1,600**
Baby Clown, 1955 **$1,200**
Bible Characters
David **$11,000**
Queen Esther **$11,000**
Billy or Bobby,
1955-1963 **$450-$500**
Bride, 1955-1960 **$350**
Bridesmaid, pink 1955 **$900**
Cherry Twin, 1957 **$900 each**
Cousin Grace, 1957. Boxed **$1,600**
Cousin Marie, 1963 **$475**
Davy Crockett Boy or
Girl, 1955 **$600**
Easter Wendy, 1953 **$1,000**
Edith, 1958 **$650**

12in (31cm) hard plastic/cloth *Baby Genius,* all original except shoes. *H & J Foulke, Inc.*

14in (36cm) *Little Women Amy* with floss wig, all original. *H & J Foulke, Inc.*

Groom, 1956-1972	**$450**
Guardian Angel, 1954	**$550**
Hiawatha, 1967-1969	**$350**
Little Madeline, 1953	**$775**
Little Minister, 1957	**$1,500**
Little Southern Girl, 1953	**$850**
Little Victoria, 1954	**$1,300**
Maypole Dance, 1954, boxed	**$650**
McGuffey Ana, 1964-1965	**$350**
Miss USA, 1966-1968. Boxed	**$425**
My Shadow, 1954	**$1,500**
Nurse, 1956-1965.$	**450-$500**
Parlour Maid, 1956	**$1,000**
Pocahontas, 1967-1969	**$350**
Prince Charles, 1957	**$800**
Princess Ann, 1957	**$800**
Priscilla or Colonial Girl, 1962-1970	**$350**
Scarlett, 1965-1972	**$400**
Southern Belle, 1963	**$450**
Wendy Can Read, 1957. Boxed	**$950**
Wendy Does Highland Fling, 1955	**$400**
Wendy Dude Ranch, 1955	**$600**

Wendy in Easter Egg, 1965	**$1,700**
Wendy Ice Skater, 1956	**$450**
Wendy Loves to Waltz, 1955	**$625**
Wendy in Riding Habit, 1965. Boxed	**$550**

International Costumes:

Bent-knee walker	**$150-$200**
Bent-knee nonwalker, 1965-1972	**$75-$100**
Korea, Africa, Hawaii, Vietnam, Eskimo, Morocco, Ecuador, Bolivia	**$300-$400**
Straight-leg, rosy cheeks, 1973-1976	**$60**
Straight-leg, pinched lips, 1982-1987	**$40-$45**
Current face, 1988-on	**$40-$50**

Storybook, Ballerinas & Brides:

Bent-knee nonwalker	**$75-$100**
Straight-leg, rosy cheeks, 1973-1976	**$60-$70**
Straight-leg, pinched lips, 1982-1987	**$40-$45**
Current face, 1988-on	**$45-$55**

Little Women: Set of 5.

Straight-leg walker, 1955	**$1,500**
Bent-knee walker, 1956-1964	**$1,200**
Bent-knee nonwalker	**$650-$750**
Straight legs	**$300-$350**
1994 FAO Schwarz movie outfits	**$600**

Exclusive and Special Editions:

Enchanted Doll House, 1980-1981	**$250-$275**
Wendy, 1989. MADC Exclusive	**$175**
Navajo Woman, 1994. MADC Convention	**$350**
Bobbie Sox, 1990. Disney	**$175**
David & Diana, 1989. FAO Schwarz, Set	**$175**

21in (53cm) *Cissy,* all original.
H & J Foulke, Inc.

Mouseketeer, 1991. Disney $100
Easter Bunny, 1991.
Child at Heart $350
Cowboy, 1987.
MADC Convention $450
Little Miss Magnin, 1992. I. Magnin
with tea set and teddy bear $150
Tippi Ballerina, 1988.
CU Gathering $350-$400
Little Emperor, 1992.
UFDC Luncheon $500
Anne of Green Gables, trunk set.
Neiman-Marcus $275
Sailor Boy, UFDC $750

Little Genius: 1956-1962. Baby with
short curly wig, 8in (20cm).
Basic or simple outfit $175-$200
Fancy outfit $250
Christening outfit $300

Lissy Face: 1956-1958.
12in (31cm) Lissy $400-$500
Boxed with trousseau $1,200-$1,500
Schwarz Exclusive $950
Bridesmaid $600
Kelly, 1959 $400-$500
Little Women, 1957-1959 $250
Southern Belle, 1963 $1,200
McGuffey Ana, 1963 $1,600
Katie, 1962 $1,200
Tommy, 1962 $1,000
Cinderella, 1966 $850
Boxed Set $1,250
Laurie, 1967 $400
Pamela, 1962-1963
Boxed with wigs $1,000
Suitcase gift set $1,500

Elise: 1957-1964
16½in (42cm)
street clothes $350-$400
Ball gowns $650-$850
Bride, elaborate $750-$950
Sleeping Beauty, Disney$600-$700

25in (64cm) *Winnie Walker*, all original.
H & J Foulke, Inc.

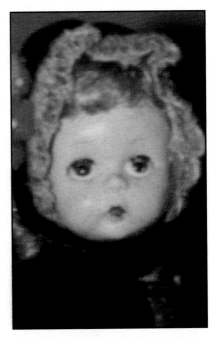

8in (20cm) *Agatha,* all original. *Terri &
Kathy's Dolls.*

16½in (42cm) *Elise,* all original.
Rosemary Kinizer.

10in (25cm) *Cissette,* all original.
H & J Foulke, Inc.

Bridesmaid	$500-$550
Ballerina	$550-$650
Vinyl head, 1964.	
(Kelly Face)	$300-$350

Cissette Face: 1957-1973.
10in (25cm) Cissette, 1957-1963.

Basic doll, mint-in-box	$350-$400
Day dresses	$275-$375
Suit and hat, boxed	$650
Evening gowns	$600-$800
Queen	$400-$450
Gold Ballerina, 1959	$450-$500
Denmark	$500-$600
Gibson Girl	$600-$700
Jacqueline, 1962	$700-$750
Margot, 1961	$600-$800
Sleeping Beauty, 1959-1960.	$350-$400
Mardi Gras, 1992 Spiegel	$60
Diamond Lil, 1993 ADC	$190
Lady Hamilton #975, 1957	$1,200
Cinderella, 1989 Disney	$600-$700
Miss Unity, 1991 UFDC	$400

Portrettes: 1968-1973

Godey, 1968-1970	$300-$350
Scarlett, 1968-1973	$300-$350
Renoir, 1968-1970	$325-$375
Agatha, 1968	$350-$375
Southern Belle, 1968-197	$300-$350
Melinda, 1968-1970	$300-$350
Jenny Lind, 1969	$500-$550
Melanie, 1969-1970	$375-$400
Queen, 1972-1973	$250-$350

Shari Lewis: 1959.

14in (36cm)	$400-$500
21in (53cm)	$700-$800

Maggie Mixup: 1960-1961

16½in (42cm)	$400-$450
8in (20cm)	$450-$550
8in (20cm) angel	$800-$1,000
Little Lady	$350
Little Lady Gift Set	$1,000

VINYL DOLLS. Original tagged clothing; excellent never-played-with condition, bright color.

Kelly Face: 1958-1965. 15in (38cm)

Kelly	$275-$300
Pollyana	$275-$300
Marybel with complete case	
	$325-$375
Edith	$250-$275
Elise	$325-$375

Jacqueline: 1961-1962

21in (53cm) suit and hat	$550-$650
Riding habit	$550-$600
Brocade gown #2130, 1962	$900-$1,000
10in (25cm)	$700-$750

Portraits: 1962-current. 21in (53cm)

Scarlett, 1968.	
Cotton print	$900-$1,000
1975-1982. Green velvet or taffeta	$350
1978. Satin print	$500
Melanie, 1967-74	$400-$500
Queen, 1968	$700-$750
Godey, 1969	$500-$550
Bride, 1969	$650-$700
Madame Pompadour, 1970	
	$900-$1,000
Mimi, 1971	$450-$500
Gainsborough, 1973	$350-$400
Madame Alexander, 1984-1990	$300
Sarah Bernhardt, 1987	$300

Caroline: 1961-1962.

15in (38cm)	$275-$325
Riding habit	$300-$375

Melinda: 1963. 14in (36cm) | $250-$350

15in (38cm) *Kelly,* all original. *H & J Foulke, Inc.*

10in (25cm) *Agatha,* all original. *Terri & Kathy's Dolls.*

17in (43cm) *Leslie,* all original. *H & J Foulke, Inc.*

14in (36cm) *Baby Ellen,* all original. *H & J Foulke, Inc.*

Janie Face: 1964-1990. 12in (31cm).

Janie, 1964-1966	**$225-$250**
Lucinda, 1969-1970	**$250-$275**
Rozy, 1969	**$275-$300**
Suzy, 1970	**$275-$300**
Muffin, 1989-1990	**$50-$60**

Brenda Starr: 1964

12in (31cm)	**$225**
Yolanda, 1965	**$225**

Betty: 1960. Smiling face, walker,

30in (76cm)	**$350**

Patty: 1965

18in (46cm)	**$250-$275**

Chatterbox: 1961. Battery-operated talker,

24in (61cm)	**$250-$275**

Smarty Face: 1962-1965. 12in (31cm).

Smarty, 1962-1963	**$200-$250**
with baby	**$300-$350**
Brother	**$225-$275**
Katie (black), 1965	**$350-$400**

Polly Face: 1965-1971. 17in (43cm).

Polly, 1965	**$225-$275**
Mary Ellen Playmate	**$275**
Leslie (black), 1965-1971	**$300-$325**

Mary Ann Face: 1965-current.
14in (36cm).

Mary Ann, 1965	**$225**
Orphant Annie, 1965-1966	**$300**
Gidget, 1966	**$275**
Little Granny, 1966	**$150**
Riley's Little Annie, 1967	**$175**
Renoir Girl, 1967-1971	**$175**
Disney Snow White, 1967-1977	**$350-$375**
Easter Girl, 1968	**$750-$850**
Scarlett, flowered gown, 1968	**$450-$500**

Madame, 1967-1975	**$150-$175**
Jenny Lind & Cat, 1969-1971	**$225**
Gone with the Wind, 1969-1986	**$75-$95**
Jenny Lind, 1970	**$275**
Grandma Jane, 1970	**$150-$175**
Goldilocks, 1978-1982	**$75**
Bonnie Blue, 1989	**$100-$110**
Discontinued dolls, 1982-1995	**$50-$90**

Babies: 1963-present. Cloth and vinyl.
Littlest Kitten, 1963. 8in (20cm).

Basic or simple outfit	**$200-$225**
Fancy outfit	**$250-$275**

Sugar Tears, 1964

14in (36cm)	**$75-$100**

Sweet Tears, 1965-1982

14in (36cm)	**$55-$65**
Layette sets	**$125 up**

Baby Ellen (black), 1965-1972.

14in (36cm)	**$100-$110**

Pussy Cat (black)

20in (51cm)	**$100-$125**

Mary Cassatt Baby, 1969-1970.

20in (51cm)	**$200-$250**

Happy, 1970. 20in (51cm) **$200-$250**
Smiley, 1971. 20in (51cm) **$200-$250**
Baby Lynn, 1973-1976

20in (51cm)	**$100-$125**

Baby Brother, 1977-1979

20in (51cm)	**$75-$100**

Baby McGuffey, 1971-1976

20in (51cm)	**$200-$250**
Mary Mine, 1977-1989	**$125-$150**

Sound of Music: Small set, 1965-1970.

Friedrich, 8in (20cm)	**$150**
Gretl, 8in (20cm)	**$150**
Marta, 8in (20cm)	**$150**
Brigitta, 10in (25cm)	**$200**
Louisa, 10in (25cm)	**$200**
Liesl, 10in (25cm)	**$200**
Maria, 12in (31cm)	**$225**

17in (43cm) *Maggie,* all original.
H & J Foulke, Inc.

14in (36cm) *Madame,* all original.
H & J Foulke, Inc.

Sound of Music: Large set. 1971-1973. Allow 100% more for sailor outfits.

Friedrich, 11in (28cm)	**$175-$200**
Gretl, 11in (28cm)	**$150-$165**
Marta, 11in (28cm)	**$150-$165**
Brigitta, 14in (36cm)	**$125-$150**
Louisa, 14in (36cm)	**$125-$150**
Liesl, 14in (36cm)	**$125-$150**
Maria, 17in (43cm)	**$275**
Kurt, 11in (28cm) sailor suit	**$350**

Coco: 1966. Right leg bent slightly at knee.

21in (53cm)	**$1,800-$2,000**
1966 Portrait Dolls	**$1,800-$2,200**
Scarlett, #2061 white gown	**$2,500**

Elise Face: 1966-1991. Redesigned vinyl face. 17in (43cm).

Elise Portrait Doll,	
1972-1973	**$125-$150**
Ballerinas	**$75-$85**
Brides	**$65-$75**
Formals	**$65-$75**
Marlo, 1967	**$550-$650**
Maggie, 1972-1973	**$175-$200**

Peter Pan Set: 1969

Peter Pan, 14in (36cm)	**$200-$225**
Wendy, 14in (36cm)	**$200-$225**
Michael, 11in (28cm)	**$250**
Tinker Bell, 10in (25cm)	**$300-$350**

Nancy Drew Face: 1967-1994. 12in (31cm)

Nancy Drew, 1967	**$200-$225**
Renoir Child, 1967	**$125-$150**
Pamela with wigs,	
late 1960s	**$400-$500**
Poor Cinderella, 1967	**$125-$150**
Little Women, 1969-1989	**$60-$65**
Romantic Couples, pair	**$75**
Discontinued dolls	**$30-$35**

First Ladies: 1976-1989

14in (36cm) each	**$50-$75**

AMERICAN CHARACTER

Marked Petite or American Character Mama Dolls: 1923-on. Composition/cloth; original clothes; all in good condition.

16-18in (41-46cm)	**$225-$265**
24in (61cm)	**$325-$375**

Baby Petite, 12in (31cm)   **$200**

Puggy: 1928. All-composition, frowning face; original clothes; all in good condition.

12in (31cm)	**$525-$575**

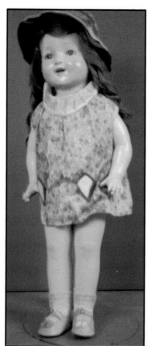

21in (53cm) *Petite Sally,* all original. *H & J Foulke, Inc.*

FACTS

American Character Doll Co., New York, N.Y. 1919-on.
Trademark: Petite

Marked Petite Girl Dolls: 1930s. All-composition; original clothes; all in good condition with nice coloring and perfect hair.

16-18in (41-46cm)	**$325-$350**
24in (61cm)	**$400-$425**

Sally: 1930. All-composition. Painted eyes and molded hair or wigged with sleeping eyes; original clothes; all in good condition with nice coloring.

12in (31cm)	**$225-$250**
16in (41cm)	**$275-$325**

Sally-Joy: 1930. Composition/cloth.

18in (46cm)	**$350-$375**
21in (53cm)	**$375-$400**
with extensive wardrobe	**$595**

Carol Ann Beery, 1935. All-composition. "Two-Some Doll" with special crown braid, matching playsuit and dress.

13in (33cm)	**$450-$500**
16½in (42cm)	**$600-$650**

Toodles: 1956. Hard rubber baby, drinks and wets; original clothes; excellent condition.

18½in (47cm)	**$225-$250**

Toodles Toddler: 1960. Vinyl and hard plastic, "Peek-a-Boo" eyes.

24in (61cm)	**$275-$300**
30in (76cm)	**$350-$375**

Tiny Tears: 1950s. Hard plastic head with tear ducts; drinks and wets; original clothes; excellent condition.

Rubber body,	
12in (31cm)	**$150-$165**
18in (46cm)	**$200-$225**
Original box and accessories	**$350**
All vinyl, 1963.	
12in (31cm)	**$65**
15in (38cm)	**$85**
Boxed with accessories	**$150-$175**

Sweet Sue: 1953. All-hard plastic or hard plastic and vinyl, some with walking mechanism, some fully-jointed including elbows, knees and ankles; original clothes; all in excellent condition, with perfect hair and pretty coloring.

14in (36cm)	**$275-$300**
18-21in (46-53cm)	**$325-$350**
24in (61cm)	**$325-$375**
20in (51cm) pink gown, boxed,	
at auction	**$525**

15in (28cm) *Tiny Tears,* boxed with layette. *H & J Foulke, Inc.*

17in (43cm) *Sweet Sue,* all original. *H & J Foulke, Inc.*

Annie Oakley, 1955
    14in (36cm)   **$450**
Alice in Wonderland, 18in (46cm)
    Boxed, at auction   **$690**
Sweet Sue Sophisticate, vinyl head,
    20in (51cm)   **$275-$325**

Toni, vinyl head:
    10½in (26cm)   **$190-$210**
    20in (51cm)   **$275-$325**

Ricky, Jr., 1955. All vinyl:
    14in (36cm)   **$95-$110**
    21in (53cm)   **$150-$175**
    16in (41cm) boxed, at auction   **$285**

Eloise: Ca. 1955. All-cloth, yellow yarn hair; original clothing; in excellent condition. Designed by Bette Gould from the fictional little girl "Eloise" who lived at the Plaza Hotel in New York City.
    21in (53cm)   **$450-$500**

Whimsies: 1960. Characters, original clothing; excellent condition. **Hedda Get Bedda (3 faces), Wheeler the Dealer, Lena the Cleaner, Polly the Lady, Bessie the Bashful Bride, Dixie the Pixie,** and others.
    19-21in (48-53cm)   **$90-$110**
    Mint-in-box with tag   **$225**

Little Miss Echo: 1962. Recorded voice; original clothing, excellent condition.
    Boxed, 30in (76cm)   **$250-$300**
    Out of box   **$150**

Tressy: 1963-1965. Growing hair:
    12½in (32cm) boxed   **$100-$125**
    Doll only   **$60-$70**
    Black   **$400**
Pre-teen Tressy, 1963. Growing hair.
    14in (36cm) boxed   **$100-$125**
Cricket, 1965. Boxed   **$50-$55**
Mary Make-up: 1965. Boxed   **$125**

ARRANBEE

16in (41cm) *Nancy,* all original. *H & J Foulke, Inc.*

11in (28cm) *Nancy Lee* Skating doll. *Kathy & Terri's Dolls.*

FACTS

Arranbee Doll Co., New York, N.Y., U.S.A. 1922-1960.
Mark: "ARRANBEE" or "R & B."

My Dream Baby: 1924. Bisque head/cloth body. See Armand Marseille infant on page 153 for description and prices.

Storybook Dolls: 1930s. All-composition; original storybook costumes; all in excellent condition, with perfect hair and pretty coloring.

9-10in (23-25cm)	**$175-$195**
Boxed	**$275**

Bottletot: 1926. All-composition; molded celluloid bottle in hand; appropriate clothes; all in good condition.

13in (33cm)	**$195**

Nancy: 1930. All-composition; original clothes; all in good condition, with pretty coloring.

12in (31cm) molded hair, painted eyes	**$240-$265**
12in (31cm) with trousseau in wardrobe trunk	**$500-$550**
16in (41cm) sleep eyes, wig, open mouth	**$400-$425**

Debu'Teen and Nancy Lee: 1938-on. All-composition; original clothes; all in good condition with perfect hair and pretty coloring.

11in (28cm)	**$225**
14in (36cm)	**$350**
18in (46)	**$425**
21in (53cm)	**$500**

Skating Doll, 18in (46cm)	**$500**
Brother, 14in (36cm)	**$350-$375**
WAC, 18in (46cm)	**$500**

Little Angel Baby: 1940s. Composition/cloth; original clothes; all in good condition.

16-18in (41-46cm)	**$300-$350**
Hard plastic, 18in (46cm)	**$350**

Nanette and Nancy Lee: 1950s. All-hard plastic; original clothes; all in excellent condition, with rosy cheeks.

14in (36cm)	**$400-$450**
17in (43cm)	**$500-$550**
20in (51cm) Skater	**$650**
15in (38cm) boxed with wardrobe, at auction	**$1,300**

Cinderella, 14in (36cm)	**$500-$600**
Floss wig, evening gown, 14in (36cm)	**$400-$450**

Littlest Angel: 1956. All-hard plastic jointed knee, walker; original clothes; all in excellent condition.

10-11in (25-28cm)	**$135-$165**
Boxed	**$200-$250**
Boxed outfits	**$40-$60**

Little Angel: 1950s

12in (31cm)	**$125-$150**

Coty Girl: 1958. All-vinyl, fashion body, high-heeled feet.

10½in (27cm) boxed	**$175-$200**

10in (25cm) *Littlest Angels,* all original. *Rosemary Kinizer.*

ARTIST DOLLS
TRADITIONAL

Traditional Artists: Many members of NIADA or ODACA. All dolls original and excellent.

Armstrong-Hand, Martha, porcelain
babies and children **$2,500**
all-bisque with jointed body
at auction **$3,700**
Barrie, Mirren, cloth historical
children **$95**
Beckett, Bob & June, carved wood
children **$300-$375**
Blakeley, Halle, high-fired
clay lady dolls **$550-$750**
Brandon, Elizabeth, porcelain children.
Theola, Joshua,
Joi Lin, Jael **$300-$500**
Bringloe, Frances, carved wood.
American Pioneer Children,
6¼in (16cm) pair **$600**

Bullard, Helen, carved wood.
Holly **$125-$135**
Hitty **$350**
American Family Series
(16 dolls) **$225-$250 each**
Clear, Emma, porcelain, china and
bisque shoulder head dolls **$350-$500**
Danny **$450**
George & Martha
Washington **$500-$600 pair**
Gibson Girl **$350-$400**
DeNunez, Marianne,
10in (25cm) Bru Jne **$300**
Florian, Gertrude, ceramic
composition dressed ladies **$300**
Heiser, Dorothy, cloth sculpture.
Fashion Pair of 1770s **$2,800**
Queens
10-13in (25-33cm) **$1,100-$1,500**
Mary, Mary 16in (41cm) **$3,100**
Hale, Patti, carved
wood heads **$200-$300**
Hitty, all wood **$300**
Johnson, Sharon, porcelain children.
Elizabeth, Lil Jewel **$125**
Kane, Maggie Head, porcelain.
Gypsy Mother **$400-$450**
Ling, Tita. Phillipines.
Carved wood 12in (30cm) **$650**
Oldenburg, Mary Ann,
porcelain children **$200-$250**
Park, Irma, wax-over-porcelain miniatures, depending upon detail **$175 up**
Parker, Ann,
historical characters **$275**
Redmond, Kathy,
porcelain shoulder heads
Victoria Set, 4 dolls **$1,500**

12½in (32cm) Kathy Redmond *Flower Girl*, all original. *H & J Foulke, Inc.*

Henry VIII	**$600**
Henry's Wives	**$450 each**
Elizabeth I & Edward	**$250 each**
Medieval Ladies	**$450**
Children	**$350-$400**

Saucier, Madeline, cloth.

15in (38cm)	**$450**

Shreve Island Plantation, flat wood, painted underwear,

Julie Ann, 3¾in (9cm)	**$45-$50**

Smith, Sherman, carved wood,

5-6in (13-15cm)	**$250-$300**
Pinocchio, 7½in (19cm)	**$350-$400**
Hitty	**$300**
Miss Unity, 12½in (31cm)	**$550**

Sorensen, Lewis, wax.

Father Christmas	**$1,200**
Toymaker	**$800**
Gibson Girls	**$350-$375**
Sweet, Elizabeth, 18in (46cm)	
Amy, 1970	**$250**

13in (33cm) Martha Thompson ceramic man, all original. *H & J Foulke, Inc.*

Thompson, Martha, porcelain.

Princess Caroline, Prince Charles, Princess Ann	**$800-$900 each**
Little Women	**$600-$700**
Betsy	**$800-$900**
McKim Child (not bisque)	**$800**
Royal Ladies	**$1,500 up**

Tuttle, Eunice, miniature porcelain

children	**$500-$600**
Angel Baby	**$400-$425**
Vargas, Black wax characters	**$400**

Walters, Beverly, porcelain, miniature fashions

	$500 up

Wyffels, Berdine, porcelain.

6in (15cm) girl, glass eyes	**$195**

Zeller, Fawn, porcelain.

One-of-a-kind Dolls	**$2,000 up**
Angela	**$800-$900**
Jeanie	**$600-$800**
Jackie Kennedy	**$800**
Polly Piedmont, 1965	**$600-$800**
Holly,	
U.S. Historical Society	**$500-$600**
Polly II, 1989.	
U.S. Historical Society	**$200-$225**

17in (43cm) Fawn Zeller *Jackie,* all original. *H & J Foulke, Inc.*

ARTISTS DOLLS
UFDC

U.F.D.C. National & Regional Souvenir Dolls: Created by doll artists in limited editions and distributed to convention attendees as souvenirs. Before 1982, most dolls were given as kits; after 1982, most dolls were fully made up and dressed. Except as noted, dolls have porcelain heads, arms and legs; cloth bodies. A few are all porcelain.

Alice in Wonderland: Yolanda Bello, 1990 Region 10. Complete doll. **$165**

Alice Roosevelt: Kathy Redmond, 1990 National. Complete doll. **$125-$135**
Companion doll **Eleanor** **$225-$250**

Baby Stuart: Pat Robinson. 1996 National. Complete doll. **$135**

Bo-Peep: carved wood, Fred Laughton, 1989 Region 15. with staff and sheep. **$85**

Charity: Fred Laughon, peg wood. 1995 National **$100-$125**

Cookie. Linda Steele. 1987 Regional. Complete doll **$225**

Crystal Faerie: Kazue Moroi and Lita Wilson, 1983 Midwest Regional. Complete doll **$85**

Emma: Rappahannock Rags, cloth. 1993 National **$95**

Father Christmas: (Kit) Beverly Walters, 1980 National. Fully made up **$400**

Gibson Girl Bathing Beauty: Phyllis Wright. 1993 Regional, with bathing costume and beach chair **$85**

Janette: Fawn Zeller, 1991 National. Complete doll, undressed **$300-$350**

Kate: All cloth by Anili, 1986 National. With original box **$165-$185**

Ken-Tuck: (Kit) Janet Masteller, 1972 Regional. Fully made up **$65-$75**

Laurel: Lita Wilson and Muriel Kramer. 1985 Regional. Fully made up **$75-$85**

Li'l Apple: Faith Wick, 1979 National. Fully made up with romper suit **$50**
Companion doll **Apple Lil** **$75**

Little Miss Sunshine: (Kit) 1974 Florida Regional. Fully made up **$65-$75**

Louise. 1977 National. Complete doll **$135**

Mary: Linda Steele, 1987 National. Fully made up **$90-$100**
Companion doll **Lewis** **$125-$150**

Miami Miss: (Kit) Fawn Zeller, 1961 National. Fully made up **$200-$250**
Dressed. **$300-$350**

Nellie Bly: Muriel Kramer, 1985 Pittsburgh Regional. Complete doll **$85-$95**

Osceola: X. Kontis, composition. Early convention doll **$100-$125**

PaPitt: X. Kontis, composition, 1958 National **$100-$125**

13½in (34cm) *Janette,* 1991 UFDC National Convention souvenir doll. *H & J Foulke, Inc.*

Pinky: Linda Cheek, California Regional.
Complete doll   **$250-$300**
Portrait of a Young Girl: Jeanne Singer,
1986 Rochester Regional.
Complete doll   **$200-$300**
Precious Lady: Maori Kazue, 1972
National. Fully made up   **$95**
Princess Kimimi: (Kit) 1977 Ohio
Regional. Fully made up   **$85-$95**
Queen Victoria. 1994 National. Complete
doll   **$135**
Rose O'Neill: Lita Wilson, 1982
National. Complete doll   **$150-$165**
Scarlett: Beverly Walters, 1976 Regional.
Half doll, fully made up   **$135**
Scarlett: Lita Wilson and Muriel Kramer,
1989 Florida Regional. Half doll, fully
made up   **$125-$135**
Sunshine: Lucille Gerrard, 1983 National.
Complete doll   **$75-$85**
Companion doll **Wain**   **$90-$100**
Tammy: Jeanne Singer. 1989 Western
N.Y. Doll Club. Complete doll   **$85**
Trick or Treat. Dana Martindale. 1991
Regional. Complete doll with
"Nose."   **$125**

Grace by Robert Tonner, 1996, limited
edition of 750. *Rae-Ellen Koenig, The
Doll Express.*

ARTISTS DOLLS
COMMERCIAL

Commercial Doll Artists: Prices are for
a factory perfect doll, never played with,
including all accessories, wrist tag, certificate and box if any.

Anri, carved wood.
  Ferrandiz, Gabriel, Marie
    14in (36cm)   **$350**
  Sarah Kay, 7in (18cm)   **$290-$330**

Dolfi, carved wood. 13in (33cm)   **$275**

Dolls by Jerri (McCloud), porcelain
  Little Women, 1983-1984.
    14in (36cm)   **$75-$100**

Good-Krueger, Julie, vinyl.
  Children, 21in (53cm)   **$125-$165**
  Anne with an E   **$300**
  Sew Much Love (Club Doll) **$200**

Gunzel, Hildegard, wax-over-porcelain.
  Wax over porcelain
    Mara Lee, 1998,
      30in (76cm)   **$2,600**
    Stephana, 1998,
      36in (91cm)   **$3,350**
  Vinyl
    For Alexander Doll Co.
      Megan, 1993   **$165**
      Marissa, 1991   **$135**
      Monica, 1990   **$125**
    Marie Caprice with her doll,
      30in (76cm)   **$650**
    Binella   **$650**
    Tricia, 1990, 27in (69cm) **$225**
    Chipie Baby, 1998,
      21in (53cm)   **$300-$325**
    Lamponi, 22in (56cm) **$320-$360**
    Matthias, 1988, 30in (76cm) **$250**
    Piccolina II, 1998, 25in (63cm)**$450**
    Ilse, 1996, 26in (56cm)   **$395**

Heath, Philip
    Lauren, 40in (102cm)   **$650**
    Imre baby, 33in (83cm)   **$650**
    World of Children Collection
                $450-$450

Heller, Karin, all cloth.
    Children   **$250-$300**

Iacono, Maggie, all cloth.
    Children   **$400-$450**

Middleton, Lee, vinyl
    Sugar Britches, Honey Love, other
      babies and toddlers   **$100-$125**

Roche, Lynne & Michael, porcelain and wood
    17-20in (43-51cm)$ **1,200-$1,500**
    Small Emily and Hannah, fully
      jointed porcelain   **$700-$800**

Sandreuter, Regina, carved wood.
    17in (43cm) children   **$700-$800**

Scattolini, Laura, cernit, one-of-a-kind.
    22-24in (56-61cm)   **$350-$450**

Schrott, Rotrout for Gadco.
    Martina, porcelain, 1988,
      28in (71cm)   **$400**
      Vinyl   **$250**
    Marlene, porcelain, 28in (71cm)**$400**
      Vinyl   **$250**
    Puyi, 1989, 26in (66cm)   **$125-$150**
    Suzi, 1989, 28in (71cm)   **$125-$150**
    Riccardo, 1991   **$200**

Spanos, FayZah, vinyl
    Babies   **$175-$225**
    Theodora, 31in (79cm)   **$300**
    Serene, 30in (76cm)   **$300**

Tonner, Robert.
    Models, 19in (48cm)   **$175-$200**
    Michelle   **$400**
    Claudia, 1995 (25 dolls) **$1,000 up**
    Grace, 1996, vinyl (750 dolls)**$275**

Treffeisen, Ruth.
    Porcelain
      Children,
        25-30in (64-76cm) **$1,700-$2,200**
    Vinyl
      Children   **$300-$400**
    Ilsa, 23in (58cm)   **$200**
    Aimee   **$250**
    Olivia & Oliver, babies,
      1999, pair   **$350-$400**
    Inya, 16in (41cm)   **$155**
    Aurore, 26in (66cm)   **$475**
    Leslie, 1995, 25in (63cm)   **$450**

Turner, Judith, vinyl for Hasbro.
    Real Baby, 1984   **$55-$65**
    Sleeping version   **$95**

Turner, Virginia, vinyl
    Large Children,
      30-32in (76-81cm)   **$250-$280**
    Small Children,
      21in (53cm)   **$110-$125**

Woods, Robin, vinyl.
    Camelot Collection,
      14in (36cm)   **$75-$125**
    Let's Play Dolls (Alexander Doll Co.),
      13in (33cm)   **$75-$95**
    Dancer's Recital, trunk and
      wardrobe   **$125**
    Anne of Green Gables
      (Royal Doll Co.)   **$125-$150**
    Dee Dee (Disney), 1989   **$150**
    Fantasia Fairy, 1994   **$190**
    Children   **$65-$85**

ASHTON-DRAKE

Designer: Yolanda Bello:
Picture Perfect Babies

Jason (1st)	$250-$350
Heather (2nd)	$100-$125
Jennifer (3rd)	$75-$100
Matthew (4th) (1987)	$75-$85
Amanda (1988)	$50-$60
Sarah (1989)	$40-$50
Jessica (1989)	$40-$50
Lisa (1990)	$40-$50
Michael (1990)	$65
Emily (1991)	$40-$50
Danielle (1991)	$40-$50

Playtime Babies

Lindsey (1994)	$40
Shawna (1994)	$40
Todd	$40

Lullaby Babies

Amy (3rd)	$55

Moments to Remember

Jill (1993)	$45-$55
Justin (1991)	$45-$55

Magical Moments of Summer

Whitney (1995)	$35-$45

Designer: Wendy Lawton:
Little Women $100-$125

Designer: Joan Ibarolle:
Little House on the Prairie characters
(1992-1995) $85-$115

Designer: Diana Effner:
Heroines from the Fairy Tale Forest,
16in (41cm) $50-$70
Goldilocks
Cinderella
Rags Cinderella

Snow White
Red Riding Hood
Rapunzel
Mother Goose Series, 14in (36cm)

Mary, Mary (1991)	$50-$60
Curly Locks (1993)	$40-$50

Classic Collection, 15in (38cm)

Hillary	$50-$55

Babies

Sugar Plum (1994)	$60

Designer: Julie Good-Kruger:
Amish Blessings

Rebeccah	$40
Rachael	$40

All I Wish for You
(Angel Series) $80-$85

Heather from Picture Perfect Babies
Series by Yolanda Bello.
Rae-Ellen Koenig, The Doll Express.

Designer: Mary Tretter
Wizard of Oz $65-$75
Dorothy
Scarecrow
Cowardly Lion
Tinman

Designer: Brigette Duval:
Fairy Tale Princesses $50-$60
Snow Queen

Cinderella
Sleeping Beauty

Designer: Titus Tomescu
From This Day Forward
(Brides) (1994)
Elizabeth $50-$60

Others:
American Fashion on Parade (1990),
16in (41cm) $35-$55
Elvis (1994) $50

For Walt Disney:
Snow White $60-$70
Dopey $60

Designer Mel Odom:
Gene
Premiere, 1996 $550-$650
Holiday Magic, 1996, 1st Christmas
outfit only $250-$350
Atlantic City Convention Package,
bathing outfit and all handouts
given at the convention $2,000
Blossoms in the Snow, 1997, 2nd
Christmas outfit only $225
My Favorite Witch, 1997
Convention doll $1,250-$1,500
Midnight Romance, 1997 FAO
Schwarz exclusive $150-$225
White Hyacinth, 1997 FAO
Schwarz exclusive $150
Night at Versaille, 1997 FAO
Schwarz exclusive $175-$200
Broadway Melody,
1998 Convention doll $475-$575
King's Daughter $350-$400

Gene in **Teatime at the Plaza,**
FAO Schwarz exclusive.
Sidney Jeffrey Collection.

BARBIE®

FACTS

Mattel, Inc., Hawthorne, Calif., U.S.A. 1959 to present. Hard plastic and vinyl.
11½–12in (29-31cm).
Mark: 1959-1962: Barbie TM/Pats. Pend ©MCMLVIII/by/Mattel, Inc.
1963-1968: Midge TM/© 1962/Barbie® /© 1958/by/Mattel, Inc.
1964-1966: © 1958/Mattel, Inc./U.S. Patented/U.S. Pat. Pend.
1966-1969: © 1966/Mattel, Inc./U.S. Patented/U.S. Pat.
Pend./Made in Japan.

Pricing Note: Condition is extremely important in pricing BARBIE® dolls. Mint condition means the doll has never been played with, coloring is beautiful, hair is perfect, all accessories are present. Rule of thumb dictates that to price out-of-original-box dolls and accessories, deduct 50%; for lightly played with items, deduct an additional 25%.

BARBIE® is a registered trademark of Mattel, Inc.

First BARBIE®: 1959. Vinyl, solid body; very light complexion, white irises, pointed eyebrows, ponytail, black and white striped bathing suit, holes in feet to fit stand, gold hoop earrings; mint condition.

11½in (29cm) boxed	**$6,000-$8,000***

Doll only, no box or accessories

Mint	**$3,500-$4,500**
Very good	**$2,500**
Stand	**$1,200**
Shoes	**$50**
Hoop earrings	**$65**

Dressed display boxed doll

#862 Barbie-Q	**$13,500**

Second BARBIE®: 1959-1960. Vinyl, solid body; very light complexion, same as above, but no holes in feet, some wore pearl earrings; mint condition. Made 3 months only.

11½in (29cm) boxed	**$6,000-$7,000***

Doll only, no box or accessories, very good **$3,000-$4,000**

*Brunette harder to find than blonde.

Third BARBIE®: 1960. Vinyl, solid body; very light complexion, same as above, but with blue irises and curved eyebrows; no holes in feet; mint condition.

11½in (29cm) boxed	**$900-$1,200**
Doll only, mint	**$500-$600**

Dressed display boxed doll

#892 Golden Elegance	**$4,400**

Fourth BARBIE®: 1960. Vinyl; same as #3; but with solid body of flesh-toned

BARBIE #2. *Sidney Jeffrey Collection.*

American Girl BARBIE® in Gold and Glamour. *Sidney Jeffrey Collection.*

Bubble Cut BARBIE®. *Courtesy of McMasters Doll Auctions.*

vinyl; mint condition.

11½in (29cm) boxed	**$650-$750**
Doll only, mint	**$350**
Dressed display boxed doll	
#881 **Busy Gal**	**$2,800**

Fifth BARBIE®: 1961. Vinyl; same as #4; ponytail hairdo of firm Saran; mint condition.

11½in (29cm) boxed	**$450-$550**
Doll only, mint	**$275-$325**

Bubble Cut BARBIE®, 1961 on.

Mint-in-box	**$300-$325***
Doll only, mint	**$150-$175***

Bubble side part,

Doll only, mint	**$300**

Fashion Queen BARBIE®, 1963.

Mint-in-box	**$500**
Doll only with 3 wigs	**$125-$135**

Miss BARBIE®, 1964.

Mint-in-box	**$1,300**

Swirl Ponytail BARBIE®, 1964.

Mint-in-box	**$500-$600***
Doll only, mint	**$250-$350***

*Allow 25% extra for platinum or white ginger hair.

Bendable Leg BARBIE®, 1965 and 1966.
American Girl, center part,

mint-in-box	**$1,500-$2,400**

Side part, mint-in-box	**$3,500-$4,500**
High color face, mint-in-box	**$3,400**

Color Magic BARBIE®, 1966.

Mint-in-box, brunette	**$1,600-$2,200**
blonde	**$1,200-$1,800**
Doll only, mint, brunette	**$1,300**
blonde	**$850**

Twist 'n Turn BARBIE®, 1967.

mint-in-box	**$375**

Talking BARBIE®, 1970.

mint-in-box	**$225-$250**

Living BARBIE®, 1970.

mint-in-box	**$225**

Hair Happenin's BARBIE®, 1971.

mint-in-box	**$1,200**

Montgomery Ward BARBIE®, 1972.

mint doll	**$250-$300**

Growin' Pretty Hair, 1971-1972	**$375**

Gift Set, mint-in-box.

Fashion Queen BARBIE® & Ken,	
1964	**$1,200**
Wedding Party, 1964	**$1,900**
On Parade (*BARBIE®, Ken* and	
Midge), 1964	**$1,100**
Skipper Party Time, 1964	**$550**
Little Theatre, 1964	**$7,500**
Pep Rally (no dolls), 1964	**$800**

Outfits: All never removed from package. Deduct 50% for *complete* but out-of-package outfits.

Roman Holiday	$3,000 up
Gay Parisienne	$2,000 up
Easter Parade	$2,500 up
Shimmering Magic	$1,500 up
Here Comes the Bride	$950 up
Pan Am Stewardess	$2,000 up
Barbie® Baby Sits	$300 up
Dogs & Duds	$300 up
Enchanted Evening	$400 up
1600 Series and Jacqueline Kennedy-style outfits	$295 up
Dinner at 8	$250
Commuter Set	$1,500
Picnic Set	$295
Sorority Meeting	$150
Silken Flame	$135 up
Midnight Blue	$500 up
Miss Astronaut	$750 up
Red Flare	$200
Cruise Stripes	$225

Dinner at Eight	$130
Senior Prom	$275

Accessories: Mint in package.

BARBIE® doll's First Car	$250-$300
BARBIE® doll's First Dreamhouse	$150
Fashion Shop	$300
Little Theatre	$500
Cases	$25 up
BARBIE® doll's Bed	$100

Other Dolls:

Ken #1 1961. Mint-in-box	$225
Bendable legs, mint-in-box	$300-$325
Dressed boxed doll	$275 up
Midge, 1963. Mint-in-box	$195
1966. Bendable legs, mint-in-box	$550
Allan, 1964-1966.	
Mint-in-box, bendable legs	$350
straight legs	$175

Color Magic BARBIE®. *Courtesy of McMasters Doll Auctions.*

Growin' Pretty Hair BARBIE®. *Courtesy of McMasters Doll Auctionns.*

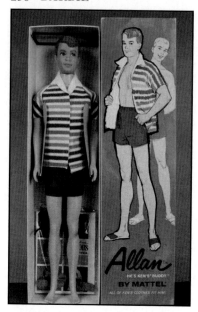

Allan. *Courtesy of McMasters Doll Auctions.*

Growin' Pretty Hair Francie.
Courtesy of McMasters Doll Auctions.

Skipper 1964. Straight legs,
  Mint-in-box   **$175**

Ricky, 1965. Mint-in-box   **$200**

Scooter, 1965. Straight legs,
  Mint-in-box   **$200**

Francie, 1966-1967.
  Doll only, mint bendable leg   **$185**
    straight legs   **$200**
    Twist 'n Turn   **$235**

  Black, 1967. Mint-in-package   **$1,500**
  Doll only, mint   **$850**
  "No Bangs", 1970.
    Mint-in-box   **$1,500**
    Doll only, mint   **$900 up**
    Growin' Pretty Hair   **$270**
Hair Happenin's, 1970.
  Mint-in-box   **$275**

Casey, 1967. Mint-in-box   **$275-$300**

Twiggy, 1967.
  Mint-in-box   **$325-$375**

Christie, 1968-1972. (Black) Twist 'n Turn
  Mint-in-box   **$350**

Stacey, 1968-1971. Twist 'n Turn
  Mint-in-box   **$350**

P.J., 1969-1971. Twist 'n Turn
  Mint-in-box   **$225-$275**
  Live Action on Stage, mint-in-box **$215**

Truly Scrumptious, 1969.
  Mint-in-box   **$525**
  Doll only, mint   **$300**

Julia, 1969.
  Mint-in-box, one-piece
    uniform   **$285**
  Mint-in-box, two-piece uniform **$300**
  Talking, mint-in-box   **$200**

Tutti, 1967-1970. Mint-in-box   **$150**
Chris, 1967-1970. Mint-in-box   **$210**
Todd, 1967-1970. Mint-in-box   **$200**

Pretty Pairs,
  Angie 'N Tangie $250-$300
  Nan 'N Fran $225-$250
  Lori 'N Rori $250-$275

Bob Mackie BARBIE® Dolls:
  1990 Gold   **$500 up**
  1991 Platinum   **$450 up**
  1991 Starlight Splendor (black)**$400 up**
  1992 Empress Bride   **$600 up**
  1992 Neptune Fantasy   **$600 up**
  1993 Masquerade Ball   **$300**
  1994 Queen of Hearts   **$200**
  1995 Goddess of the Sun   **$175**

Christmas BARBIES®:
  1988, English language box   **$650**
  1989   **$225**
  1990   **$175**
  1991   **$150**
  1992   **$100**
  1993   **$120**
  1994   **$100**
  1995   **$55**
  1996   **$50**
  1997   **$35-$45**
  1998   **$25**

Exclusive Store Specials:
  1990 Winter Fantasy
    (FAO Schwarz)   **$175**
  1993 Little Debbie   **$50**
  1993 Rockettes (FAO Schwarz) **$160**
  1994 Nicole Miller (Bloomingdales) **$95**
  1994 Victorian Elegance (Hallmark)**$100**
  1994 Silver Screen (FAO Schwarz)**$150**
  1994 Tooth Fairy (WalMart)   **$25**
  1995 Shopping Chic (Speigel)   **$85**
  1995 Jeweled Splendor
    (FAO Schwarz)   **$200**
  1995 Circus Star (FAO Schwarz) **$100**
  1995 International Traveller
    (Duty Free Shops)   **$75**

Talking Julia with oxidized hair.
Courtesy of McMasters Doll Auctions.

Black Francie. *Sidney Jeffrey*

Twist 'n Turn Francie. *Courtesy of McMasters Doll Auctions.*

Live Action P.J. on Stage. *Courtesy of McMasters Doll Auctions.*

1995 Donna Karan	
(Bloomingdales)	**$100**
1995 Royal Enchantment	
(J.C. Penney)	**$50**
1995 Statue of Liberty	
(FAO Schwarz)	**$75**
1997 Pink Ice (Toys R Us)	**$80**

Timeless Creations:
(now BARBIE® Collectibles)

Stars and Stripes Collection:

1990 Air Force BARBIE®	**$55**
1991 Navy BARBIE®	**$50**
1992 Marine BARBIE®	**$50**
1992 Marine Gift Set	**$85**
1993 Army Gift Set	**$75**
1994 Air Force Gift Set	**$60**

Classique Collection:

1992 Benefit Ball	**$150**
1993 Opening Night	**$85**
1993 City Style	**$90**
1994 Uptown Chic	**$90**
1994 Evening Extravaganza	**$75**
1994 Evening Extravaganza	
(black)	**$90**
1995 Midnight Gala	**$85**

Nostalgia Series:

1994 35th Anniversary	
(blonde)	**$40**
(brunette)	**$55**
1994 Gift Set	**$125**
1994 Solo in the Spotlight	**$35**
1995 Busy Gal	**$65**
1996 Enchanted Evening	**$35**
1996 Poodle Parade	**$30**
1997 Fashion Luncheon	**$40**

Scarlett Series, 1994 & 1995.

Green Velvet	**$75**
Red Velvet	**$75**
Barbecue	**$75**
Honeymoon	**$85**
Ken as Rhett Butler	**$60**

Great Eras:

1993 Gibson Girl	**$125**
1993 1920s Flapper	**$145**
1994 Egyptian Queen	**$125**

1994 Southern Belle	$100
1995 Medieval Lady	$60
1996 Grecian Goddess	$60
1997 Chinese Empress	$50

Other BARBIE® Dolls:

1986 Blue Rhapsody (porcelain)	$700
1988 Mardi Gras	$80
1989 Pink Jubilee	$1,500 up
1990 Wedding Fantasy	$50
1992 My Size	$125
1994 Snow Princess	$140
1994 Gold Jubilee	$700-$800
1994 Evergreen Princess	$100
1994 Evergreen Princess (red hair)	$400
1995 Peppermint Princess	$75
1995 Starlight Waltz	$100
1995 Dior, 1st	$100
1995 50th Anniversary (porcelain)	$350
1996 Pink Splendor	$500
1996 Jewel Princess	$35
1996 Jewel Princess (Disney brunette)	$150
1996 Escada	$55
1996 Dior, 2nd	$85
1997 Bill Blass	$60
1997 Midnight Princess	$45
1997 Midnight Princess (Disney, brunette)	$110

Truly Scrumptious. *Courtesy of McMasters Doll Auctions*

Angie 'n Tangie, Nan 'n Fran, Lori 'n Rori. *Courtesy of McMasters Doll Auction.*

BETSY M^cCALL

American Character Doll Co.: 1957.
All hard plastic, molded eyelashes, jointed knees, rooted Saran hair on wig cap; original clothes, excellent with rosy cheeks.

8in (20cm) basic, (undergarment, shoes and socks)	**$150-$175**
mint-in-box, basic	**$325-$375**
in dresses	**$200-$250**
in gowns	**$300-$400**
Designer Studio Set	**$925**

Clothes, clean and in very good condition:

dresses	**$30-$50**
shoes and socks	**$35**
Boxed outfits	**$85-$125**

American Character, 1960. All vinyl, lashed sleep eyes, slender limbs; original clothes; excellent condition.

14in (36cm)	**$350-$375**

20in (51cm)	**$450**
30in (76cm)	**$550-$600**
36in (91cm)	**$650-$750**
Boxed, all original	
14in (36cm)	**$650-$750**
20in (51cm)	**$850-$950**

Jointed at wrists, waist, knees and ankles:

22in (56cm)	**$400-$450**
30in (76cm)	**$625-$675**

Ideal Novelty & Toy Co., 1948. Vinyl head, hard plastic body; original clothes; excellent condition

14in (36cm)	**$250-$300**
mint-in-box	**$500**

Ideal Novelty & Toy Co., 1959. All vinyl; original clothes; excellent condition.

36in (91cm) **Betsy McCall**	**$550-$650**
38in (96cm) **Sandy McCall**	**$500-$600**

Uneeda, 1959-1961.

All vinyl, 11½in (29cm)	**$100-$125**

Horsman, 1974.

All vinyl, 29in (73cm) boxed	**$225-$275**

Tomy, 1984. Porcelain/cloth. All original and boxed, Four Seasons.

16in (41cm)	**$40-$50**

Tonner, Robert. 1997. Porcelain, all original,

"Stamp Doll," 11in (28cm)	**$50-$55**

Large *Betsy McCall,* all original.
Norman & June Verro.

BOUDOIR DOLLS

Boudoir Doll: Head of composition, cloth or other material, painted features, mohair wig, composition or cloth stuffed body, unusually long extremities, usually high-heeled shoes; original clothes elaborately designed and trimmed; all in excellent condition.

1920s Art Doll, cloth head, exceptional quality, silk hair,
28-30in (71-76cm)   **$400-$500**

Standard quality, cloth head, dressed,
28-30in (71-76cm)   **$175-$225**
undressed   **$90-$110**
1940s composition head,
dressed   **$125**

Lenci, 24-28in (61-71cm)   **$1,500 up**
faded color   **$1,000-$1,250**

Smoking Doll, 25in (64cm)   **$450-$500**

Poured Wax, 22in (56cm)   **$600**

FACTS
Various French, U.S. and Italian firms. Early 1920s into the 1940s.

24in (61cm) Poir-type boudoir doll.
H & J Foulke, Inc.

BUDDY LEE

Marked Buddy Lee: Molded hair, painted eyes to side; jointed at shoulders, stiff hips, legs apart; dressed in original Lee clothes; all in very good condition.
Composition, 1920-1948.
13in (33cm)   **$450-$550**
Hard Plastic, 1949-1962.
13in (33cm)   **$450-$550**
Coca Cola uniform, white   **$625**
tan   **$650**
Gasoline Station Uniform **$350-$400**

FACTS
H.D. Lee Co., Inc. garment manufacturers of Kansas City, MO. 1920-1962.
Mark: "Buddy Lee" embossed on back

Hard plastic **Buddy Lee** in Phillips 66 uniform. *H & J Foulke, Inc.*

CAMEO DOLL COMPANY

14in (36cm) *Newborn Miss Peep,* 1962. *McMasters Doll Auctions.*

11in (28cm) *Bundie,* all original. *H & J Foulke, Inc.*

Kewpie: 1913. (See page 130.)

Bundie: 1918-1925. All composition.

11in (28cm)	**$300****

Scootles: 1925. Designed by Rose O'Neill. All-composition; appropriate clothes; all in very good condition.

7in-8in (18-20cm)	**$500-$600**
12-13in (31-33cm)	**$550-$600**
15-16in (38-41cm)	**$700-$750**
20in (51cm)	**$1,000-$1,200**

Sleep eyes:

12in (31cm)	**$700-$750**
20in (51cm)	**$1,250-$1,500**

Black,

13-14in (33-36cm)	**$750-$850**

All-bisque, marked on feet:

5-6in (13-15cm), Germany$	**650-$750**
6-7in (15-18cm), Japan$	**500-$550**

Baby Bo Kaye: 1925. (See page 42.)

Wood Segmented Characters: Designed by Joseph L. Kallus. Composition head, segmented wood body; undressed; all in very good condition.

Margie, 1929. 10in (25cm)	**$225-$250**
15in (38cm)	**$400-$450**
17in (43cm)	**$550**
Pinkie, 1930. 10in (25cm)	**$250-$275**
Joy, 1932. 10in (5cm)	**$250-$275**
15in (38cm)	**$375-$400**

Betty Boop, 1932.

12in (31cm)	**$650-$750**

With molded bathing suit and composition legs; wearing a cotton print

dress	**$750-$850****
Pop-Eye, 1935	**$300****
Hotpoint Man, 16in (41cm)	**$800****
RCA Radiotron, 16in (41cm)	**$800****

Bandy, General Electric,

18in (46cm)	**$800****

13in (33cm) black *Scootles,* all original. *H & J Foulke, Inc.*

16in (41cm) *Scootles,* 1973 Ltd. Ed., all original. *H & J Foulke, Inc.*

Pete the Pup, 9in (23cm) **$300**

Giggles: 1946. Designed by Rose O'Neill. All-composition; original romper; all in very good condition.
14in (36cm) **$650-$750****

Little Annie Rooney: 1925. Designed by Jack Collins. Composition, painted eyes, yarn wig, all original.
16in (41cm) **$700****

Baby Blossom: 1927. Composition and cloth, 19-20in (48-51cm) **$550-$650****

Champ: 1942. Composition, molded hair, freckles, all original.
16in (41cm) **$500-$600****

Vinyl Dolls:
Miss Peep, 1957. All original,
16-18in (41-46cm) **$85**
Boxed **$135**

Newborn Miss Peep, 1962.
14in (36cm), boxed **$65**

Baby Mine, 1961. All original,
20in (51cm)boxed **$175-$225**

Margie, 1958. All original,
17in (43cm)boxed **$175-$225****

Scootles, 1964. All original,
14in (36cm) **$165-$185**
1973 Ltd. Ed. (Maxines)
16in (41cm) **$200-$225**
1980s. (Jesco), all original,
12in (31cm) **$40-$60**
**Not enough price samples to compute a reliable range.

FACTS

Cameo Doll Company, New York, N.Y., later Port Allegany, Pa. Original owner: Joseph L. Kallus. 1922-on.

CAMPBELL KIDS

12in (33cm) Horsman 1948 *Campbell Kid,* all original with desirable Campbell Soup outfit and label. *Private Collection.*

E.I. Horsman Co., 1910-1914. Designed by Grace Drayton. Composition head, molded and painted bobbed hair; original cloth body; appropriate or original clothes; all in good condition.

Mark: On head: **E.I.H. © 1910**

Cloth label on sleeve:

The Campbell Kids Trademark by Joseph Campbell. Mfg. by E.I. Horsman Co

10-13in (25-33cm)	**$275-$325**
16in (41cm)	**$400-$450**

American Character & E.I. Horsman Co., 1923. Designed by Grace Drayton, sometimes called *Dolly Dingle*. All composition, molded bobbed hair, painted eyes to side; original clothes; all in good condition.

12in (31cm)	**$550-$650**

E. I. Horsman Co., 1948. All composition, molded bobbed hair, painted eyes to side, watermelon mouth; original clothes; all in good condition.

12in (31cm)	**$450-$475**
With Campbell Soup outfit and label	**$600**

All Vinyl, 1971. Original clothes, bright color, unplayed with condition.

8in (20cm)	**$25-$30**
11in (28cm)	**$40-$45**

All Cloth, 1980s. Perfect, unplayed with condition | **$20-$25** |

Porcelain, 1997. Soldier in a Soup Can.

11½in (29cm)	**$65-$70**

12in (31cm) Horsman 1910 *Campbell Kid,* all original. *H & J Foulke, Inc.*

DEWEES COCHRAN

Dewees Cochran Doll: Latex with jointed neck, shoulders and hips; human hair wig, painted eyes, character face; dressed; all in good condition.

15-16in (38-41cm) Cindy,
  1947-1948 **$800-$900**
Grow-up Dolls: Stormy, Angel, Bunnie, J.J. and Peter Ponsett each at ages 5, 7, 11, 16 and 20, 1952-1958 **$2,200-$2,500**
Look-Alike Dolls
  (6 different faces) **$2,200-$2,500**
Individual Portrait
  Children **$2,500-$4,500**
  Baby, 9in (23cm) **$1,500**
Composition American Children (see Effanbee, page 263.).

Dewees Cochran Portrait Child, all original. *Private Collection.*

COMPOSITION
(AMERICAN)

Condition: Unless otherwise noted, all dolls should be all original with perfect hair, good coloring, original clothes; light crazing acceptable.

All-Composition Child Doll: 1912-1920. Various firms, such as Bester Doll Co., New Era Novelty Co., New Toy Mfg. Co., Superior Doll Mfg. Co., Artcraft Toy Product Co., Colonial Toy Mfg. Co. Ball-jointed composition body; appropriate clothes; all in good condition. These are patterned after German bisque head dolls.
  22-24in (56-61cm) **$300-$350**
Character baby, all-composition
  19in (48cm) **$275-$300**

Early Composition Character Doll: Ca. 1912. Composition head with molded hair and painted features; appropriate clothes.
  12-15in (31-38cm) **$150-$200**
  18-20in (46-51cm) **$250-$300**
  24-26in (61-66cm) **$350-$450**
Two-face toddler,
  14in (36cm) **$275-$300**

Molded Loop Dolls: Ca. 1930s. Composition head with molded bobbed hair and loop for tying on a ribbon; quality is generally mediocre.
  12-15in (31-38cm) **$150-$175**

Patsy-type Girl: Ca. 1930s. All-composition with molded bobbed hair; of good quality.
  9-10in (23-25cm) **$165-$185**
  14-16in (36-41cm) **$275-$325**
  20in (51cm) **$375-$400**

23in (58cm) composition/
cloth mama doll,
all original.
H & J Foulke, Inc.

28in (71cm) early
composition/cloth
mama doll,
all original.
H & J Foulke, Inc.

16in (41cm)
Patsy-type doll,
all original.
H & J Foulke, Inc.

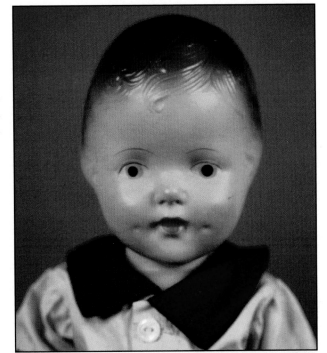

14in (36cm)
composition/cloth
infant, all original.
H & J Foulke, Inc.

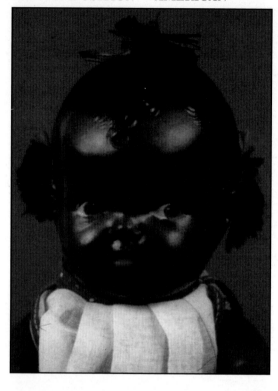

13in (33cm) black *Topsy.*
H & J Foulke, Inc.

Mama Dolls: Ca. 1920-on. Composition head with hair wig; composition lower limbs; cloth body.

16-18in (41-46cm)	**$250-$275**
20-22in (51-56cm)	**$350-$375**
24-26in (61-66cm)	**$450-$475**

Babies and Infants: Ca. 1920 on. Composition head with molded hair, composition lower arms, cloth body (may have composition lower legs).

14-16in (36-41cm)	**$175-$225**
18-20in (46-51cm)	**$250-$300**

Dionne-type Doll: Ca. 1935. All-composition with molded hair or wig; of good quality.

7-8in (18-20cm) baby	**$135**
13in (33cm) toddler	**$250-$275**
18-20in (46-51cm) toddler	**$350-$375**

Alexander-type Girl: Ca. 1935. All-composition; of good quality.

13in (33cm)	**$225-$250**
16-18in (41-46cm)	**$300-$350**
22in (56cm)	**$350-$400**

Shirley Temple-type Girl: Ca. 1935-on. All-composition; of good quality.

16-18in (41-46cm)	**$400-$500**

Costume Doll: Ca. 1940. All-composition. 11in (28cm)

Excellent quality	**$150-$175**
Standard quality	**$65-$75**

Miscellaneous Specific Dolls:

Carmen (Miranda), Eegee.

14in (36cm)	**$225**
20in (51cm)	**$350**

Cat, Rabbit or **Pig head,** naked,

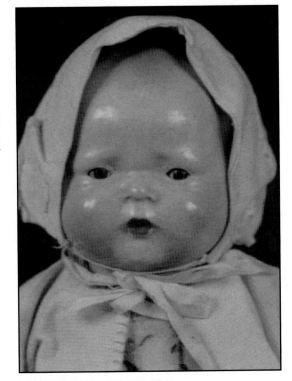

14in (36cm) Unmarked composition/cloth baby, all original. *H & J Foulke, Inc.*

10-11in (25-28cm)	**$350-$400**
David, Bible Doll Co. of America,	
11in (28cm) boxed	**$285**
The Emma Doll, character boy	
16in (41cm)	**$400****
Famlee, 1921. Boxed with 6 heads and	
6 costumes	**$1,000**
G.G. Drayton,	
14in (36cm)	**$450-$500****
Hedwig/DiAngeli	
Elin, Hannah, Lydia, Suzanne,	
14in (36cm)	**$625-$675**
Indian child, 1940s.	
8in (21cm) boxed	**$60**
Jack and Jill,	
11in (28cm) pair	**$275**
Jackie Robinson	
13½in (34cm)	**$700****
Jerry Mahoney, Juro Novelty.	
24in (61cm)	**$275-$325**
Kewpie-type characters,	
12in (31cm)	**$80-$90**
Little Miss Movie, Eegee.	
27in (69cm)	**$700-$800**
Lone Ranger,	
16in (41cm)	**$700-$750**
MBC, 1940s.	
7in (18cm)	**$50-$60**
Miss Curity,	
18in (46cm)	**$450-$500**
Monica, 1941-1951.	
18in (46cm)	**$450-$550**
P.D. Smith,	
22in (56cm)	**$2,600****
Paris Doll Co. Peggy,	
28in (71cm) walker	**$350-$400**
Pinocchio, Crown Toy, 1939.	
12in (31cm)	**$250-$300**

**Not enough price samples to compute a reliable range.

13in (33cm) *Ritzy Chubby Baby*
Dionne-type toddler, all original.
H & J Foulke, Inc.

Puzzy, 1948. H. of P.,
　　15in (38cm)　　　　　$350-$400
Royal "Spirit of America,"
　　15in (38cm) with original box
　　　and outfits　　　　$300-$350
Santa Claus,
　　19in (48cm)　　　　$450-$500
Sizzy, 1948. H. of P.,
　　14in (36cm)　　　　$250-$300
Sterling Doll Co. Sports Dolls,
　　29in (74cm) all original　$300-$350
Trudy 3 faces, 1946.
　　14in (36cm)　　　　$275-$295
Three Pigs and Wolf boxed set,
　　all original　　　$800-$1,000

Black Composition Doll: Ca. 1930. Original or appropriate clothes; some have three yarn tufts of hair on either side and one top of the head; all in good condition. (See photograph on page 250.)

14in (36cm)
Alexander-type
girl, all original.
H & J Foulke, Inc.

"Topsy" "Baby:
  10-12in (25-31cm) $160-$175
  16in (41cm) $250-$275
Toddler,
  15-16in (38-41cm) $300-$350
Girl, 17in (43cm) $350-$400
1910 character,
  13½in (34cm) $300-$350
Patsy-type,
  13-14in (33-36cm) $300-$350

Tony Sarg Mammy with Baby,
  17in (43cm) **$1,000-$1,100**

Ming Ming Baby: Quan-Quan Co., Los Angeles and San Francisco, Calif. Ca. 1930. All-composition baby; original Oriental costume of colorful taffeta with braid trim; feet painted black or white for shoes.
  10-12in (25-31cm) $200-$225

8in (21cm) Indian child, all original. *H & J Foulke, Inc.*

12in (31cm) unmarked Eugenia black toddler, all original. *H & J Foulke, Inc.*

COMPOSITION
(GERMAN)

All-Composition Child Doll: Socket head with good wig, sleep (sometimes flirty) eyes, open mouth with teeth; jointed composition body; appropriate clothes; all in good condition, of excellent quality.

12-14in (31-36cm)	**$225-$275**
18-20in (46-51cm)	**$375-$425**
22in (56cm)	**$450-$500**

Character face,

18-20in (46-51cm)	**$425-$525**

Double-Face Googly,

14in (36cm)	**$425-$475**

Black Composition Doll: All composition; molded hair or wig, glass eyes (sometimes flirty); appropriate clothes; all in good condition.

11in (28cm)	**$350**
16-18in (41-46cm)	**$650-$750***
Patsy-type, 11in (28cm)	
all original	**$650**

Dora Petzoldt Child: 1919 on. Molded composition (sometimes cloth) head, closed mouth, pensive character face, painted eyes, mohair wig; cloth body, sometimes with long arms and legs; original clothing; all in very good condition.

19-22in (48-56cm)	**$850-$950**
Moderate wear, redressed	**$400-$450**

Character Baby: Composition head with good wig, sleep eyes, open mouth with teeth; bent-limb composition baby body or hard-stuffed cloth body; appropriate clothes; all in good condition, of excellent quality.

All-composition baby,	
16-18in (41-46cm)	**$375-$425**
Cloth body,	
18-20in (46-51cm)	**$300-$350**
All composition toddler,	
16-18in (41-46cm)	**$450-$500**

FACTS
Various German firms such as König & Wernicke, Kämmer & Reinhardt and others. Ca. 1920s on.

14in (36cm) double-faced googly, all original. *H & J Foulke, Inc.*

COMPOSITION
(JAPANESE)

COSMOPOLITAN

9in (23cm) *Dionne Quintuplet* baby.
H & J Foulke, Inc.

Japanese Composition Doll: All-composition with molded hair, painted features; dressed (may have original rayon panties with "Japan" stamp) or undressed; all in excellent condition.

Dionne Quintuplets:
Baby, 7in (18cm)	**$165-$185**
Baby, 9in (23cm)	**$250-$300****
Toddler, 7-1/2in (19cm)	**$165-$185**
9in (23cm)	**$250-$300**
Choir Boy, with book molded in hands,	
10in (25cm)	**$135-$150**
Toddler, 8in (20cm),	
all original	**$125-$135**
Shirley temple. See page 303.	

**Not enough price samples to compute a reliable average.

FACTS
Unidentified Japanese Companies,
1920-1940
Mark: "Japan" incised or stamped
on back torso.

Ginger. 1954 on. All-hard plastic walker, sleep eyes; original clothes; excellent condition with good color and perfect hair. Unmarked. 8in (20cm)

Unmarked. 8in (20cm)	**$150-$175**
Mint-in-box	**$225**
Trunk with doll and 10 outfits,	
light wear	**$600**
Roundup, Mouseketeer, or	
Davy Crockett	**$225-$250**
Disneyland Costumes	**$300-$350**
Girl Scout or **Brownie**	**$175-$225**
Boxed outfits	**$30-$60**
Boxed wig	**$135**
Dresser	**$190**
Vinyl head, all original	**$50-$60**

Miss Ginger: 1957 on. Vinyl head, hard plastic body with adult figure, high-heeled feet; original clothes; excellent condition. **Mark:** "GINGER" on head.

10½in (27cm)	**$190-$210**
Dresses	**$20-$30**
Boxed outfits	**$75**

Little Miss Ginger: 1958 on. Vinyl head, rigid vinyl body, adult figure with high-heeled feet; original clothes; excellent condition, eyes not askew. **Mark:** "GINGER" on head.

8in (20cm)	**$75-$85**
Shoes	**$20**
Dresses	**$20-$30**

FACTS
Cosmopolitan Doll & Toy Corp.,
Jackson Heights, NY.

8in (21cm) *Ginger,* all original. *Terri & Kathy's Dolls.*

DELUXE READING

Bride Dolls, 1958. All vinyl, fashion doll. Complete original bride clothes.

24-29in (61-74cm)	**$75-$85**

Candy, 1962. All vinyl fashion doll, 3 extra costumes, hats and accessories. Boxed.

20in (51cm)	**$125-$135**

Penny Brite, 1963. All vinyl child doll with accessories and wardrobe sold separately.

8in (20cm) original dress	**$20-$25**
Boxed doll	**$40**
Boxed outfit	**$15-$40**
Beauty Salon	**$35**

Kitchen Set	**$35**
3 Rooms Boxed Set, at auction	**$360**

Dawn, 1969 on. Topper. All vinyl play doll with accessories, wardrobe and friends.

6in (15cm)	**$30-$40**
Boxed doll	**$55-$75**
Boxed or packaged outfit	**$35-$40**
Flower Fantasy, boxed	**$200**
Dancing Glori (no bangs)	**$165**

Suzy Homemaker, 1964. Vinyl and hard plastic, jointed knees.

21in (53cm)	**$65**

Candy, all original and boxed. *McMasters Doll Auctions.*

EFFanBEE

Metal Heart Necklace or Bracelet with chain **$45-50**

Metal Pinback Button **$65-75**

Early Characters: Composition character face, molded painted hair; cloth stuffed body; appropriate clothes; in good condition. Some marked **"Deco."** 12-16in (30-41cm).

Baby Grumpy, 1912. Molds 172, 174 or
 176 **$375-$425**
Miss Coquette, Naughty Marietta,
 1912 **$400 -$425**
Pouting Bess, 1915,
 162 or 166 **$350-$375**
Billy Boy, 1915 **$350-$375**
Whistling Jim, 1916 **$350**
Harmonica Joe, 1924 **$400-$450**
Katie Kroose, 1918 **$400-$450**
Buds, 1915-1918. 7in (18cm) **$175-$195**
 Black **$200-$225**
Aunt Dinah, 1915. 16in (41cm) **$600**

Johnny Tu-Face, 1912 **$400-$450**
Betty Bounce, 1913 **$350-$400**
Baby Huggins, 1915 **$300**
**Not enough price samples to compute a reliable average.

19in (48cm) *Mary Ann,* all original.
H & J Foulke, Inc.

16in (41cm) *Lovums*, all original. *H & J Foulke, Inc.*

FACTS

EFFanBEE Doll Co., New York,
N.Y., 1912-on.
Marks: Various, but nearly always
marked "EFFanBEE" on torso or
head, sometimes with doll's name.
Wore a metal heart-shaped bracelet;
later a gold paper heart label.

Effanbee

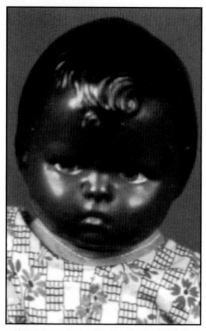

14in (36cm) black *Baby Grumpy*, *H & J Foulke, Inc.*

16in (41cm) *Tommy Tucker*, all original. *H & J Foulke, Inc.*

Shoulder Head Dolls: Composition shoulder head; cloth torso, composition arms and legs; original clothes; all in good condition.
Baby Grumpy, 1925-1939.

12in (31cm) white	**$300-$325**
Black	**$375-$400**

Pennsylvania Dutch Dolls, 1936-1940.
All original and excellent. **$225**
Baby Dainty, 1912-1922.

15in (38cm)	**$250**

Patsy, 1925. 15in (38cm) **$350**
Rosemary, 1925; **Marilee**, 1924; and other name dolls.

14in (36cm)	**$275-$300**
17in (43cm)	**$350-$400**
25in (64cm)	**$450-$550**
30in (76cm)	**$650-$750**

Mary Ann, 1928.

19-20in (48-51cm)	**$375-$425**
All-composition	**$450-$500**

Mary Lee, 1928.

16-17in (41-43cm)	**$325-$375**
All-composition	**$375-$425**

Mae Starr, 1928.

30in (76cm) phonograph doll	**$600-$700**

Babies: Composition head; cloth body, original clothes; all in good condition, with perfect hair and good coloring, light crazing acceptable.
Bubbles, 1924.
Mark:

16-18in (41-46cm)	**$400-$450**
20-22in (51-56cm)	**$500-$550**
25-26in (63-66cm)	**$650-$750**
20in (51cm) appropriately redressed	**$325-$350**

Baby Evelyn, 18in (46cm) **$250-$275**

7in (18cm) *Baby Tinyette* Quintuplets, all original. *H & J Foulke, Inc.*

15in (38cm) *Katie,* all original. *H & J Foulke, Inc.*

Lovums, 1928.

Mark:

EFFANBEE
LOVUMS
©
PAT N⁰. 1,283,558

16-18in (41-46cm)	**$350-$400**
22-24in (56-61cm)	**$500-$550**
28in (71cm)	**$650-$700**

Mickey, Baby Bright Eyes, Tommy Tucker, Katie, 1939-1949.

16-18in (41-46cm)	**$350-$385**
22-24in (56-61cm)	**$450-$500**
Twins in Boxed Set, 14in (36cm)	**$900**

Sweetie Pie, 1942.

16-18in (41-46cm)	**$350-$385**
22-24in (56-61cm)	**$450-$500**
Boxed with layette, 23in (58cm)	**$750**

Baby Effanbee, 1925.

12in (31cm)	**$160-$180**

Lambkin, 1930s.

16in (41cm)	**$450-$475**
Boxed with pillow	**$650-$700**

Sugar Baby, 1936. Caracul wig,

16-18in (41-46cm)	**$300-$350**

Babyette, 1943. eyes closed,

13in (33cm) boxed with pillow	
	$550-$600

Pat-O-Pat, (clap hands), 1925.

13in (33cm)	**$150-$165**

Patsy Family: 1928-on. All-composition; original or appropriate old clothes; may have some light crazing.

Mark:

EFFANBEE
PATSY JR.
DOLL

EFFANBEE
PATSY
DOLL

Wee Patsy, 6in (15cm)	**$425-$475**
boxed with extra outfits	**$650-$700**
Sewing set, boxed set	**$650**
Storybook Doll, all original	**$600**
Baby Tinyette, 7in (18cm)	**$325-$350**
Quintuplets, set of 5, boxed,	
all original	**$2,200**

22in (56cm) *Patsy Lou.* H & J Foulke, Inc.

Tinyette Toddler, 8in (20cm)	$325-$350
Patsy Babyette, 9in (23cm)	$325-350
Patsyette, 9in (23cm)	$425-$450
Brown	$650
Hawaiian	$650
George and Martha Washington,	$650 pair
Patsy Baby,	
11in (28cm)	$375-$425
Boxed	$650-$675
Brown	$550-$600
Patsy Jr., Patsy Kins, Patricia Kin,	
11in (28cm)	$425-$475
Patsy, 14in (36cm)	$525-$575
Oriental	$850
1946, unmarked	$400-$450
Boxed	$500
On Patricia body	$600
Patricia, 15in (38cm)	$525-$575

14in (36cm) *Patsy.*
H & J Foulke, Inc.

Patsy Joan, 16in (41cm)	$525-$575
Brown	$750
1946 (different mold)	$475
Patsy Ann, 19in (48cm)	$575-$625
Brown	$950
Patsy Lou, 22in (56cm)	$575-$625
Patsy Ruth, 26in (66cm)	$1,200-$1,300
Patsy Mae,	
30in (76cm)	$1,300-$1,500

Skippy: 1929.
14in (36cm)

Soldier, Sailor	$450-$500
Boy's Suit	$550-$600
White Horse Inn outfit	$700
Cowboy, at auction	$1,050
Redressed	$350-$400
Brown	$900-$1,100

19in (48cm) *Patsy Ann*. *H & J Foulke, Inc.*

14in (36cm) *Patsy Baby* head on *Patsy* body, all original "White Horse Inn" clothes. This is a factory assembled doll. *H & J Foulke, Inc.*

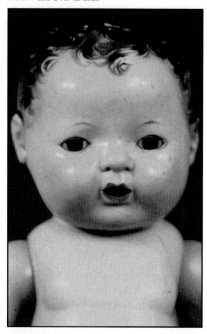

15in (38cm) all-rubber *Dy-Dee Baby. H & J Foulke, Inc.*

17in (43cm) *Anne Shirley,* all original. *H & J Foulke, Inc.*

Dy-Dee Baby: 1933-on.
Mark:

> "EFF-AN-BEE
> DY-DEE BABY
> US PAT.-1-857-485
> ENGLAND-880-060
> FRANCE-723-980
> GERMANY-585-647
> OTHER PAT PENDING"

Hard rubber head with applied rubber ears, soft rubber body; appropriate old clothes; good condition.

9in (23cm)	**$275-$300**
11in (28cm)	**$175-$200**
13in (33cm)	**$200-$225**
15in (38cm)	**$250-$275**
20in (51cm)	**$375-$400**
24in (61cm)	**$450**
With box and layette,	
13in (33cm)	**$525**
15in (38cm)	**$575**
Carded 5-piece nursery set with **Dy-Dee**	
booklet	**$110-$135**
Dy-Dee pajamas	**$25-$28**
Bottle	**$15-$18**
Book: **Dy-Dee Dolls Days**	**$75**

Hard Plastic Head with applied ears, soft rubber body; appropriate old clothes; good condition.

11in (28cm)	**$125-$150**
15in (38cm)	**$225-$250**
20-21in (51-53cm)	**$325-$350**

All-Composition Children: 1933-on. Original clothes; all in very good condition, with nice coloring and perfect hair.

Anne Shirley, 1935-1940; **Little Lady,** 1940-1949.

14-15in (36-38cm)	**$275-$300**
17-18in (43-46cm)	**$300-$325**
21in (53cm)	**$400-$450**
27in (69cm)	**$500-$550**

Boxed with trousseau, 18in (46cm) **$700**

WAAC outfit, 14in (36cm) **$650**

American Children, 1936-1939.
Closed mouth. 19-21in (48-53cm) marked
head on **Anne Shirley** body,

painted eyes	**$2,200**
sleep eyes	**$2,000**

17in (43cm) boy, unmarked,

painted eyes **$1,800****

Open mouth, unmarked.

Barbara Joan, 15in (38cm) **$700-$750**

Ice Queen (skater) **$750**

Barbara Ann, 17in (43cm) **$750-$800**

Barbara Lou, 21in (53cm) **$900-$950**

Birthday Doll, Music box in torso,

17in (43cm) **$1,050**

Suzette, 1939. Painted eyes,

11½in(29cm) **$350-$400**

Suzanne, 1940.

14in (36cm) **$350-$400**

Portrait Dolls, 1940. Ballerina, **Bo-Peep**, **Gibson Girl**, bride, groom, dancing couple, colonial.

11in (28cm) **$300-$350**

**Not enough price samples to compute a reliable average.

Candy Kid, 1946. Toddler, molded hair.

12in (31cm) **$350-$400**

"The Champ," at auction **$630**

Betty Brite, 1933. Caracul wig.

16½in (42cm) **$325-$375**

Butin-Nose, 1939.

9in (23cm) **$275-$300**

Oriental **$500**

Brother and Sister, 1943. Yarn hair, 16in (41cm) and 12in (31cm) each **$250-$300**

Charlie McCarthy: 1937. Strings at back of head to operate mouth; original clothes; all in very good condition.

17-20in (43-51cm) **$650-$750**

Mint-in-box with button **$850-$950**

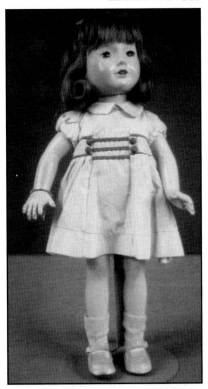

15in (38cm) *Barbara Joan,* all original.
H & J Foulke, Inc.

20in (51cm) *American Child*, all original. *H & J Foulke, Inc.*

14in (36cm) *Suzanne* with magnetic hand, all original. *H & J Foulke, Inc.*

Historical Dolls: 1939. All-composition. Three each of 30 dolls portraying the history of American fashion, 1492-1939. "American Children" heads with elaborate human hair wigs and painted eyes; elaborate original costumes using velvets, satins, silks, and brocades; all in excellent condition.

Mark: On Head:

"EFFanBEE AMERICAN
CHILDREN"

21in (53cm)	**$1,500-$1,800**

Historical Doll Replicas: 1939.

14in (36cm)	**$500-$600**
Boxed	**$700-$750**

Hard Plastic Dolls:

Howdy Doody: 1949-1950. Hard plastic head and hands, molded hair, sleep eyes; cloth body; original clothes; all in excellent condition.

19-23in (48-58cm)	**$300-$400**
Mint-in-box	**$525-$575**

Honey: 1949-1955. All-hard plastic; original clothes; all in excellent condition. Later dolls have walking mechanism.
Mark:

EFFANBEE

14in (36cm)	**$325-$350**
18in (46cm)	**$375-$425**
24in (61cm)	**$500**
In Schieparelli outfits 18in (46cm)	**$500**
Prince Charming	**$500-$600**
Cinderella	**$500-$600**
Alice	**$400-$450**

Tintair Honey,

14in (36cm)	**$400-$450**
In original box with accessories	**$600-$650**

Vinyl Dolls: All original and excellent condition.
Mickey, 1956.

10-11in (25-28cm)	**$125-$135**

Champagne Lady, 1959.

19in (48cm)	**$250-$300**
Fluffy*, 1957 on. 8in (20cm)	**$35-$40**
11in (28cm)	**$40-$50**
Boxed Outfits	**$20-$25**

Patsy Ann, 1960 on.

15in (38cm)	**$100-$125**
Suzette, 1962. 15in (38cm)	**$75-$100**

*For girl scouts, see page 272.

Mary Jane, 1959 on.

32in (81cm)	**$225-$275**
Nurse	**$275-$325**

Little Lady, 1958.

19in (48cm)	**$125-$150**

Fashion Lady, Ca. 1958.

19in (48cm)	**$250**

Most Happy Family, 1958. (Mother, Sister, Brother, Baby.)

Boxed 8-21in (20-53cm)	**$250-$300**

Alyssa, Ca. 1960. 23in (58cm)   **$225**

Bud, Ca. 1960. 24in (61cm) **$200-$225**

Happy Boy, 1961.

10½in (27cm)	**$50-$60**

Half Pint, 1982 on.

11in (28cm) toddler	**$25-$35**

Boudoir Lady, 1961.

30in (76cm) Boxed	**$275**

Dy-Dee Darlin', 1971, 18in (46cm)**$100**

Baby Lisa, 1980, Designed by Astry Campbell. In basket with accessories,

11in (28cm)	**$100**

Disney Dolls, 1977. 14in (36cm)   **$175**

   Alice in Wonderland

   Cinderella

   Snow White

   Sleeping Beauty

   1985, 12in (31cm) Cinderella &

Prince Charming Set	**$95**

Hagara, Jan. 1984., 15in (38cm)

Christina with Teddy	**$125**
Laurel	**$100**

Hibel, Edna, 1984,

Flower Girl of Brittany	**$85**
Contessa Isabella	**$85**

Suzie Sunshine, 1961-1979. Designed by Eugenia Dukas

18in (46cm) boxed	**$110**

Sugar Pie, 1962-1964

18in (46cm) boxed	**$125**

Effanbee Club Limited Edition Dolls:

1975 **Precious Baby**	**$200-$300**
1976 **Patsy**	**$200-$225**
1977 **Dewees Cochran**	**$75-$100**

14in (36cm) *Tintair Honey,* all original and boxed. *H & J Foulke, Inc.*

30in (76cm) *Boudoir Lady,* all original. *H & J Foulke, Inc.*

12in (31cm) *Sister,* all original. *H & J Foulke, Inc.*

20in (51cm) *Charlie McCarthey*, all original. *H & J Foulke, Inc.*

14in (36cm) Historical Doll *Monroe Doctrine 1816,* all original. *H & J Foulke, Inc.*

1978 Crowning Glory	$750-$60
1979 Skippy	$200-$225
1980 Susan B. Anthony	$60-$65
1981 Girl with Watering Can	$65-$75
1982 Princess Diana	$100-$125
1983 Sherlock Holmes	$75-$85
1984 Bubbles	$55-$65
1985 Red Boy	$55-$60
1986 China Head	$25-$35

Legend Series: Mint-in-box.

W.C. Fields, 1980	$200
John Wayne, (cowboy), 1981	$250
John Wayne, (cavalry), 1982	$250
Mae West, 1982	$95
Groucho Marx, 1983	$95
Judy Garland, 1984	$125
Lucille Ball, 1985	$125
Liberace, 1986	$250
James Gagney, 1987	$65
Humphrey Bogart, 1988	$65

George Burns, 1996	**$50-$60**
Gracie Allen, 1996	**$50-$60**
Carol Channing	**$50**

Presidents: Mint-in-box.

Abraham Lincoln, 1983	**$75**
George Washington, 1983	**$75**
Teddy Roosevelt	**$95**
Franklin D. Roosevelt	**$75**

Personalities: Mint-in-box.

Mark Twain, 1984	**$60**
Louis Armstrong, 1984-5	**$95**
Sir Winston Churchill, 1984	**$75**
Eleanor Roosevelt	**$75**
Babe Ruth	**$200**

Pride of the South: 1981-1983.

13in (33cm) mint-in-box	**$50-$60**

Grande Dames: 1976-1983.

15in (38cm) mint-in-box	**$50-$60**

Gigi: 1979-1980.

11in (28cm) mint-in-box	**$40**

International & Storybook: 1976 on.

11in (28cm) mint-in-box	**$20-$30**
Wizard of Oz, 1994,	
6 dolls, set	**$125**
Mary Poppins, 1985	**$35-$40**
Heidi, 1984	**$40-$50**
Peter Pan, 1994.	
3 dolls, set	**$50**

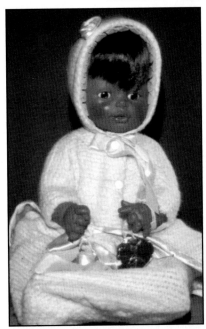

18in (46cm) *Dy-Dee Darlin'*, all original. *Kathy & Terri's Dolls.*

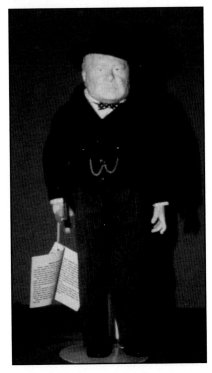

15in (38cm) *Sir Winston Churchill,* all original. *McMasters Doll Auctions.*

FREUNDLICH

15in (38cm) *WAAC*, all original. *H & J Foulke, Inc.*

General Douglas MacArthur: Ca. 1942. All-composition portrait doll, molded hat, original khaki uniform; all in good condition.
Mark: Cardboard tag:
   "General MacArthur"
   18in (46cm)   **$450-$500**

Military Dolls: Ca. 1942. All-composition with molded hats; original clothes. Soldier, Sailor, WAAC, and WAVE, all in good condition.
   15in (38cm)   **$275-300**

Baby Sandy: 1939-1942. All-composition; appropriate clothes; all in good condition.
   8in (20cm)   **$200-$225**
   12in (31cm)   **$300-$350**
   14-15in (36-38cm)   **$450-$500**
   20in (51cm) boxed   **$850**

Other Composition Dolls:
Orphan Annie & Sandy,
   12in (30cm) pair with tags   **$575**
Red Ridinghood, Wolf &
Grandmother Set, all original
   9in (23cm)   **$650-$750**
Dionne Quints and
   Nurse Set, all original   **$650-$750**
Dummy Dan, 15in (38cm)   **$125**
Goo Goo Eva and others,
   20in (51cm)   **$90-$110**
Goo Goo Topsy (black),
   20in (51cm)   **$110-$135**
Wolf, 11in (28cm) naked   **$250-$350**

FACTS
Freundlich Novelty Corp., New York, N.Y., U.S.A. 1923-on.

11in (28cm) Wolf. *H & J Foulke, Inc.*

G.I. JOE®

G.I. Joe Action Soldiers. *Courtesy of McMasters Doll Auctions.*

Action Soldiers of the World, French Resistance Fighter. *Courtesy of McMasters Doll Auctions.*

Marked G.I. Joe: Molded and painted hair and features, scar* on right cheek; fully-jointed body; complete original outfit; all in perfect condition. Dolls less than perfect sell for considerably less.

*All **G.I. Joe** dolls have a scar on the right cheek except **Foreign** dolls and the **Nurse**.

Action Soldier, all original, boxed	**$285-$300**
Action Sailor (painted hair), boxed	**$450**
Action Marine, boxed	**$350**
Action Pilot, boxed	**$600**
Action Soldier Black (painted hair), boxed	**$1,500**

Naked Dolls:

Action Soldier (painted hair)	**$95**
Adventure Team (flocked hair*)	**$75**
Adventure Team (flocked hair and beard*)	**$70**
Black Action Soldier (painted hair)	**$400 up**

*Hair must be in excellent condition.

Action Soldiers of the World (painted hair, no scars):

German Soldier,	
boxed, large box	**$1,200**
boxed, small box	**$600**
dressed doll only, no accessories	**$225-$250**
Russian Infantry Man:	
boxed, large box	**$1,200**
boxed, small box	**$600**
dressed doll only, no accessories	**$225-$250**

FACTS

Hasbro (Hassenfeld Brothers, Inc.) Pawtucket, RI, U.S.A. 1964 - 1979. Hard plastic and vinyl. 12in (31cm) fully-jointed.
Mark: G.I. Joe   After 1967 added: Copyright 1964   Pat. No. 3,277,602
By Hasbro
Patent Pending
Made in U.S.A.

British Commando:

boxed, large box	**$1,250**
boxed, small box	**$500**
dressed doll only,	
no accessories	**$200-$225**

French Resistance Fighter:

boxed, large box	**$900**
boxed, small box	**$500**
dressed doll only,	
no accessories	**$200-$225**

Australian Jungle Fighter:

boxed, large box	**$750**
boxed, small box	**$400**
dressed doll only,	
no accessories	**$150-$175**

Japanese Imperial Soldier (unique model used only for this type):

boxed, large box	**$1,300**
boxed, small box	**$800**
dressed doll only,	
no accessories	**$275-$300**

Talking Action Soldier, boxed	**$400**
Talking Action Sailor, boxed	**$575**
Talking Action Marine, boxed	**$475**
Talking Action Pilot, boxed	**$800**

Nurse Action Girl, boxed	**$3,000**
dressed doll only	**$1,200**
naked doll	**$350**
Adventurer (lifelike hair) Black,	
boxed	**$300**
Man of Action (lifelike hair),	
boxed	**$250**

Man of Action with Kung-Fu Grip (lifelike hair), boxed **$225**

Talking Man of Action (lifelike hair), boxed **$225-$250**

Land Adventurer (lifelike hair and beard), boxed **$185-$200**

Air Adventurer (lifelike hair and beard), boxed **$240-$265**

Sea Adventurer (lifelike hair and beard), boxed **$225-$250**

Talking Astronaut (lifelike hair),

boxed	**$400-$425**
dressed doll	**$275-$300**

Accessories:

Footlocker, green	**$40**
Space Capsule, boxed	**$350**
Five Star Jeep, boxed	**$500**
Desert Patrol Jeep, boxed	**$1,900**
Motorcycle, boxed	**$250**

Outfits in unopened packages:

#7532 Green Beret Special Forces	**$600**
#7521 Military Police (brown)	**$400**
#7521 Military Police (aqua)	**$1350**
#7531 Ski Patrol	**$250**
#7620 Deep Sea Diver	**$300**
#7710 Dress Parade Set	**$225**
#7824 Astronaut Suit	**$250**
#7537 West Point Cadet	**$1,500**
#7624 Annapolis Cadet	**$1,400**
#7822 Air Cadet	**$1,400**
#7612 Shore Patrol	**$300**
#7807 Scramble Set	**$275**

G.I. Joe Land Adventurer and *Talking G.I. Joe. Courtesy of McMasters Doll Auctions.*

GINNY-TYPE DOLLS*

Prices are for dolls in excellent overall condition with perfect hair, pretty coloring and original outfits. All dolls are hard plastic and about 7-8in (18-20cm) tall.

A & H Doll Mfg. Corp.

Gigi	**$45-$50**
Boxed doll	**$85**
Outfits	**$10-$15**
Boxed outfits	**$25**
Julie	**$35-$35**

Doll Bodies, Inc.

Mary Lu	**$40-$50**

Fortune Doll Co.

Pam	**$60-$65**
Outfits	**$10-$15**
Boxed Outfits	**$25**
Pam Ballerina (pointed toes)	**$80-$85**
Ninette	**$40-$50**

Hollywood Doll Mfg. Co.

Girl	**$40-$45**
Rock-a-Bye Baby, boxed	**$50-$60**

Virga *Lolly-Pop* with blue hair, all original. *Terri & Kathy's Dolls.*

Stashin Doll Co.

Andrea, molded white strap shoes	**$50-$60**

**Virga (Beechler Arts), molded
    white strap shoes**

Lolly-Pop colored hair	**$60-$80**
Boxed	**$95-$110**
Lucy	**$60-$65**
Play-Mates	**$60-$65**
Boxed	**$95-$110**
Schiaparelli (GoGo)	**$100-$125**

*See separate entries for Cosmopolitan **Ginger**, Vogue **Ginny**, Nancy Ann Storybook **Muffie**, and Alexander **Wendy**.

Virga *Play-Mates*, all original and boxed. *H & J Foulke, Inc.*

GIRL SCOUT

Prices are for dolls in excellent overall condition with perfect hair and original clothes, including hat, scarf, belt, shoes and socks.

Georgene Novelties, Inc., all cloth, 1930s and 1940s.
Girl Scouts and Brownies
    Flat face, 15in (38cm) **$350-$400**
    Molded cloth face, 13in (33cm) **$250**
    Molded plastic face, 13in (33cm)**$100**

Terri Lee Sales Corp., hard plastic. Ca. 1950.
Girl Scouts and Brownies
    Terri Lee, 16in (41cm) **$400-$450**
    Dress and hat only **$90**
    Tiny Terri Lee,
      10in (25cm) **$200-$225**
    Ginger, 8in (20cm) **$175-$225**

Vogue Dolls, Inc., hard plastic. Ca. 1956.
Girl Scouts and Brownies
    Ginny, painted lash walker,

8in (20cm) **$275-$325**
Outfit only **$125**
80th Anniversary, 8in (20cm)
    boxed **$100**
    Black, boxed **$125**

Uneeda Doll Co., vinyl head/ hard plastic body, "U" on head. Ca. 1960.
    Janie, 8in (20cm) **$125-$150**
    Carry Case **$100**

Effanbee Doll Co., vinyl, Ca. 1960 through 1970s
    Patsy Ann, 15in (38cm)
      Girl Scout **$350-$400**
      Brownie **$500**
      Blue Bird, Camp Fire **$550****
    Suzette, 15in (38cm)
      Girl Scout **$500 up**
      Brownie **$500 up**
      Blue Bird, Camp Fire **$550****
    Fluffy, 8in (20cm)
      Girl Scout, Brownie **$125-$150**
      Boxed **$175**
      Camp Fire, Blue Bird **$175**
      Camp outfit or bathing suit sold
        separately **$50-$75**
    Punkin, 11in (28cm)
      Girl Scout, Brownie **$125-$135**
      Camp Fire, Blue Bird **$150-$175**

Jesco, Inc., vinyl. Ca. 1985
    Katie, 9in (23cm) **$75-$85**

Madame Alexander, hard plastic. 1992.
    8in (20cm) **$100-$125**
      (blonde harder to find)

8in (20cm) Uneeda *Janie* with carry case. *H & J Foulke, Inc.*

GODEY'S LITTLE LADY DOLLS

7in (18cm) #220P *Little Miss Debutante in Luncheon Party Dress,* all original. *H & J Foulke, Inc.*

Ruth Gibbs Doll: Pink or white china head; cloth body with china limbs and painted slippers; original clothes.

7in (18cm)	**$90-$110**
7in (18cm) boxed	**$150-$165**
Black, boxed	**$300-$350****
10in (25cm) skin wig	**$295**
12in (31cm) original underclothes	**$145-$160**
12in (31cm) boxed	**$215-$235**
Little Women, set of 5	**$850**
Trousseau, boxed set (4 outfits)	**$575**
Fairy Tale, boxed	**$575**

**Not enough price samples to compute a reliable average.

FACTS
Ruth Gibbs, Flemington, N.J., U.S.A. 1946.
Designer: Herbert Johnson.
Mark: Paper label inside skirt
"Godey's Little Lady Dolls;" "R.G."
incised on back plate.

HALLMARK

Tagged Hallmark Cloth doll: Printed on cloth with an article of separate clothing, usually a coat or skirt, stitch-jointed shoulders, hips and knees, shaped shoes and hats. All original and excellent.
6½-7½in (17-19cm)
1976 Bicentennial Commemorative Series: George Washington, Martha Washington, Betsy Ross, Benjamin Franklin, boxed   **$45-$50 each**
1979 Series I: Amelia Earhart, Annie Oakley, G. W. Carver, Chief Joseph, Babe Ruth, Susan B. Anthony,
boxed   **$15-$18**
Holiday Dolls: Little Drummer Boy, Santa Claus, Winifred Witch, Indian Maiden, boxed   **$16-$18**
Series II: Davy Crockett, Molly Pitcher, Mark Twain, P. T. Barnum, Clara Barton, never had boxes   **$6-$8**
Juliette Low (founder of the
Girl Scouts)   **$65-$75**

FACTS
Hallmark Cards, Inc., Kansas City, MO.
1976-1979.
Mark: Cloth label on each doll

Santa Claus with original box. *H & J Foulke, Inc.*

HARD PLASTIC DOLLS

17in (43cm) unmarked bride, all original. *H & J Foulke, Inc.*

10in (25cm) Block Doll Corp. *Answer Doll,* all original. *Kathy & Terri's Dolls.*

Marked "Made in U.S.A." or with various letters: Ca. 1950s. All hard plastic; sleep eyes; perfect wig; original cloths; all in excellent condition with very good coloring.

Alexander-type

14in (36cm)	**$225-$250**
18in (46cm)	**$275-$300**
24in (61cm)	**$300-$325**

Miscellaneous Specific Dolls: All original clothes including underwear, shoes and socks; excellent condition with lovely complexion and perfect hair; unmarked except as indicated.

Answer Doll, 1951. Block Doll Corp.; toddler with yes/no button,

10in (25cm)	**$75**

Baby Walker, 1950s. Block Doll Corp.; toddler, 10in (25cm) **$55-$65**

Duchess Doll Corp., 1950s. Slender storybook and fashion dolls in various costumes.

Marked on back, 7-8in (18-20cm)**$8-$10**

Walt Disney's **Peter Pan** and

Tinkerbelle	**$20-$25 each**
boxed	**$95-$100**

Gigi Perrau, 1952, Goldberger Doll Mfg. Co.; portrait doll of the movie star with smiling mouth and teeth, dynel hair, hard plastic body, vinyl head, excellent face color,

20in (51cm)	**$600 up****

Haleoke, 1950s. Roberta Doll Col. 18in (46cm), with accessories and additional clothing. **$450**

Heddi Stroller, 1952. Belle Doll & Toy Corp.; walker, saran braids,

20in (51cm)	**$165-$195**

Hollywood Doll Mfg. Co., 1947 on. Storybook and fashion dolls in various costumes; marked on back,

4½-5½in (12-14cm), boxed	**$25-$35**
Rockaby Baby, boxed	**$50-$60**

LuAnn Simms, 1953. Roberta, Horsman & Valentine; **Mark:** "Made in U.S.A." or "180", walker, 14in(36cm) **$250-$300**

Marion, 1949. Monica Studios; rooted hair, sleep eyes, 18in (46cm) **$400****

Mary Jane, 1955. G.H.&E. Freydberg, Inc. Terri Lee-type doll,
17in (43cm) **$275-$300**

Miss Gadabout, 1950s. Artisan Doll Co., **Mark:** "Heady Turny" label; walker,
20in (51cm) **$165-$195**

Paris Doll Co. 1951.
Rita, walker. 29in (74cm) **$250**
24in (61cm) child walker, boxed **$175**

Raving Beauty, 1953. Artisan Doll Co. Tag on some clothing: "Original Michelle//California." Separate clothing was available. Open mouth, walker,
20in (51cm) **$325-$350**

Susan Stroller, 1953, Goldberger Doll Mfg. Co.
Mark: "Eegee." Walker, saran hair,
23in (58cm) **$165-$195**

Wanda the Walking Wonder, 1950s. Advance Doll Co.,
17-19in (43-48cm) **$150-$200**

**Very few price samples available for comparison.

Italian Hard Plastic: Ca. 1950 on. Bonomi, Ottolini, Ratti, Furga, Magda and others. **Mark:** usually on head. Heavy, fine quality hard plastic, human hair wig, sleep eyes, sometimes flirty; original clothes; all in excellent condition.
12in (31cm)	**$125**
15-17in (38-43cm)	**$150-$200**
19-21in (48-53cm)	**$225-$250**
25in (64cm) fashion	**$275**

English Black Hard Plastic Characters: 1950s. Pedigree and others. Curly black wig sometimes over molded hair.
16in (41cm)	**$150-$175**
21in (53cm)	**$225-$275**

17in (43cm) Magda *Liliana,* all original. *H & J Foulke, Inc.*

23in (58cm) Impo walker, all original. *H & J Foulke, Inc.*

HASBRO

Little Miss No Name, 1965. Large round eyes, molded tear, forlorn expression, original ragged clothes; all in excellent condition.

15in (38cm)	**$90-$110**
boxed	**$200-$250**

Aimee, 1972. All vinyl; original clothing; all in excellent condition **$45-$55**

Charlie's Angels, 1977. Gift Set,

Boxed	**$195**

Jem Series, 1986-1987. All-vinyl fashion dolls; original clothing; all in excellent condition, in original box. Deduct one-third for an out-of-box doll.

12½in (32cm)

Jem	**$25-$35**
Kimber	**$35-$45**
Aja	**$45-$50**
Roxy	**$45**
Pizazz	**$55-$60**
Stormer	**$35-$45**
Rio	**$25-$30**
Boxed outfits	**$25-$30**

G.I. Joe: See page 269.

Raggedy Ann: See page 170.

Charlie's Angels Gift Set, boxed.
Rosemary Kanizer.

HIMSTEDT

Marked Himstedt Doll: Hard vinyl head swivels on long shoulder plate, cloth lower torso, vinyl arms and curved legs; inset eyes with real eyelashes, painted feathered eyebrows, molded upper eyelids, open nose, human hair wig; original cotton clothing, bare feet. All in excellent condition with original box and certificate.

Barefoot Children, 1986. 26in (66cm)

Ellen	**$700-$800**
Kathe	**$700-$800**
Paula	**$600-$650**
Fatou	**$900-$1,000**
Lisa	**$650-$700**

American Heartland Dolls, 1987.
19-20in (48-51cm)

Timi and **Toni**	**$400-$450 each**

The World Children Collection, 1988.
31in (79cm)

Kasimir	**$1,500-$1,600**
Malin	**$1,200-$1,400**
Michiko	**$1,000-$1,200**
Frederike	**$1,200-$1,400**
Makimura	**$900-$1,000**

FACTS

1986 on. Hard vinyl and cloth.
Designer: Annette Himstedt
Distributor: Mattel, Inc., Hawthorne, CA., U.S.A. Dolls made in Spain.
Mark: Wrist tag with doll's name; cloth signature label on clothes; signature on lower back plate and on back of doll's head under wig.

Reflections of Youth, 1989. 26in (66cm)

Adrienne	**$750-$850**
Janka	**$750 -$850**
Ayoka	**$800-$900**
Kai	**$750-$850**

1990:

Fiene	**$650-$750**
Taki (baby)	**$900-$1,000**
Annchen (baby)	**$550-$650**

1991:

Liliane	**$850-$950**
Neblina	**$950-$1,050**
Tinka	**$1,000-$1,100**
Freeke & Bibbi	
(club doll)	**$900-$1,000**

1993:

Kima	**$500-$550**
Lona	**$500-$550**
Tara	**$550-$600**
Jule	**$850-$950**

1994:

Panchita, Pancho, Melvin,	
Elke	**$450-$500**

1998:

Baby Leischen (club doll)	**$500-$600**

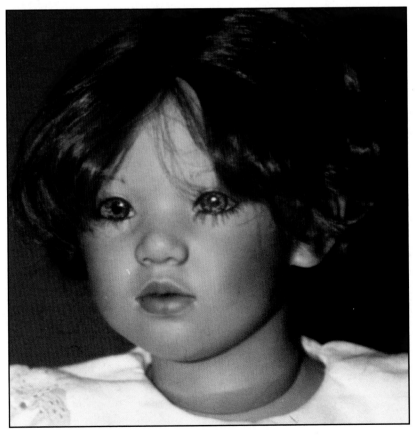

Liliane, all original. *Jensen's Antique Dolls.*

HORSMAN

Early Composition Dolls: Original or appropriate old clothes; all in good condition.

Billiken: 1909. Composition head, velvet or plush body. **Mark:** cloth label.

12in (31cm)	**$350-$400**

"Can't Break 'Em" Characters: Ca. 1911. Character head, hard stuffed cloth body. **Mark:** "E.I.H. 1911".

11-13in (28-33cm)	**$200 up**
Polly Pru, 13in (33cm)	**$350-$375****

Little Mary Mix-Up,

15in (31cm)	**$350-$375****

Cotton Joe, black,

13in (33cm)	**$425-$475**

Uncle Sam's Kid, 1917, Composition/cloth. All original.

16in (41cm)	**$400-$450**
Baby Bumps	**$250**
Black	**$300**

Puppy & Pussy Pippin: 1911. Grace G. Drayton. Plush body, composition head, cloth label.

8in (20cm) sitting.

Puppy Pippin	**$400-$450****
Pussy Pippin	**$500-$600****

Peek-a-Boo: 1913-1915. Grace G. Drayton. Composition head, arms, legs and lower torso, cloth upper torso. **Mark:** cloth label on outfit.

7½in (19cm)	**$150-$175**

Baby Butterfly: 1911-1913. Oriental doll, composition head, cloth body, original costume.

13in (33cm)	**$500****

Peterkin: 1914-1930. All-composition, various boy and girl clothing or simply a large bow.

11in (28cm)	**$325-$375**

Gene Carr Characters: 1916. Composition/cloth. **Snowball** (black boy); **Mike** and **Jane** (eyes open); **Blink** and **Skinney** (eyes closed). Designed by Bernard Lipfert from Gene Carr's cartoon characters.

13-14in (33-36cm)	**$325-$375**
Black Snowball	**$450-$550**

Jackie Coogan: 1921. Composition/cloth; appropriate old clothes.

14in (36cm)	**$550-$600**

HEbee-SHEbee: 1925. All-composition; blue shoes indicate a **HEbee**; and pink ones a **SHEbee**.

11in (28cm	**$600-$650**
Fair condition, some peeling	**$325-$375**
Mint, all original	**$800-$900**

All Bisque. See page 23.

**Not enough price samples to compute a reliable average.

FACTS

E.I. Horsman Co., New York, NY. Manufacturer; also distributor of French and German dolls. 1878-on.

13in (33cm) Gene Carr *Mike*, all original with label. *H & J Foulke, Inc.*

Ella Cinders: 1925. Composition/cloth. From the comic strip by Bill Conselman and Charlie Plumb for Metropolitan Newspaper Service.
Mark: "1925©MNS."
 18in (46cm) **$650-$750**
Baby Dimples: 1928. Composition/cloth; appropriate old clothes.
Mark: ©
 E.I.H. CO. INC.
 16-18in (41-46cm) **$275-$325**
 22-24in (56-61cm) **$400-$450**
 19in (48cm) with trunk and extensive wardrobe and accessories **$600**
Mama Dolls: late 1920s on. Composition/cloth.
Mark: HORSMAN or E.I.H. CO. INC.
 Babies, including **Brother** and **Sister**
 12-14in (31-36cm) **$175-$200**
 18-20in (46-51cm) **$275-$300**
 Girls, including **Rosebud** and **Peggy Ann**
 14-16in (36-41cm) **$250-$275**
 22-24in (56-61cm) **$325-$375**

Tynie Baby: 1924. Slightly frowning face; cloth/composition; appropriate clothes. Designed by Bernard Lipfert.
Mark: © 1924
 E.I. Horsman Inc.
 Made in
 Germany
 Bisque head,
 8½–9½in (22-24cm) h.c. **$550-$650**
 11-12in (28-31cm) h.c. **$750-$850**
 Composition head,
 15in (38cm) long **$300-$325**
 19in (48cm) **$400-$425**
 All-bisque, swivel neck, glass eyes, wigged or molded hair.
 8-10in (20-25cm) **$2,200-$2,500**
 Vinyl, 1950. 15in (38cm),
 boxed **$90-$110**

All Composition Child Dolls: 1930s and 1940s. Original clothes; all in very good

9½in (24cm) all-bisque *Tynie Baby. H & J Foulke, Inc.*

25in (64cm) *Jackie*, all original. *H & J Foulke, Inc.*

condition; may have "Gold Metal Doll" tag.

Mark: "HORSMAN"

13-14in (33-36cm)	**$225-$250**
16-18in (41-46cm)	**$275-$325**
15in (38cm) boxed	**$375**

Chubby toddler,

16-18in (41-46cm)	**$300-$350**

Jo-Jo, 1937. (See photograph on page 278.)

12in (31cm)	**$275-$300**
Jeanne, 1937. 14in (36cm)	**$300**

Naughty Sue, 1937.

16in (41cm)	**$425-$475**
Roberta, 1937. 16in (41cm)	**$425-$475**

Bright Star, 1940.

17-20in (43-51cm)	**$450-$500**

All-Hard Plastic Dolls: 1950s. Original clothing; perfect hair; good coloring; all in excellent condition.

Cindy: 1950-1955. Open mouth with teeth and tongue, synthetic wig, walker body. **Mark:** "160, 170 or 180 Made in U.S.A."

16-18in (41-46cm)	**$250-$300**

LuAnn Simms: Ca. 1953. Long brunette wig with front and side hair pulled to back, blue eyes. Mold number **180** or **170**.

18in (46cm)	**$350-$400**

Vinyl Dolls: Original clothing; all in excellent condition with perfect hair and excellent color.

Rene Ballerina, 1957. Fully jointed with high-heeled feet, rooted hair.

Mark: "82//HORSMAN"

19in (48cm)	**$150-$165**

20in (51cm) mama doll, all original.
H & J Foulke, Inc.

15in (38cm) pigtail girl, all original.
H & J Foulke, Inc.

Cindy, 1957. Fashion Doll.
19in (21cm) **$200-$225**
Cindy Strutter. Child.
23in (58cm) boxed **$135**
Tweedie, 1958. Slender limbs, short hair.
Mark: "38 Horsman."
14½in (37cm) **$50-$100***
Couturier Doll, 1958. Fashion doll with
stuffed vinyl body.
20in (51cm) boxed **$225-$250**

Jackie Kennedy, 1961. Rooted black
hair, blue sleep eyes, pearl jewelry.
Mark: "HORSMAN//19 © 61//JK25."
25in (64cm) **$165-$185**
Poor Pitiful Pearl, 1963. Cartoon character.
Mark: "1963//Wm Steig//Horsman"
11-12in (28-31cm) **$95-$100**
boxed **$195**
16in (41cm) **$150**
boxed **$250**
Hansel & Gretel, 1963. Character faces.
Mark: Michael Meyerberg, Inc.
15in (38cm) **$200-$225**
Walt Disney's Cinderella Set. 1965.
Extra head and costume for "poor" doll.
Mark: "H"
11½in (29cm), boxed **$150-$165**
Mary Poppins: 1964. Several different
costumes.
12in (31cm) **$30-$40**
boxed set with 7in (18cm) **Jane** and
Michael **$150-$165**
Flying Nun: 1965. 12in (31cm) **$95**
boxed **$175-$185**
Patty Duke: 1965. Gray flannel pants, red
sweater, 12in (31cm) **$85**
boxed **$150-$175**
Elizabeth Taylor: 1976.
11½in (29cm) **$55**
Angie Dickinson, Police Woman: 1970s.
9in (23cm) boxed **$38**

MARY HOYER

Marked Mary Hoyer: Original tagged
factory clothes or garments made at home
from Mary Hoyer patterns; all in excellent
condition.
Composition: 14in (36cm) **$350-$450**
Hard plastic:
14in (36cm)
In knit outfit **$400-$425**
In tagged Hoyer outfit **$425-$525**
In tagged gown **$500-$600**
14in (36cm) boy with
caracul wig **$500-$550**
18in (46cm), **Gigi**
In tagged dresses **$1,600**
In tagged gowns **$1,600-$2,000**
Vinyl: Playdoll,
14in (36cm) **$95-$110**

FACTS
The Mary Hoyer Doll Mfg. Co.,
Reading Pa., U.S.A. Ca. 1925-on.
Mark: Embossed on torso:
"The Mary Hoyer Doll"
or in a circle:
"ORIGINAL
Mary Hoyer Doll"

14in (36cm)
hard plastic
Mary Hoyer,
all original
and boxed.
*H & J Foulke,
Inc.*

IDEAL

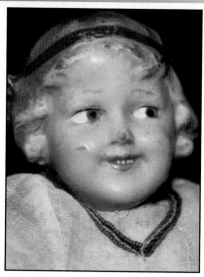

11in (28cm) *Naughty Marietta. Jensen's Antique Dolls.*

18in (46cm) *Peter Pan*, all original with tag. *H & J Foulke, Inc.*

Early Composition Dolls: 1910-1929. Composition heads, cloth bodies, composition lower arms, some with molded composition shoes; original or appropriate old clothes; all in good condition, some wear acceptable.

Head Mark:

Happy Hooligan: 1910. Comic character,
21in (53cm)   **$500****
Snookums: 1910. Plush body.
14in (36cm)   **$600**
Ty Cobb: 1911. Baseball outfit **$500****
Naughty Marietta (Coquette): 1912.
Molded hair with ribbon
band   **$350-$400**
Captain Jenks: 1912.
Khaki uniform   **$275-$325**
Uneeda Kid: 1914-1919. Molded black
boots; original bloomer suit, yellow
slicker and rain hat, carrying a box of
Uneeda Biscuits, showing some wear.
16in (41cm)   **$475-$500**
24in (61cm)   **$650-$700****
Bronco Bill: 1915. Cowboy outfit with
gun and holster   **$325**
ZuZu Kid: 1916-1917. Original clown
suit. National Biscuit Co.
16in (41cm)   **$400-$450**
Liberty Boy: 1917. Molded clothes,
cloth hat; some wear.
12in (31cm)   **$350-$375**
Soozie Smiles: 1923. Two faces, crying
and smiling   **$400-$425**
**Not enough price samples to compute a reliable average.

FACTS
Ideal Novelty & Toy Co., Brooklyn, NY. 1907-on.

Flossie Flirt: 1924-1931. Eyes move side to side.

14in (36cm)	**$225-$250**
20in (51cm)	**$300-$350**

Buster Brown: 1929. Red suit with hat,

17in (43cm)	**$325-$375**

Peter Pan: 1929. Original felt suit and hat, 18in (46cm).

Excellent with label	**$550-$600**
Good, some wear	**$300-$400**

Early Children:

12-15in (31-38cm)	**$225-$250**

Early Babies: Baby Mine, Prize Baby, etc. 15-16in (38-41cm) **$225**

Composition Babies: 1930s and 1940s. Composition heads and lower limbs, cloth bodies; original or appropriate clothes; all in good condition with nice coloring; light crazing acceptable.

Tickletoes: 1930-1947. Soft rubber arms and legs, flirty eyes.

16in (41cm)	**$325-$375**

Baby Smiles: 1931. Toddler with rubber arms. 17in (43cm) **$250-$275**

Snoozie: 1933. Designed by Bernard Lipfert; yawning mouth, may have rubber arms.

Mark: ©

By B. LIPFERT

16-20in (41-51cm)	**$350-$400**

Cuddles: 1933. Rubber limbs.

22in (56cm)	**$350-$400**

Bathrobe Baby: 1933. Rubber body.

12in (31cm)	**$100-$125**

Princess Beatrix: 1938. Magic eyes.

16in (41cm)	**$250-$300**
22in (56cm)	**$350-$400**

Betsy Wetsy: 1937-on. Drink and wet baby. **Head Mark:** IDEAL

Composition or hard rubber head/rubber body,

14-16in (36-41cm)	**$160-$185**

Hard plastic head/rubber body,

12-14in (31-36cm)	**$110-$135**

21in (51-53cm) *Judy Garland* in gown from MGM motion picture *Strike up the Band. Courtesy of Edward R. Pardella.*

13in (33cm) *Little Princess*, all original. *H & J Foulke, Inc.*

25in (63cm) *Deanna Durbin,* all original. *H & J Foulke, Inc.*

15½in (39cm) *Pigtail Sally,* all original. *H & J Foulke, Inc.*

Boxed with layette,
early vinyl body **$475**
All vinyl, 12in (31cm) **$55-$65**

Composition Children: 1935-1947. All composition in excellent condition with perfect hair and good cheek color; original clothes.

Shirley Temple: 1935. See page 302.

Snow White: 1937. Black wig, gown with rayon skirt showing figures of 7 dwarfs.

Torso Mark: SHIRLEY TEMPLE

Dress tag: An Ideal Doll

11-13in (28-33cm)	**$500-$550**
18in (46cm)	**$650-$750**
All cloth, 16in (41cm)	**$525-$575**
Mint-in-box	**$750**

Deanna Durbin: 1938. Smiling mouth with teeth. Metal button with picture.

Head Mark: Deanna Durbin
Ideal Doll, USA

14in (36cm)	**$650-$750**
20-21in (51-53cm)	**$1,000-$1,200**
24in (61cm)	**$1,500-$1,600**
21in (53cm) mint-in-box	**$1,700**

Judy Garland as Dorothy from *The Wizard of Oz:* 1939.

Head Mark: IDEAL DOLL
MADE IN USA

16in (41cm)	**$1,500-$1,650**
Replaced clothes	**$1,000-$1,100**

Betty Jane, Little Princess, Pigtail Sally, Ginger, Cinderella: 1935-1947.

14in (36cm)	**$325-$375**
18in (46cm)	**$425-$475**

Soldier: Ca. 1942. Character face; army uniform with jacket and hat.

13in (33cm)	**$325-$375**

Miss Curity: Ca. 1945. Nurse uniform.

18in (46cm)	**$450-$500**

Flexy Dolls: 1938 on. Wire mesh torso, flexible metal cable arms and legs.

12in (31cm).

Baby Snooks (Fanny Brice)	$250-$275
Mortimer Snerd	$250-$275
Soldier	$200-$225
Children	$200-$225

Judy Garland from *Strike up the Band:* 1940. (See photograph on page 283.)

Head Mark: MADE IN U.S.A.

Body Mark: IDEAL DOLL

[backwards 21]

21in (53cm)	$1,000-$1,200

Composition and Wood Segmented Characters: 1940. Label on front torso.

Pinocchio, 10½in (27cm)	$450-$475
20in (51cm)	$800-$900
King Little, 1in (36cm)	$275-$325
Jiminy Cricket, 9in (23cm)	$450-$500
Gabby, 11in (8cm)	$375-$425

Magic Skin Dolls: 1940-on. Stuffed latex rubber body in very good condition (subject to easy deterioration). Original clothes; all in excellent condition.

Head Mark: IDEAL

Magic Skin Baby: 1940.

14-15in (36-38cm)	$95-$110
Plassie: 1940. 16in (41cm)	$95-$110
Toddler, all-hard plastic, 14in (36cm)	$150-$175

Sparkle Plenty, 1947.

15in (38cm) Baby	$160-$185
Toddler	$150-$175

Joan Palooka, 1953.

14in (36cm)	$125-$135

Baby Coos: 1948-1952. Sounds like a baby when squeezed.

14-16in (36-41cm)	$110-$135

Brother or Sister Coos:

25-30in (64-76cm), dressed like toddlers	$200-$300

14in (36cm) *Toni,* all original. *H & J Foulke, Inc.*

21in (53cm) *Harriet Hubbard Ayer,* all original. *H & J Foulke, Inc.*

Toni Family: 1948-on. Hard plastic "Toni" home permanent doll and derivatives, nylon wig, original clothes, perfect hair, pretty cheek color; all in excellent condition.

Head Mark: IDEAL DOLL
Body Mark: IDEAL DOLL
P-90
Made in USA

Toni:

14-16in (36-41cm)	
P-90 & P-91	**$400**
Naked, untidy hair	**$70-$80**
Mint-in-box	**$550-$650**
19-21in (48-53cm)	
P-92 & P-93	**$600-$650**
22½in(57cm) P-94	**$950****
Playwave Box and contents	**$75**

Mary Hartline:

14in (36cm)	**$400**
22½in (57cm)	**$850****
Mint-in-box with accessories,	
16in (41cm)	**$700**

Harriet Hubbard Ayer: Vinyl head make-up doll.

14in (36cm)	**$200-$225**
21in (53cm)	**$400-$450****
Mint-in-box with accessories	**$400-$450**

Miss Curity: Nurse.

14in (36cm)	**$400**
Mint-in-box with accessories	**$650**

Sara Ann: Saran hair,

14in (36cm)	**$400**
21in (53cm) Bride	**$600****

Saucy Walker: 1951-1955. All-hard plastic with walking mechanism; original clothes, excellent hair and cheek color.

Mark: IDEAL DOLL

16-17in (41-43cm)	**$125-$150**
20-22in (51-56cm)	**$175-$200**
Mint-in-box	**$350-$400**

Posie: 1954-1956. Vinyl head

17in (43cm)	**$185-$210**

Saralee: 1950. Black vinyl/cloth body. Designed by Sarah Lee Creech; modeled by Sheila Burlingame. Original clothes; excellent condition.

17-18in (43-46cm)	**$300-$350**
Undressed	**$125**

Bonny Braids: 1951. Vinyl character head; hard plastic body; original clothes; excellent condition.

13in (33cm)	**$150-$200**
Mint in comic strip box	**$400**

Revlon Dolls: 1955-1959. Vinyl head, rooted hair; hard plastic body with jointed waist, high-heeled feet; perfect hair, bright cheek color; original clothing, excellent condition.

Miss Revlon,

18-20in (46-51cm)	**$200-$250**
Mint-in-box, dress	**$350 up**
Mint-in-box, gown	**$450 up**

Little Miss Revlon,

10½in (27cm)	**$125-$150**
boxed	**$225-$250**

**Not enough price samples to compute a reliable average.

18in (46cm) *Miss Revlon*, all original. *H & J Foulke, Inc.*

Patti Playpal Family: 1959-1962.

Patti, 35in (89cm)	**$425-$475**
Peter, 38in (97cm)	**$550-$650**
Daddy's Girl, 42in (107cm)	**$1,000-$1,200**
Miss Ideal, 29in (74cm)	**$400-$450**
25in (64cm)	**$375-$400**
Patti, 18in (46cm)	**$350-$450**
Bonnie & Johnny, 24in (61cm) babies	**$225-$250**
Penny, 32in (81cm)	**$275-$300**
Saucy Walker, 28in (71cm)	**$285**
30in (76cm)	**$325**
1982 Patti, mint-in-box	**$100-$125**
Black, mint-in-box	**$225**

Tammy Family: 1962-1966. Mint-in-box; deduct 50% for an out-of-box doll.

Tammy, 12in (31cm)	**$85-$115**
Pos'n Tammy, 12in (31cm)	**$125-$135**
Glamour Misty (Miss Clairol)	**$95-$110**
Ted (big brother), 12½in (32cm)	**$150**
Mom, 12½in (32cm)	**$185**
Dad, 13in (33cm)	**$150**
Pepper (sister), 9in (23cm)	**$75-$85**
Pete (little brother), 7¾in (20cm)	**$200 up**
Patti (Pepper's friend) 9in (23cm)	**$250 up**
Dodi (Pepper's friend) 9in (23cm)	**$85**
Salty (Pepper's friend) 7¾in (20cm)	**$200**
Bud (Tammy's boyfriend) 12½in (32cm)	**$200**
Boxed outfits	**$55-$65**

Miscellaneous Vinyl Dolls. All original, excellent coloring, perfect condition.

Lori Martin (National Velvet), 38in (97cm), 1961	**$750-$800**
Magic Lips, 1955. 24in (61cm)	**$125-$150**
Thumbelina, 1961. Vinyl and cloth; wriggles like a real baby. 14in (36cm)	**$100-$125**
19in (48cm)	**$160-$185**
Mint-in-box, at auction	**$350**

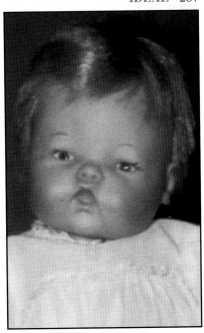

14in (36cm) *Thumbelina,* original dress. *Terri & Kathy's Dolls.*

18in (46cm) *Posie,* all original. *H & J Foulke, Inc.*

Kissy, 1961-1964. Toddler,
22in (56cm) **$90-$110**
Boxed **$135-$150**
Bam Bam, 1963. 12in (31cm)**$45-$50**
16in (41cm) **$60-$75**
Pebbles, 1963. 8in (20cm) **$25-$30**
12in (31cm) **$45-$50**
15in (38cm) boxed **$135**
Betty Big Girl, 1968. 32in (81cm),
boxed **$350**
Little Lost Baby, 1968. Three faces.
22in (56cm) **$95-$110**
Flatsy, 1968-1970. Each with
accessory **$20-$25**
boxed **$40-$50**
Early style,
boxed with frame **$75-$95**
Joey Stivic, 1976. Archie Bunker's
grandson, 15in (38cm) **$65**
Dorothy Hammil, 1977.
11½in (29cm) **$25**
Diana Ross, 17½in (45cm) **$150-$175**
Giggles, 16in (41cm) **$65-$75**
Hopalong Cassidy, 25in (63mc) **$375**

Crissy and Family: 1968-1974. Growing
hair dolls. All original and excellent.
Crissy, Beautiful Crissy **$35-$45**
Black Crissy **$100**
Velvet **$30-$40**
Black Velvet **$65**
Cinnamon **$20-$25**
Mia **$40-$45**
Kerry **$40-$45**
Tressy **$50-$60**
Brandi **$45-$50**
Dina **$45-$50**
Cricket **$20-$25**
Baby Crissy **$55-$65**
Crissy Beauty Parlor, boxed **$50**
Crissy Clothes Rack and Closet Set,
boxed **$65**
Packaged clothes **$15-$40**

Tiffany Taylor, 1974. 19in (48cm) **$35-$40**
Boxed **$55**
Black **$75**

Flatsy Dewie, boxed. *Rosemary Kanizer.*

12½in (32cm) *Tammy's
Mom,* all original.
H & J Foulke, Inc.

KENNER

Dusty, 1974. Smiling face, freckles.

    12in (31cm), boxed **$50-$60**

    Outfits **$25**

Skye, 1974. Black skin. 12in (31cm),

    boxed **$50-$60**

    Outfits **$25**

Cover Girls, 1978-1980. Fashion doll with bendable elbows and knees, jointed wrists. 12in (31cm)

    Darci **$55-$65**

    Erica (auburn) **$150-$175**

    Dana (black skin) **$75-$85**

    Outfits **$30-$40**

Hardy Boys, 1978. Mint-in-box dolls.

Shaun Cassidy, Parker Stevenson **$28**

Star Wars: 1974-1978. Mint-in-box dolls. For excellent out-of-box dolls, deduct 50%.

    Darth Vader, 15in (38cm) **$150-$175**

    Han Solo, 12in (31cm) **$450-$475**

    Luke Skywalker,

      12in (31cm) **$250-$275**

    Princess Leia,

      11½in (29cm) **$175-$225**

    Stormtrooper, 12in (31cm) **$200-$225**

    Obi Wan Kenobi,

      12in (31cm) **$125-$135**

      R2D2, 7½in (19cm) **$165-$185**

      C3PO, 12in (31cm) **$125-$135**

      Boba Fett, 13in (33cm) **$250-$275**

      Jawa, 8½in (22cm) **$90-$100**

      IG88, 15in (38cm) **$550-$650**

      Chewbacca, 15in (38cm) **$150-$160**

      Yoda, 9in (23cm) **$85-$95**

Six Million Dollar Man, 1975-1978.

    13in (33cm) Boxed figures.

      Bigfoot **$55-$65**

      Steve Austin **$65-$85**

      Jaime Summers **$55-$65**

      Bionic Man, at auction **$365**

      Fembot **$165**

      Bionic Woman Classroom Playset,

        at auction **$485**

      Oscar Goldman **$60-$70**

Star Wars Princess Leia, 1977. *George Humphrey.*

Hardy Boys Shaun Cassidy, 1978. *Miriam Blankman.*

KNICKERBOCKER

15in (38cm) *Snow White*, all original.
Rhoda Shoemaker Collection.

9in (23cm) *Dopey,* all original. *Jensen's Antique Dolls.*

FACTS
Knickerbocker Doll & Toy Co.,
New York, N.Y., U.S.A. 1937.
Head Mark:
"WALT DISNEY
KNICKERBOCKER TOY CO."

Composition Snow White: 1937. All-composition; black mohair wig with hair ribbon; original clothing; all in very good condition.

15in (38cm)	**$400-$450**
20in (51cm)	**$550-$650**

With molded black hair and blue ribbon,

13-15in (33-38cm)	**$300-$400**

Set: 15in (38cm) Snow White and seven
9in (23cm) Dwarfs **$2,750**

Composition Seven Dwarfs: All-composition; individual character faces; original velvet costumes and caps with identifying names: Sneezy, Dopey, Grumpy, Doc, Happy, Sleepy and Bashful. Very good condition.

9in (23cm) **$250-$300 each**

Additional composition dolls:
Jiminy Cricket, 10in (25cm) **$450-$550**
Pinocchio, 14in (36cm) **$550-$650**
Mint-in-box, at auction **$1,500**
Blondie, 11in (28cm) all original and boxed, at auction **$1680**
Dagwood, 13in (33cm) **$650-$750**
Alexander, 9in (23cm) **$400-$450**

Additional cloth dolls:
Seven Dwarfs,
14in (36cm) **$250-$275 each**
Snow White, 16in (41cm) **$375-$425**
Donald Duck **$500 up**
Mickey Mouse, 1935 **$500 up**
Two-Gun Mickey, Mint with tag,
at auction **$3,900**
Minnie Mouse **$500 up**

Raggedy Ann &Andy. See page 170.
Little Lulu,
18in (46cm) **$300-$400****
Child Doll, 1935. Mask face (washable), original clothes,
12-14in (31-36cm) **$125-$150**
Little Orphan Annie and Sandy, 1977.
16in (41cm) **$40-$50**
**Not enough price samples to compute a reliable average.

KRUEGER

All-Cloth Doll: Ca. 1930. Mask face; oil cloth body with hinged shoulders and hips; original clothes; in excellent condition.

7in (18cm)	**$50-$60**
12in (31cm)	**$100-$125**
16in (41cm)	**$150-$165**
20in (51cm)	**$200-$225**

Pinocchio: Ca. 1940. Mask character face; cloth torso, wood jointed arms and legs; original clothes, all in good condition.

15in (38cm)	**$400-$450****

Kewpie: See page 130.

Dwarfs: Ca. 1937. All cloth, mask face.

12in (30cm)	**$175-$200**

Scootles: 1935. Rose O'Neill. All cloth, mask face, yarn hair.

10in (25cm)	**$450****
18in (46cm)	**$850****

**Not enough price samples to compute a reliable average.

12in (30cm) *Doc.,* missing glasses. *H & J Foulke, Inc.*

FACTS

Richard G. Krueger, Inc., New York, N.Y., U.S.A. 1917-on.
Mark: Cloth tag or label.

MATTEL

Condition: Unless otherwise indicated, all dolls should be in excellent, unplayed with condition, in original clothes with all accessories, perfect hair, excellent coloring.

Chatty Cathy Family: 1960-1965.

Chatty Cathy,	
20in (51cm)	**$175-$225**
boxed	**$300-$350**
Black	**$600-$800**
Charmin' Chatty,	
25in (64cm)	**$100-$125**
Chatty Baby, 18in (46cm)	**$95-$115**
Tiny Chatty Baby,	
15in (38cm)	**$60-$65**
Tiny Chatty Brother,	
15in (38cm)	**$60-$65**
Singing Chatty,	
17in (43cm)	**$100-$125**

Buffy & Mrs. Beasley: 1967. All vinyl Buffy, vinyl/cloth Mrs. Beasley.

6in (15cm) boxed	**$200**

Mrs. Beasley: Vinyl and cloth, with glasses,

16in (40cm)	**$200-$300**
boxed	**$400-$500**

Skediddles: 1966.

Mint-in-package	**$65-$85**

Star-Spangled Dolls: 1976.

New England Girl, Pioneer Daughter, Southern Belle	**$40-$45**

Sunshine Family, 1977.

Boxed set	**$75**

Guardian Goddesses: 1979.

11½in (29cm)	**$150-$175**

Toddlers and Babies. All original and excellent, unplayed with, in working condition.

Baby Secret, 1966.	
18in (46cm)	**$50-$75**
Baby First Step, 1966.	
18in (46cm)	**$50-$75**

Baby Pataburp, 1964.
    16in (41cm)   **$25-$30**
Baby Tenderlove, 1970-1972.
    Newborn, 13in (33cm)   **$15-$18**
    Living, 20in (51cm)   **$30-$35**
    Brother (sexed), 12in (31cm)**$35-$40**
Cheerful, Tearful, 1966.
    13in (33cm)   **$25-$30**
Dancerina, 1970.
    12in (31cm)   **$25-$30**
    16in (41cm)   **$45-$55**
    24in (61cm)   **$75-$85**
Hi Dottie, 1969. 17in (43cm)   **$25**
Sister Belle, 1961. 17in (43cm) **$65-$75**
Mattie Mattel, 1961. 17in (43cm)**$65-$75**
Timey Tell, 1964. 17in (43cm)
    with watch   **$25-$30**
Tippy Toes, 1967. 17in (43cm) with
    tricycle or horse, good face   **$22**

Dolls from Television Shows: All prices are for mint-in-box or package dolls.
Charlies's Angels, 1978.
    11½in (29cm)   **$50**
Debbie Boone, 1978.
    11½in (29cm)   **$65**
Dick Van Dyke, 1969.
    25in (64cm), talks   **$125**
Donny Osmond, 1978. 12in (31cm) **$35**

Marie Osmond, 1978. 12in (31cm) **$35**
Jimmy Osmond, 1979. 10in (25cm) **$45**
Grizzly Adams, 1971. 10in (25cm) **$40**
Herman Munster, 1965.
    Hand puppet   **$125**
    Full body   **$225**
How the West Was Won, 1971.
    10in (25cm)   **$30 each**
Welcome Back Kotter, 1973.
    9in (23cm)   **$50-$60 each**

Little Kiddles: 1966. Mint-in-box or package; deduct 50% for an out-of-package doll with all accessories in excellent condition.
Body Mark: 1965//Mattel, Inc.// Japan.

Sleeping Biddle	**$125**
Liddle Biddle Peep	**$165**
Peter Pandiddle	**$225**
Liddle Middle Muffet	**$185**
Liddle Red Riding Hiddle	**$185**
Sizzly Friddle	**$145**
Freezy Sliddle	**$135**
Howard Biff Boodle	**$135**
Orange Ice Cone Kiddle	**$60-$65**
Violet Kiddle Kologne	**$40-$45**
Loo Locket Kiddle	**$35-$40**
Heart Pin Kiddle	**$30-$35**
Lorelie Bracelet Kiddle	**$40-$45**

Little Kiddle Little Diddle. H & J Foulke, Inc.

Sunshine Fun Family, boxed. *Rosemary Kanizer.*

MEGO CORPORATION

Television, Movie and Entertainment Dolls: All prices are for mint-in-box or package dolls.

Batman, 1974. 8in (20cm) **$150**
Penguin, 1974. 8in (20cm) **$95**
Captain & Tenille, 1977.
12½in (32cm) **$50-$60 each**
Sonny & Cher, 1976.
12in (31cm) **$65-$75**
CHiPs, 1977. 8in (20cm) **$35-$40 each**
Diana Ross, 1977.
12½in (32cm) **$125**
Charlie's Angels, 1975.
12½in (32cm) **$40-$50 each**
Happy Days, 1976.
8in (20cm) **$50-$55 each**
KISS, 1978. 12½in (32cm) **$150 each**
Kojack, 1977. 9in (23cm) **$65-$70**
Laverne & Shirley, 1977.
11½in (29cm) **$65-$70 each**
Lenny & Squiggy, 1977.
11½in (29cm) **$75-$85**
Joe Namath, 1971. 12in (31cm)**$40-$45**
Our Gang, 1975.
5in (13cm) **$50-$60 each**
Planet of the Apes, 1974.
8in (20cm) **$85-$100 each**
Pirates, 1971. 8in (20cm) **$45-$50 each**
Robin Hood Set, 1971.
8in (20cm) **$50-$55 each**
Starsky & Hutch, 1976.
8in (20cm) **$35-$40 each**
Suzanne Somers, 1978.
12½ in (32cm) **$50-$60**
The Waltons, 1975. 8in (20cm), two
dolls in each box **$50-$60**
Wild West, 1974. **Buffalo Bill, Cochise, Davy Crockett, Sitting Bull, Wild Bill Hickok, Wyatt Earp** **$35-$40 each**
Wonder Woman, 1976.
12½in (32cm) **$100-$115**
Wizard of Oz, 1974.
Dorothy **$30-$35**

Munchkins **$60-$65**
Tin Man, Cowardly Lion **$30-$35**
Wizard with Playset **$135**
Star Trek, 1975. Fully jointed plastic. Packaged on blister card. For unpackaged dolls, deduct 50%, 8in (20cm).
Captain Kirk **$45-$50**
Mr. Spock **$45-$50**
Dr. McCoy **$100-$115**
Mr. Scott **$100-$115**
Klingon **$45-$50**
Lt. Uhura **$100-$115**
Andorian **$400-$450**
The Keeper **$175-$200**
Romulan **$625-$700**
Star Trek, 1979. Mint-in-box.
12½in (32cm)
Captain Kirk **$85**
Mr. Spock **$85**
Ilia **$85**

Star Trek Mr. Spock, 1979. *George Humphrey.*

MOLLY-'ES

NANCY

Molly-'es Composition Dolls: Beautiful original outfits; all in good condition.

Babies, 15-18in (38-46cm)	**$225-$250**
Girls, 12-13in (31-33cm)	**$175-$195**
Toddlers, 14-16in (36-41cm)	**$275-$300**
Ladies, 18-21in (46-53cm)	**$500-$550**

Internationals: All-cloth with mask faces; all original clothes; in excellent condition with wrist tag.

13in (33cm)	**$95**
Mint-in-box	**$125**

Raggedy Ann &Andy: See page 170.
Thief of Baghdad Series, 1939. Orange hang tag.

Sabu, composition.
- 15in (38cm) **$550-$600**

Sultan, 19in (48cm) cloth **$650-$750**
Princess, 15in (38cm) composition or 18in (46cm) cloth **$600-$650**
Prince, 23in (58cm) cloth **$750**

Vinyl Dolls: All original and excellent.
Darling Little Women,
- 8in (20cm) **$50-$60** **
- 12in (31cm) **$85-$95** **

Internationals,
- 8in (20cm) **$40-$50**

Perky, 8in (20cm) **$50-$60**

**Not enough price samples to compute a reliable range.

FACTS
International Doll Co., Philadelphia, Pa. Made clothing only. Purchased undressed dolls from various manufacturers. 1920s on.
Clothes Designer: Mollye Goldman.
Mark: A cardboard tag.

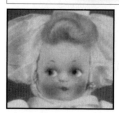

12in (31cm) Molly-'es *Suzette of France,* all original. *H & J Foulke, Inc.*

Painted Bisque Marked Storybook Doll: Mohair wig, painted eyes; one-piece body and head, jointed legs and arms; original clothes; excellent condition with sticker or wrist tag and box. Deduct 25-30% for out-of-boxed dolls. 5½–7in (13-19cm).

1936: Babies only. Gold sticker on dress; sunburst box. **Mark:** "88 Made in Japan" or "87 Made in Japan"
- 3½-4½in (8-10cm) **$450-$550**

1937-1938: Gold sticker on dress; sunburst box, gold label. **Mark:** "Made in Japan 1146," "Made in Japan 1148," "Japan," "Made in Japan" or "AMERICA" **$550-$700**

1938-1939: Gold sticker on dress; sunburst transition to silver dot box. **Mark:** "JUDY ANN USA" (crude mark), "STORY-BOOK USA" (crude mark). Molded socks/molded bangs. **Mark:** "StoryBook Doll USA" **$500-$600**

Masquerade Series, each	**$800**
Topsy and **Eva**, pair	**$1,200**
Scotch, at auction	**$950**
Judy Ann	**$600**
Oriental	**$1,700**
Gypsy	**$1,200**
Pirate	**$1,300**
Storybook Set	**$4,300**
Sports Series, each	**$1,200**

1940: Gold sticker on dress; colored box with white polka dots. Molded socks. **Mark:** "StoryBook Doll USA" **$250 up**

FACTS
Nancy Ann Storybook Dolls Co., South San Francisco, CA. 1936-on.

ANN STORYBOOK DOLLS

Margie Ann	**$325-$350**
"Pudgies"	**$250-$350**

1941-1942: Gold wrist tag; white box with colored polka dots; jointed legs. **Mark: "StoryBook Doll USA"** **$110-$125**

White socks	**$135-$165**
"Pudgies"	**$250-$300**

1943-1947: Gold wrist tag; white box with colored polka dots; frozen legs. **Mark: "StoryBook Doll USA"** (some later dolls with plastic arms) **$75-85**

Socket head	**$95**

Operetta Series	**$175**
All Time Hit Parade Series	**$175**
Powder and Crinoline Series	**$150-$175**
Holiday Inserts	**$100-$125**

Hard Plastic Marked Storybook Doll: Swivel head, mohair wig, painted eyes, jointed legs; original clothes, gold wrist tag; white box with colored polka dots, excellent condition.

Mark: "Story Book Doll USA"

5½-7in (13-19cm)	**$50-$60**
Topsy (black)	**$125-$150**
Holiday Inserts	**$75-$85**

Bent-limb Baby:

Star hand baby	**$150-$175**
Bisque with closed fist, open mouth	**$165-$185**
Painted bisque, hard plastic arms	**$100-$125**
Hard Plastic	**$100**
Boxed furniture	**$300 up**

Muffie: all-hard plastic, wig, sleeping eyes, 8in (12cm) tall:
Mark: "StoryBook Dolls USA" some with "Muffie."

1953: straight leg nonwalker, painted lashes, no brows, dynel wig (side part with flip); 54 complete costumes. Original clothes, excellent condition. **$250-$300***

1954: walker, molded eyelashes, eyebrows after 1955, side part flip or braided wig; 30 additional costumes. Original clothes, excellent condition. **$185-$225***

3¾in (9cm) hard plastic baby, all original. *H & J Foulke, Inc.*

6in (15cm) painted bisque *A Shower Girl for April,* all original. *H & J Foulke, Inc.*

1955-1956: hard plastic walker or bent-knee walker, rooted Saran wig (ponytail, braids or side part flip); vinyl head and hard plastic body; molded or painted upper lashes.   **$150-$165**

1968: reissued, unmarked, **Muffie Around the World,** straight leg walker, molded eyelashes, glued on wig. 12 dolls in cellophane see-through boxes.   **$110-$125**

Nancy Ann Style Show, hard plastic,
   18in (46cm)   **$650-$850**

Miss Nancy Ann, 10½in (27cm), teenage body, high-heeled feet   **$100-$125**
   Boxed outfits   **$70**

Debbie, hard plastic toddler.
   10in (25cm)   **$160-$175**
   Mint-in-box   **$350**

Little Miss Nancy Ann, 9in (23cm)
   Boxed doll with 2 boxed outfits,
      at auction   **$400**
*Allow extra for red hair.

OLD COTTAGE

Old Cottage Doll: Rubber compound or hard plastic head with hand painted features, wig, stuffed cloth body; original clothing; excellent condition.
   8-9in (20-23cm)
      Children and Storybook outfits   **$165**
         Scotch, Pearlies   **$135**
   12-13in (31-33cm),
      mint-in-box   **$350****

Tweedledee & Tweedledum,
   9in (23cm)   **$625 pair**

**Not enough price samples to compute a reliable average.

9in (23cm)
*Old Cottage
Scots Girl*,
all original.
*H & J
Foulke, Inc.*

8in (21cm) *Muffie* walker, original box.
Terri & Kathy's Dolls.

FACTS

Old Cottage Toys, Allargate, Rustington, Littlehampton, Sussex, Great Britain. 1948.
Designers: Greta Fleischmann and her daughter Susi.
Mark: Paper label - "Old Cottage Toys" - handmade in Great Britain.

PRINCESS DIANA DOLLS

Dolls must be mint-in-box, complete with all accessories and have their certificates.

Madame Alexander. 1998. Hard Plastic.
10in (25cm) **$125-$140**

Ashton Drake, 1998. Porcelain. Designed by Titus Tomescu, in blue, red or green evening gown. **$95-$115**

Danbury Mint, 1982. Porcelain. Wedding gown. 19in (48cm) **$350-$400**
Royal Wardrobe Collection, Doll
with 9 outfits **$150-$200**

Effanbee, 1982, Vinyl.
Wedding gown. **$100-$125**

Franklin Mint. 1998. Porcelain. Beaded gown and others. 17in (43cm)**$125-$150**
People's Princess, 1998, 16in (41cm)
vinyl, blue suit, doll only **$80-$100**

Gadco, 1998. Young Diana, red coat and hat. 35in (89cm) **$260-$310**

Royal Britannia Collection. 1997 reissue of 1982 doll, wdding gown
12in (3cm) boxed **$40**

Royal Diana. Set of 8 boxed dolls. **$100**

Society for Preservation of History, Inc. 1997. Porcelain.
18in (46cm) blue satin gown **$70**

Street Players Holding Corp. Vinyl.
1997, wedding gown **$25**
1998, black dress **$25**

Peggy Nisbet, 1982
Wedding gown **$65**
Boxed **$125**

8in (20cm) *H.R.H. Princess of Wales*, P1005 Wedding Model by Peggy Nisbet, all original. *H & J Foulke, Inc.*

RALEIGH

RAVCA

Raleigh Doll: All heavy composition; appropriate clothes; all in good condition. Child:

11in (28cm) wigged	**$450-$500**
13in (33cm) molded hair	**$600-$650**
18in (46cm) molded hair	**$950-$1050**
22-24in (56-61cm) shoulder head on cloth body, compo arms	**$350-$450**

Baby:

12in (30cm)	**$400**

FACTS
Jessie McCutcheon Raleigh,
Chicago, Ill. 1916-1920.
Designer: Jessie McCutcheon
Raleigh.
Mark: None.

11in (28cm) Raleigh *Goldilocks,* all original. *H & J Foulke, Inc.*

Bernard Ravca Doll: Paris, France, 1924-1939; New York, 1939 on. Stockinette face individually needle sculpted; cloth body and limbs; original clothes; all in excellent condition.

Mark: Paper label: "Original Ravca Fabrication Française"

10in (25cm) French peasants	**$100-$125**
13in (33cm)	**$150-$165**
21in (53cm)	**$350-$400**

American Historical Figures: George Washington, Betsy Ross, Ben Franklin, etc.

9in (23cm)	**$175-$225**

Crepe paper dolls, hand painted faces.

6½in (16cm)	**$10-$12**

Composition heads. Bendable bodies.

7½in (19cm)	**$35-$40**

Ravca-type fine quality peasant man or lady. 17in (43cm) **$225-$265 each**

Frances Diecks Ravca Doll: New York, 1935 on.

36in (91cm) 1952. **Queen Elizabeth II** and others	**$650-$850**
12in (30cm) **"Easter Sunday"** 1973, Black child	**$250**

21in (53cm) Ravca peasant man, all original. *H & J Foulke, Inc.*

RELIABLE TOY CO.

Marked Reliable Doll: All-composition or composition shoulder head and lower arms, cloth torso and legs, sometimes composition legs; painted features; original clothes; all in good condition, some light crazing acceptable.

Barbara Ann Scott (Ice Skater),
15in (38cm)   **$400-$500**
Canadian Mountie,
17in (43cm)   **$300-$350**
Clicquot Club Soda Eskimo,
14in (36cm)   **$250-$275**
Her Highness, 15in (38cm)**$350-$375**
Hiawatha or **Indian Maiden,**
13in (33cm)   **$85-$110**
Military Man, 14in (36cm)**$225-$275**
Scots Girl or **Boy,**
14in (36cm)   **$85-$110**
Shirley Temple, 22in (56cm)   **$1,200**

FACTS
Toronto, Canada. 1920 on.
Mark:
RELIABLE//MADE IN//CANADA

REMCO INDUSTRIES

Littlechap Family, 1963. Basic doll, unplayed with, in original box. Deduct 50% for out-of-box dolls.

Dr. John, 14½in (37cm)   **$85-$95**
Lisa, 13½in (34cm)   **$85-$95**
Judy, 12in (31cm)   **$85-$95**
Libby, 10½in (27cm)   **$85-$95**
Rooms   **$300**
Office   **$300**
Tagged clothes
(packaged outfits)   **$30-$75**

Television Programs & Personalities: All prices are for dolls that are mint, in original box.

Addams Family,
5½in (14cm)   **$100-$125**
I Dream of Jeannie, 6in (15cm)**$50-$60**
Laurie Partridge (Susan Dey), 1973.
19in (48cm)   **$85-$95**
Orphan Annie, 1967. 15in (38cm) **$45**
Beatles, 1964.
4½in (11cm) with guitars   **$400**

15in (38cm)
Reliable *Her Highness,* all original. *H & J Foulke, Inc.*

Littlechap Family brochure.
Rosemary Kanizer.

SANTONS

SANDRA SUE

Santons: Figures representing the elderly people of Provence. Clay character heads, clay hands and legs, wire armature bodies. Authentic costumes, many representing various occupations and activities; all original, excellent condition.

7in (18cm)	**$55**
10-12in (25-31cm)	**$100-$125**

FACTS

1930s to present
Simone Jouglas, J.P. Marinacei,
Syndicat de Satonniers de Provence
and others.
Provence, France.

Sandra Sue: 1952 on. All hard plastic, slender, Saran wig, molded eyelashes, unmarked.

8in (20cm) basic doll (camisole, panties, half slip, shoes and socks)	**$125-$140**
Boxed	**$225**
In street dresses	**$135-$160**
In gowns	**$175-$225**
Little Women	**$225**
Outfits, packaged	**$30-$85**
Bridal gown	**$125**
Communion dress	**$110**

Cindy Lou: 1951. All-hard plastic walker, saran wig. Many outfits matched **Sandra Sue's.**

14in (36cm) basic doll (camisole, panties, half slip, shoes and socks)	**$275**
In street dresses	**$325**

FACTS

Richwood Toys, Inc.,
Annapolis, MD. 1952 on.
Designer: Ida H. Wood

12in (31cm) Santons by Simone Jouglas. *H & J Foulke, Inc.*

8in (20cm) *Sandra Sue,* all original. *Miriam Blankman Collection.*

SASHA

Sasha: All-vinyl of exceptionally high quality, long synthetic hair; original clothing, tiny circular wrist tag; excellent condition.

16in (41cm)	**$210-$225**
Boxed	**$250**
In cylinder package	**$350-$400**

Gregor (boy)	**$210-$225**
Boxed	**$250**
Cora (black girl)	**$250-$275**
Caleb (black boy)	**$250-$275**

Black baby	**$200**
White baby	**$165**
Sexed baby, pre 1979	**$250-$275**
Packaged clothes	**$85**

Early cloth-faced **Sasha,** all original. *H & J Foulke, Inc.*

Limited Edition Dolls:

1980 **Velvet Dress**	**$350-$375**
1982 **Pintucks Dress**	**$350-$375**
1983 **Kiltie**	**$350-$375**
1984 **Harlequin**	**$350-$375**
1985 **Prince Gregor**	**$350-$375**
1986 **Princess**	**$1,000-$1,500**
1986 **Sari**	**$725-$775**

"Serie Sasha": (For photograph see *12th Blue Book,* page 316.)
Götz model, 1965-69. All original.

16in (41cm)	**$1,500-$1,800**

Early model 1950s – 1960s.

20-21in (51-53cm) child	**$7,500-$12,500**
13in (33cm) baby, at auction	**$3,800**

Götz: 1995 on. Boxed   **$200-$225**

16in (41cm) **Sasha,** all original. *H & J Foulke, Inc.*

FACTS

Trendon Toys, Ltd., Reddish, Stockport, England. 1965-1986.
Designer: Sasha Morgenthaler.

SHIRLEY TEMPLE

All-Composition Child: 1934 through late 1930s. Marked head and body, jointed composition body; all original including wig and clothes; entire doll in very good condition. Sizes 11-27in (28-69cm).

Mark: On body:

SHIRLEY TEMPLE
13

On head:

13
SHIRLEY TEMPLE

On cloth label:

Genuine
SHIRLEY TEMPLE
DOLL
REGISTERED U.S. PAT OFF
IDEAL NOVELTY & TOY CO
MADE IN USA

11in (28cm)	$900-$1,100*
13in (33cm)	$850-$900*
15-16in (38-41cm)	$850-$900*
18in (46cm)	$1,000-$1,100*
20-22in (51-56cm)	$1,200*
25in (64cm)	$1,400*
27in (69cm)	$1,800-$2,000*
Button	$135
Dress, tagged	$150 up
Shoes	$75-$125
Trunk	$175-$200
Carriage	$600-$650

Hawaiian Shirley,
18in (46cm)	$900-$100

Baby Shirley: Composition/cloth; original clothing; good condition.
16-18in (41-46cm)	$1,200-$1,300

FACTS

Ideal Novelty Toy Corp., New York, N.Y. 1934 to present.
Designer: Bernard Lipfert.

18in (46cm) composition *Shirley Temple,* all original. *H & J Foulke, Inc.*

16in (41cm) composition/cloth *Baby Shirley Temple,* redressed. *H & J Foulke, Inc.*

Other Composition Shirley Temples:

Made in Japan,
7½in (19cm)   **$275-$325**

Reliable (Canada), all original and boxed,
18-22in (46-56cm)   **$1,200**

Vinyl and Plastic: Excellent condition, original clothes.

1957, 12in (30cm)	**$225-$235**
Boxed	**$325-$425**
15in (38cm)	**$300-$325**
17in (43cm)	**$375-$400**
19in (48cm)	**$425-$450**
36in (91cm)	**$1,500-$1,800**
Script name pin	**$40**
Name purse	**$25**
Tagged or Boxed dress	**$65 up**
Black Plastic Curler Box	**$80**
1973, 16in (41cm) size only	**$100-$110**

Boxed	**$150-$165**
Boxed dress	**$35**

1972, Montgomery Ward	
14in (36cm)	**$225-$250**
1982, 1983.	
8in (20cm)	**$40-$50**
12in (30cm)	**$70-$80**
1984, Doll, Dreams & Love,	
36in (91cm)	**$250-$300**

*Allow 50-100% more for mint-in-box doll. Also allow extra for a doll with unsual outift, such as *Texas Ranger, Little Colonel,* and *Captain January.*

Porcelain:

1986, Danbury Mint	
14in (36cm)	**$75-$85**

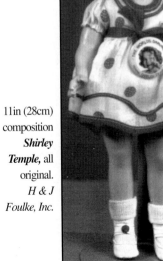

12in (30cm) 1957 vinyl ***Shirley Temple,*** all original. *H & J Foulke, Inc.*

11in (28cm) composition ***Shirley Temple,*** all original. *H & J Foulke, Inc.*

SKOOKUM INDIANS

Skookum Indian Doll: Composition character face, dark eyes painted to the side, black mohair wig; clad in an Indian blanket (fold in the blanket represents arms), cotton print dress or cotton shirt and felt trousers, headband with one or more feathers, beads, suede boots; all very colorful. Excellent, unplayed with condition.

6in (15cm)	**$45-$55**
9-10in (23-25cm)	**$100-$150**
12in (31cm)	**$200-$250**
16in (41cm)	**$400-$450**
20in (51cm)	**$650-$750**
36in (91cm)	**$1,200-$1,500**

FACTS
Created and designed by Mary McAboy, Missoula, Montana and Denver, Colorado. Dolls made by various companies including Arrow Novelty Co., New York and H.H. Tammen Co., New York, Denver and Los Angeles. 1913 on.
Mark: Sometimes a paper label on the sole of the foot.
Trademark: Skookum (Bully Good)

17in (43cm) *Skookum*, all original, missing headband. *H & J Foulke, Inc.*

SUN RUBBER CO.

Silly and **Popo.** 1937. Comic characters with molded clothes. 10in (25cm)   **$55-$65****

Minnie Mouse. 1937.
10½in (27cm) in red-and-white polka dot sundress.   **$125-$150****

Bonnie Bear, Wiggy Wags, Happy Kappy, Rompy. 1940s. One-piece squeeze dolls with molded clothes and hats. Designed by Ruth E. Newton.
6-8in (15-20cm)   **$15-$25****
So-Wee. 1941. Designed by Ruth E. Newton with painted or sleeping eyes, molded hair. Excellent.
10-12in (25-31cm)   **$65-$75**

Sunbabe. 1950. Drink and wet baby with painted eyes and molded hair. Excellent.
11-13in (28-33cm)	**$45-$55**
in original box	**$110-$125**
Sewing set, boxed	**$150-$175**

Baby Bannister. 1954. All vinyl drink-and-wet doll based on the famous baby photographs by Constance Bannister. Excellent.
12 in (31cm) in original box **$100-$125**

Gerber Baby. 1955. All rubber with inset eyes and molded hair, open/closed mouth. Excellent.
11-13in (28-33cm)	**$100-$125**
in original box	**$275-$325**

**Not enough price samples to compute a reliable range.

TERRI LEE

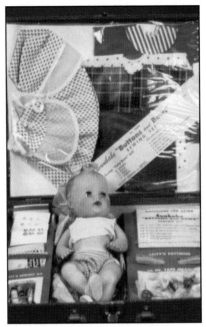

Terri Lee Child Doll: Original wig, painted eyes; jointed at neck, shoulders and hips; all original tagged clothing and accessories; very good condition.

16in (41cm)

Composition, stiff hair	**$450-$500****
Hard Plastic:	
Pat. Pending	**$500**
Terri Lee only	**$375-$425**
Mint-in-box	**$500-$600**
Boxed otuftis	**$85-$125**
Talking Terri, boxed	**$700-$750**
Patty-Jo (black)	**$900-$1,100**
Jerri Lee, 16in (41cm)	**$525-$625**
Benji (black)	**$700-$800****

Sunbabe Sewing Set, original box.
H & J Foulke, Inc.

FACTS
Barberton, Ohio. 1930s on.
Marks: Sun Rubber Co. with various numbers, names and dates

16in (41cm) patent pending *Terri Lee,*
all original, with her monkey *Penelope,*
redressed. *Courtesy of Susan Babkowski.*

Tiny Terri Lee, inset eyes.

10in (25cm)	$185-$210
Boxed	$250-265

Tiny Jerri Lee, inset eyes,

10in (25cm)	$185-$210
Connie Lynn	$375-$425
Boxed, at auction	$630
Gene Autry, at auction	$3,100
Linda Baby, 10in (25cm)	$165-$185
Ginger Girl Scout,	
8in (20cm)	$175-$225

**Not enough price samples to compute a reliable range.

TINY TOWN

Tiny Town Dolls: Molded felt faces with painted eyes and mouths, mohair wigs of various styles and colors; wrapped cloth bodies over wire armatures, felt hands, weighted white metal shoes; original clothes; excellent condition.

4in (10cm)*	$65-$75
Boxed	$110

*Other known sizes are 5in (13cm) and 7¼in (19cm) but no prices are available.

FACTS
Alma LeBlane dba Lenna Lee's Tiny Town Dolls, San Francisco, CA. Trademark registered January 11, 1949.
Mark: Some have a gold octagonal wrist tag with **Tiny Town Dolls** on one side and name of doll on the other.

FACTS
TERRI LEE Sales Corp., V. Gradwohl, Pres. 1946-Lincoln, Neb.; then Apple Valley, Calif., from 1952-Ca. 1962.
Mark: First dolls:
"TERRI LEE
PAT. PENDING"
raised letters
Later dolls: "TERRI LEE"

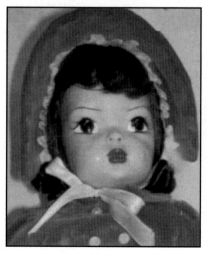

16in (41cm) *Terri Lee,* all original. *Courtesy of Susan Babkowski.*

4in (10cm) *Tiny Town Alice,* all original. *H & J Foulke, Inc.*

UNEEDA DOLL CO.

Composition Dolls:
Lucky Lindy (Charles Lindbergh): 1927. Composition/cloth; brown aviator suit, good condition.

    14in (36cm)   **$350-$450****

Rita Hayworth: 1939. All-composition, red mohair wig, all original clothes, excellent.

    14in (36cm)   **$450-$500**

Toddler: Ca. 1940. All-composition, all original clothes, very good condition.

    13in (33cm)   **$250-$275**

**Not enough price samples to compute a reliable average.

Hard Plastic and Vinyl Dolls: Excellent, unplayed with condition with original clothes, perfect hair, rosy cheeks.

Dollikin: 1957. Fully jointed hard plastic.
    8in (20cm) mint-in-box   **$35**
    11in (28cm) mint-in-box   **$50-$60**
    19in (48cm)   **$110-$135**

Baby Dollikin: 1958. Jointed elbows and knees, 21in (53cm)   **$150**

Saranade: 1962. With phonograph and record, 21in (53cm)   **$150**

Pollyana: 1960. Haley Mills in pink-and-white checked outfit.
    10½in (27cm)   **$35-$40**
    17in (43cm)   **$50-$60**
    31in (79cm)   **$295**

Wee Three: Mother, daughter and baby brother. Set   **$125**
    Boxed set   **$200**

21in (53cm) *Saranade, McMasters Doll Auction.*

31in (79cm) *Pollyana,* all original. *McMasters Doll Auction.*

FACTS
New York. 1917 on.

VINYL

VINYL DOLLS

All dolls must be in excellent condition with perfect hair, excellent coloring, no discoloration and crisp original clothes.

14R Fashion Dolls, 1957-1965. All vinyl, excellent quality ladies.

  19-20in (48-51cm)   **$80-$90**

Dick Clark, 1958-!959. Juro Novelty Co. Personality portrait doll, original clothes.

  26in (66cm) at auction   **$405**

Debutante, Ca. 1960. Goldberger. High-heeled fashion doll, vinyl and hard plastic.

  29in (74cm)   **$90-$110**

Puppetrina, 1963. Goldberger. Vinyl head, cloth body, hand puppet doll.

  22½in (57cm)   **$65**

Honey West, 1965. Gilbert Toys. Hard plastic and vinyl, painted eyes.

  11½in (29cm)   **$125**

Man from U.N.C.L.E., 1965. Gilbert Toys. Characters from T.V. Series.

  12½in (31cm) boxed   **$100**

James Bond, Secret Agent 007. Gilbert Toys. Movie character.

  12½in (31cm) boxed   **$75**

Hello, Dolly, 1961. Kaysam. All vinyl, 21in (53cm) costume from musical.

      $75-$100

Carol Channing, 1960. Nasco. All vinyl, 11½in (29cm) costume from musical

      $45-$55

Angela Cartwright, 1961. Natural Doll Co. Featured as Linda Williams on The Danny Thomas Show.

  14in (36cm) smiling character face

      $75-$85

Sally Starr, 1960s. Philadelphia T.V. personality. 10½in (26cm) cowgirl outfit

      $25-$35

Lonely Lisa, 1964. Royal Doll Co. Vinyl and cloth, large painted eyes.

  20in (51cm)   **$90-$100**

Miss America, 1957-1959. Sayco Doll Co. Vinyl fashion doll.

  18in (46cm)   **$90-$110**

  10in (25cm)   **$55-$65**

Queen for a Day, 1957. Valentine. Vinyl fashion doll.

  20in (51cm) in taffeta gown and

    velvet cape   **$90-$110**

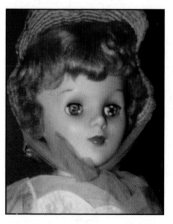

29in (74cm) Eegee (Goldberger) **Debutante,** all original. *McMasters Doll Auctions.*

20in (51cm) *Lonely Lisa,* Royal Doll Co. *Doodlebug Dolls.*

VOGUE

All-composition Girl: 1940s. Original clothes; all in good condition, with perfect hair.

Mark: None on doll; round silver sticker on front of outift. May have name stamped on sole of shoe.

13in (33cm)	**$400-$450**
19in (48cm)	**$525-$575**

All-composition Toddles: 1937-1948. Painted eyes looking to side; original clothes; all in good condition.

Mark: "VOGUE" on head
"DOLL CO." on back
"TODDLES" stamped on sole of shoe

7-8in (18-20cm)   **$275***

*Allow extra for unusual outfits, such as cowboy and Unde Sam.

Hard Plastic Ginny: Original wig and tagged clothes; all in excellent condition with perfect hair and pretty coloring.

Mark:
On strung dolls: "VOGUE DOLLS"
On walking dolls: "GINNY//VOGUE DOLLS"

7-8in (18-20cm)
1948-1949:

Painted eyes	**$350-$400***
Half-Century Series	**$1,000**
Boxed in complete outfit including	
coat and hat, at auction	**$850**

8in (21cm) *Ginny Tiny Miss #44,* all original. *Terri & Kathy's Dolls.*

FACTS

Vogue Dolls, Inc., Medford, Mass.
Creator: Jennie Graves.
Clothes Designer:
Virginia Graves Carlson.
Clothes Label: "Vogue," "Vogue Dolls," or
VOGUE DOLLS, INC.
MEDFORD, MASS. USA
® REG U.S. PAT OFF

8in (21cm) *Steve #35,* all original and boxed. *Terri & Kathy's Dolls.*

Crib Crowd Baby | $700-$800
Easter Bunny Baby | $1,200

1950-1953:

Painted eyelashes, strung | $350-$450*
Caracul wig, poodle cut | $500-$550*
Beryl, Cheryl, Tiny Miss Kindergarten, Boxed | $1,000-$1,500
Queen Elizabeth II | $900
Black **Ginny,** at auction | $1900

1954:

Painted eyelashes, walks | $300-$350*

1955-1957:

Molded eyelashes, walks | $225-$275*
Davy Crockett | $450-$500
Girl Scout or **Brownie** | $275-$325
Bon Bon, boxed | $400-$450
Tiny Miss, Debs, boxed | $350-$400
Nun | $350

1957-1962:

Molded eyelashes, walks, jointed knees | $150-$200*

1962 on.

Vinyl head, hard plastic body with jointed knees | $90

*Allow extra for mint-in-box dolls and desirable outfits, such as **Tiny Miss Series** and **Kindergarten Series.**

Accessories: All in excellent condition:

Ginny's Pup | $225-$275
Cardboard suitcase with contents | $50
Parasol | $15-$18
Gym set | $450-$500
Dresser, bed, rocking chair, wardrobe | $55-$65 each
Trousseau Tree | $150-$175
School bag | $75-$85
"Hi I'm Ginny" pin | $75
Ginny's First Secret book | $125
Swag bag, hat box, auto bag and garment bag | $35 each
Roller skates in cylinder | $25
Hats | $10-$15
Headband | $8
Dress and panties, tagged | $35-$55
Glasses | $4-$5
Shoes, center snap | $50-$75
Shoes, plastic | $9-$10
Locket & chain | $65
Purse (Ginny) | $6
Christmas Stocking (no doll), at auction | $900
Boxed clothing, 1950-1954. | $75-$150

Vinyl Ginny: 1972.

Children and internationals | $35-$40
Gift Set | $65-$75

Vinyl Ginny: 1977 on.

8in (20cm) children | $40-$50
International costumes | $35-$40
Sasson | $35
Black Ginette | $15-$20

10in (25cm) *Jan,* all original. *Terri & Kathy's Dolls.*

Other Dolls: All must be in excellent condition with perfect hair, excellent coloring and original clothes.

Jill: 1957. All-hard plastic, adult body.
10in (25cm)	**$175-$225**
Boxed Outfits	**$75-$105**

Jeff: 1957. Vinyl head.
10in (25cm)	**$75-$95**
Boxed	**$150**

Jan: 1958. All vinyl
	$95-$110
Boxed	**$150**

Ginnette: 1957. All vinyl baby.
8in (20cm) boxed	**$125-$135**
Ginnette Play Set, Boxed	**$400**
Baby Tender	$50
Crib	**$75**

Jimmy: 1958.
8in (20cm) painted eyes	**$125-$135**
Boxed	**$175**

Lil Imp: 1959-1960. Vinyl head, hard plastic body with bent knees.
11in (28cm)	**$125-$150**
Boxed	**$250-$300**

Wee Imp: 1960. All hard plastic, red hair.
8in (20cm)	**$275-$325**

Baby Dear: 1960-1964. Designed by Eloise Wilken. Vinyl head and limbs, cloth body.
12in (31cm)	**$125-$150**
18in (46cm)	**$250-$300**
Top knot, at auction	**$941**

Baby Dear One, 1962-1963.
25in (63cm)	**$300-$400**

Miss Ginny, 1962. 16in (41cm) **$65-$75**

Ginny, 1960. 36in (91cm) **$300-$500****

Brikette, 1961. 16in (41cm) **$150**
Doll with 6 boxed costumes, at auction	**$294**
22in (56cm)	**$175-$185**

Love Me Linda, 1965. All vinyl.
16in (41cm)	**$65-$75**

WRIGHT, R. JOHN

Cloth Dolls: All boxed and in perfect condition.

Adult Characters
(no boxes)	**$1,200-$1,500**
Children	**$750-$1,500**
Timothy, Rosemary	**$2,000 each**

Snow White & 7 Dwarfs, matching
numbered set, at auction	**$6,600**
Golliwog, 10in (25cm)	**$425**

Hans & Gretel Brinker,
20in (51cm)	**$950 each**

Pinocchio & Geppeto,
17in (43cm)	**$2,000**

Christopher Robin & Winnie the Pooh
17in (43cm)	**$2,000-$2,400**
12in (30cm)	**$1,000**

Winnie the Pooh
18in (46cm)	**$1,300-$1,500**
14in (36cm) with honeypot	**$700**
Pocket Pooh	**$400**

Piglet with Violets **$375-$425**
Pocket Piglet	**$200**

Christopher Robin & Winnie the Pooh, all original. *H & J Foulke, Inc.*

BIBLIOGRAPHY

Anderton, Johana.
Twentieth Century Dolls. North Kansas City, Missouri: Trojan Press, 1971.
More Twentieth Century Dolls. North Kansas City, Missouri: Athena Publishing Co., 1974.

Angione, Genevieve. *All-Bisque & Half-Bisque Dolls*. Exton, Pennsylvania: Schiffer Publishing Ltd., 1969.

Borger, Mona. *Chinas, Dolls for Study and Admiration*. San Francisco: Borger Publications, 1983.

Cieslik, Jürgen and Marianne.
German Doll Encyclopedia 1800-1939. Cumberland, Maryland: Hobby House Press, Inc., 1985.

Coleman, Dorothy S., Elizabeth Ann and **Evelyn Jane.** *The Collector's Book of Dolls' Clothes*. New York: Crown Publishers, Inc., 1975.
The Collector's Encyclopedia of Dolls, Vol. I & II. New York: Crown Publishers, Inc., 1968 & 1986.

Corson, Carol. *Schoenhut Dolls, A Collector's Encyclopedia*. Cumberland, Maryland: Hobby House Press, Inc., 1993.

Foulke, Jan.
Blue Books of Dolls & Values, Vol. I-XIII. Cumberland, Maryland: Hobby House Press, Inc., 1974-1997.
Doll Classics. Cumberland, Maryland: Hobby House Press, Inc., 1987.
Focusing on Effanbee Composition Dolls. Riverdale, Maryland: Hobby House Press, 1978.
Focusing on Gebrüder Heubach Dolls. Cumberland, Maryland: Hobby House Press, Inc., 1980.
Kestner, King of Dollmakers. Cumberland, Maryland: Hobby House Press, Inc., 1982.
Simon & Halbig Dolls, The Artful Aspect. Cumberland, Maryland: Hobby House Press, Inc., 1984.
Treasury of Madame Alexander Dolls. Riverdale, Maryland: Hobby House Press, 1979.
China Doll Collecting. Grantsville, Maryland: Hobby House Press, Inc., 1995.
German 'Dolly' Collecting. Grantsville, Maryland: Hobby House Press, Inc., 1995.
Doll Buying &Selling. Grantsville, Maryland: Hobby House Press, Inc., 1995.

Gerken, Jo Elizabeth.
Wonderful Dolls of Papier-Mâché. Lincoln, Nebraska: Doll Research Associates, 1970.

Hillier, Mary.
Dolls and Dollmakers. New York: G. P. Putnam's Sons, 1968.

The History of Wax Dolls. Cumberland, Maryland: Hobby House Press, Inc.; London: Justin Knowles, 1985.

Izen, Judith.
Collector's Guide to Ideal Dolls. Paducah, Kentucky: Collector Books, 1999.

Izen, Judith and Carol Stover.
Collector's Encyclopedia of Vogue Dolls. Paducah, Kentucky: Collector Books. 1999.

Judd, Polly and Pam.
Hard Plastic Dolls. Cumberland, Maryland: Hobby House Press, Inc., 1985.
Hard Plastic Dolls II. Cumberland, Maryland: Hobby House Press, Inc., 1989.
Glamour Dolls of the 1950s &1960s. Cumberland, Maryland: Hobby House Press, Inc., 1988.
Compo Dolls 1928-1955. Cumberland, Maryland: Hobby House Press, Inc., 1991.
Compo Dolls, Volume II. Cumberland, Maryland: Hobby House Press, Inc., 1994.

Mandeville, A.Glenn.
5th Doll Fashion Anthology. Grantsville, Maryland: HobbyHouse Press, Inc., 1996.

Mathes, Ruth E. and **Robert C.**
Dolls, Toys and Childhood. Cumberland, Maryland: Hobby House Press, Inc., 1987.

McGonagle, Dorothy A. *The Dolls of Jules Nicolas Steiner*. Cumberland, Maryland: Hobby House Press, Inc., 1988.

Merrill, Madeline O. *The Art of Dolls, 1700-1940*. Cumberland, Maryland: Hobby House, Inc., 1985.

Mertz, Ursula R.
Collector's Encyclopedia of American Composition Dolls, 1900-1950. Paducah, Kentucky: Collector Books, 1999.

Pardella, Edward R. *Shirley Temple Dolls and Fashions*. West Chester, Pennsylvania: Schiffer Publishing, Ltd., 1992.

Richter, Lydia. *Heubach Character Dolls and Figurines*. Cumberland, Maryland: Hobby House Press, Inc., 1992.

Schoonmaker, Patricia N.
Effanbee Dolls: The Formative Years 1910-1929. Cumberland, Maryland: Hobby House Press, Inc., 1984.
Patsy Doll Family Encyclopedia, Volumes I & II. Cumberland, Maryland: Hobby House Press, Inc., 1992.

Tabbat, Andrew.
Collector's World of Raggedy Ann & Andy. Volumes I & II. Annapolis, Maryland: Gold Horse Publishing, 1997.

Tarnowska, Maree. *Fashion Dolls*. Cumberland, Maryland: Hobby House Press, Inc., 1986.

ABOUT THE AUTHOR

The name Jan Foulke is synonymous with accurate information. As the author of the *Blue Book of Dolls & Values*®, she is the most quoted source on doll information and the most respected and recognized authority on dolls and doll prices in the world.

Born in Burlington, New Jersey, Jan Foulke has always had a fondness for dolls. She recalls, "Many happy hours of my childhood were spent with dolls as companions, since we lived on a quiet county road, and until I was ten, I was an only child." Jan received a B.A. from Columbia Union College, where she was named to *Who's Who in American Colleges & Universities* and was graduated with high honors. Jan taught for twelve years in the Montgomery County school system in Maryland and also supervised student teachers in English for the University of Maryland where she did graduate work.

Jan and her husband, Howard, who photographs the dolls presented in the *Blue Book*, were both fond of antiquing as a hobby, and in 1972 they decided to open a small antique shop of their own. The interest of their daughter, Beth, in dolls sparked their curiosity about the history of old dolls—an interest that quite naturally grew out of their love of heirlooms. The stock in their antique shop gradually changed and evolved into an antique doll shop.

Early in the development of their antique doll shop, Jan and Howard realized that there was a critical need for an accurate and reliable doll identification and price guide resource. In the early 1970s, the Foulkes teamed up with Hobby House Press to produce (along with Thelma Bateman) the first *Blue Book of Dolls & Values*®, originally published in 1974. Since that time, the Foulkes have exclusively authored and illustrated the thirteen successive editions, and today the *Blue Book* is regarded by collectors and dealers as the definitive source for doll prices and values.

Jan and Howard Foulke now dedicate all of their professional time to the world of dolls: writing and illustrating books and articles, appraising collections, lecturing on antique dolls, acting as consultants to museums, auction houses and major collectors, and selling dolls by mail order, the internet, and exhibits at major shows throughout the United States. Mrs. Foulke is a member of the United Federation of Doll Clubs, Doll Collectors of America, and the National Antique Doll Dealers Association. Her biography appears in *Who's Who in the East*.

Mrs. Foulke has appeared on numerous television talk shows and is often quoted in newspaper and magazine articles as the ultimate source for doll pricing and trends in collecting. Both *USA Today* and *The Washington Post* have stated that the *Blue Book of Dolls & Values* is "the bible of doll collecting."

In addition to her work on the fourteen editions of the *Blue Book of Dolls & Values*, Jan Foulke has also authored: *Focusing on Effanbee Composition Dolls; A Treasury of Madame Alexander Dolls; Kestner, King of Dollmakers; Simon & Halbig, The Artful Aspect; Focusing on Gebrüder Heubach Dolls; Doll Classics; Focusing on Dolls; China Doll Collecting, German 'Dolly' Collecting,* and *Doll Buying and Selling.* She has been a regular contributor to *Doll Reader*® magazine for 27 years (since the beginning). Her current columns are the popular *Antique Q&A* and *Guide to Antique Dolls.*

GLOSSARY

Applied Ears: Ears molded independently and affixed to the head. (On most dolls the ear is included as part of the head mold.)

Bald Head: Head with no crown opening, could be covered by a wig or have painted hair.

Ball-jointed Body: Usually a body of composition or papier-mâché with wooden balls at knees, elbows, hips and shoulders to make swivel joints; some parts of the limbs may be wood.

Bébé: French child doll with "dolly face."

Belton-type: A bald head with one, two or three small holes for attaching wig.

Bent-limb Baby Body: Composition body of five pieces with chubby torso and curved arms and legs.

Biscaloid: Ceramic or composition substance for making dolls; also called imitation bisque.

Biskoline: Celluloid-type substance for making dolls.

Bisque: Unglazed porcelain, usually flesh tinted, used for dolls' heads or all-bisque dolls.

Breather: Doll with an actual opening in each nostril, also called open nostrils.

Breveté (or Bté): Used on French dolls to indicate that the patent is registered.

Character Doll: Dolls with bisque or composition heads, modeled to look life-like, such as infants, young or older children, young ladies and so on.

China: Glazed porcelain used for dolls' heads and *Frozen Charlottes*.

Child Dolls: Dolls with a typical "dolly face," which represents a child.

Composition: A material used for dolls' heads and bodies, consisting of such items as wood pulp, glue, sawdust, flour, rags and sundry other substances.

Contemporary Clothes: Clothes not original to the doll, but dating from the same period when the doll would have been a plaything.

Crown Opening: The cut-away part of a doll head.

DEP: Abbreviation used on German and French dolls claiming registration.

D.R.G.M.: Abbreviation used on German dolls indicating a registered design or patent.

Dolly Face: Typical face used on bisque dolls before 1910 when the character face was developed; "dolly face" were used also after 1910.

Embossed Mark: Raised letters, numbers or names on the backs of heads or bodies.

Feathered Eyebrows: Eyebrows composed of many tiny painted brush strokes to give a realistic look.

Fixed Eyes: Glass eyes that do not move or sleep.

Flange Neck: A doll's head with a ridge at the base of the neck which contains holes for sewing the head to a cloth body.

Flapper Dolls: Dolls of the 1920s period with bobbed wig or molded hair and slender arms and legs.

Flirting Eyes: Eyes which move from side to side as doll's head is tilted.

Frozen Charlotte: Doll molded all in one piece including arms and legs.

Ges. (Gesch.): Used on German dolls to indicate design is registered or patented.

Googly Eyes: Large, often round eyes looking to the side; also called roguish or goo goo eyes.

Hard Plastic: Hard material used for making dolls after 1948.

Ichimatsu: Japanese play doll. See page for full description.

Incised Mark: Letters, numbers or names impressed into the bisque on the back of the head or on the shoulder plate.

Intaglio Eyes: Painted eyes with sunken pupil and iris.

JCB: Jointed composition body. See *ball-jointed body.*

Kid Body: Body of white or pink leather.

Lady Dolls: Dolls with an adult face and a body with adult proportions.

Mama Doll: American composition and cloth doll of the 1920s to 1940s with "mama" voice box.

Mohair: Goat's hair widely used in making doll wigs.

Molded Hair: Curls, waves and comb marks which are actually part of the mold and not merely painted onto the head.

Motschmann-type Body: Doll body with cloth midsection and upper limbs with floating joints; hard lower torso and lower limbs.

Open-Mouth: Lips parted with an actual opening in the bisque, usually has teeth either molded in the bisque or set in separately and sometimes a tongue.

Open/Closed Mouth: A mouth molded to appear open, but having no actual slit in the bisque.

Original Clothes: Clothes belonging to a doll during the childhood of the original owner, either commercial or homemade.

Painted Bisque: Bisque covered with a layer of flesh-colored paint which has not been baked in, so will easily rub or wash off.

Paperweight Eyes: Blown glass eyes which have depth and look real, usually found in French dolls.

Papier-mâché: A material used for dolls' heads and bodies, consisting of paper pulp, sizing, glue, clay or flour.

Parian: Very fine quality white bisque with no complexion tint, usually used to make molded hair dolls.

S.G.D.G.: Used on French dolls to indicate that the patent is registered "without guarantee of the government."

Shoulder Head: A doll's head and shoulders all in one piece.

Shoulder Plate: The actual shoulder portion sometimes molded in one with the head, sometimes a separate piece with a socket in which a head is inserted.

Socket Head: Head and neck which fit into an opening in the shoulder plate or the body.

Solid-dome Head: Head with no crown opening, could have painted hair or be covered by wig.

Stationary Eyes: Glass eyes which do not move or sleep.

Stone Bisque: Coarse white bisque of a lesser quality.

Toddler Body: Usually a chubby ball-jointed composition body with chunky, shorter thighs and a diagonal hip joint; sometimes has curved instead of jointed arms; sometimes is of five pieces with straight chubby legs.

Topsy-Turvy: Doll with two heads, one usually concealed beneath a skirt.

Turned Shoulder Head: Head and shoulders are one piece, but the head is molded at an angle so that the doll is not looking straight ahead.

Vinyl: Soft plastic material used for making dolls after 1950s.

Watermelon Mouth: Closed line-type mouth curved up at each side in an impish expression.

Wax Over: A doll with head and/or limbs of papier-mâché or composition covered with a layer of wax to give a natural, life-like finish.

Weighted Eyes: Eyes which can be made to sleep by means of a weight which is attached to the eyes.

Wire Eyes: Eyes that can be made to sleep by means of a wire which protrudes from doll's head.

INDEX

MOLD NUMBERS

100: 34, 57, 116, 136-137
101: 57, 118
102: 26, 119
103: 119, 122
104: 119
105: 119
106: 119
107: 119
1000: 33
1008: 33
1009: 58, 189-190
1010: 190
1022: 34
1024: 33
1028: 33
1032: 34
1039: 189-190
1040: 190
1046: 33
1064: 33
107: 185
1070: 127, 137
10532: 105
10586: 105
10633: 105
10727: 158
1078: 189
1079: 189
108: 119
1080: 190
109: 98, 119, 145
110: 54
111: 54, 149
11173: 105
112: 118-119
1123: 34
112x: 119
1139: 189
114: 119
1142: 33
115: 119
1159: 191-192
115A: 120
116: 120, 136
1160: 190
116A: 120
117: 17, 120
117A: 13, 120
117N: 83, 120
117X: 120-121
118A: 118

119: 98, 118
120: 26, 52, 190
121: 118, 173
1210: 33
122: 118
123: 121, 137
1235: 34
124: 121
1248: 190
1249: 58, 190
125: 34, 54, 99
1250: 190
1254: 33
126: 52, 54, 57, 99, 117, 173
1260: 190
1266: 180
1267: 180
127: 100, 121, 173
1271: 180
1272: 179-180
1276: 68
1279: 191
128: 54, 117, 122, 124
1286: 180
1288: 33
129: 54, 123-124
1294: 191
1295: 180
1296: 180
1297: 180
1299: 191
130: 99, 128
1303: 106, 192
1304: 33
1305: 192
1307: 192
1308: 192
131: 96, 136
1310: 180
132: 52
1322: 35
133: 124
1330: 151
1339: 191
134: 47, 100
1348: 84
1349: 58, 83-84
135: 121, 136
1352: 35

1357: 35
1358: 58
136: 53, 99
1361: 35
1362: 34
1369: 64
137: 46
1377: 132
138: 134
1388: 191
139: 98
1398: 191
1407: 35, 42
141: 100
1415: 64
1418: 65
142: 99, 124
1428: 191
143: 125
1431: 35
144: 124
1448: 191
145: 123
1450: 35
146: 124
1468: 192
1469: 85, 192
147: 123
1488: 191
1489: 191
149: 100, 124, 145
1498: 191-192
150: 28, 34, 99, 128, 190
1500: 145
151: 99-100, 190
152: 99, 124, 192
153: 190
154: 100, 123, 135
155: 28, 124
156: 28, 191
158: 134
159: 54, 99, 149
160: 29, 98, 124, 128, 134, 190, 280
161: 124
162: 129, 257
163: 95
164: 124, 161

165: 95, 142
166: 100, 123, 135, 137, 257
167: 124, 134, 137
168: 124
169: 100, 122, 135, 183
170: 136, 280
171: 121, 124
172: 95, 121, 128, 191, 257
173: 95, 121, 124
174: 124, 190, 257
175: 121
176: 134, 136, 190, 257
177: 127
178: 125
179: 55
180: 280
182: 125, 137
183: 46
184: 128
186: 136
188: 136
189: 94, 98, 136
1892: 150
1894: 150
1896: 83, 150
1897: 150
190: 125
1906: 182
1907: 105, 113
1909: 182-183
191: 116
192: 57, 94, 115
1923: 58
1924: 173
195: 123
196: 124
200: 44, 66, 95, 136
2000: 18, 150
201: 66, 121
202: 156
2023: 179
2025: 178-179
203: 113, 157
2033: 179
204: 44

2048: 178-179
206: 125
207: 66
2072: 179
208: 7, 66, 112-113, 125, 128
2094: 179
2096: 179
2097: 179
210: 66, 127
211: 126, 157
212: 125
214: 121, 124
215: 124
217: 66, 94
2175: 216
2176: 217
22: 54, 116, 117, 158, 173
220: 66, 125
221: 95, 113
222: 29
2235: 217
224: 44
2245: 216
225: 34
226: 126, 175
227: 175
2282: 217
2285: 216
229: 175
23: 173
230: 113, 150, 175
231: 150
232: 197
233: 152, 75-176
234: 127, 175
235: 127, 175-176
236: 175
237: 127, 175-176
238: 127, 175, 177
239: 44, 125, 175
240: 95
241: 95, 125, 126
242: 175
243: 161
244: 106

Other Titles by Author:

Blue Book® of Dolls & Values
2nd Blue Book® of Dolls & Values
3rd Blue Book® of Dolls & Values
4th Blue Book® of Dolls & Values
5th Blue Book® of Dolls & Values
6th Blue Book® of Dolls & Values
7th Blue Book® of Dolls & Values
8th Blue Book® of Dolls & Values
9th Blue Book® of Dolls & Values
10th Blue Book® of Dolls & Values
11th Blue Book® of Dolls & Values
12th Blue Book® of Dolls & Values
13th Blue Book® of Dolls & Values

Focusing on Effanbee Composition Dolls
Focusing on Treasury of Mme. Alexander Dolls
Focusing on Gebrüder Heubach Dolls
Kestner: King of Dollmakers
Simon & Halbig Dolls: The Artful Aspect
Doll Classics
Focusing on Dolls
China Doll Collecting
Doll Buying & Selling
German 'Dolly' Collecting

Out-of-print editions of the ***Blue Book® of Dolls & Values*** have become collectors' items. Out-of-print books can be found at doll shows or auctions. The following prices are for clean books with light wear on covers and corners.

Blue Book® of Dolls & Values **$135**

2nd Blue Book® of Dolls & Values **$110**

3rd Blue Book® of Dolls & Values **$75**

4th Blue Book® of Dolls & Values **$75**

5th Blue Book® of Dolls & Values **$50**

6th Blue Book® of Dolls & Values **$40**

7th Blue Book® of Dolls & Values **$40**

8th Blue Book® of Dolls & Values **$40**

9th Blue Book® of Dolls & Values **$30**

10th Blue Book® of Dolls & Values **$30**

Title page: 21in (53cm) Bruno Schmidt 2025 (529) character girl. *H. Jay Lowe Collection.* For additional information see page 178.

Back Cover: 17in (43cm) Buschow & Beck celluloid boy, all original. *H & J Foulke, Inc.*

Front Cover: Top to bottom: 14in (36cm) Mme Alexander hard plastic *"McGuffey Ana,"* all original. *Victoria's Dolls.*
18½in (47cm) A 9 T by the French firm of A. Thullier. *Private Collection.*
15½in (38cm) 1995 *"Premiere."* Courtesy *Ashton-Drake Galleries.*